# Ex Libris

# Talk *to* My Lawyer!

Publication of this book has been a project of the Calgary Bar Association with assistance from the Alberta Law Foundation.

# Talk *to* My Lawyer!

## Great Stories of Southern Alberta's Bar & Bench

JAMES H. GRAY

Hurtig Publishers Ltd.
Edmonton

Hurtig Publishers Ltd.
10560 – 105 Street
Edmonton, Alberta
Canada T5H 2W7

**Canadian Cataloguing in Publication Data**

Gray, James H., 1906–
    Talk to my lawyer!

ISBN 0-88830-325-4

1. Law — Alberta — Anecdotes, facetiae, satire,
etc.   2. Practice of law — Alberta — Anecdotes,
facetiae, satire, etc.   3. Alberta — History —
Anecdotes, facetiae, satire, etc.   4. Calgary (Alta.) —
History — Anecdotes, facetiae, satire, etc.   5. Calgary
Bar Association — History — Anecdotes, facetiae, satire,
etc.   I. Title.

KEA165.G73  1987       349.7123′0207       C87-091502-9

Designed, typeset, and manufactured in Canada

# Dedication

*William A. McGillivray (1918–1984)*
*The Late Chief Justice of Alberta*

This book was in the early planning stages when death suddenly and unkindly took the Chief Justice of Alberta, Bill McGillivray, from our midst. He had fully endorsed and assisted in the Calgary Bar Association's oral history project which led to the writing of this book. He revelled in the stories about his fellow lawyers and was always intrigued with the cases in which they were involved.

Bill McGillivray was a very special person: not only because he held the highest judicial office in the province, but because, long before that, he had always been an outstanding practising lawyer. Here was a barrister who brought far more than his considerable legal expertise to a file; he also brought humanity and understanding to each client's concerns. He lived his client's cause and always put forward his client's case forthrightly and vigorously.

As in his professional life, he was revered as a husband, father, and close friend. His relish for life and love of mankind was always evident. He never fancied pomp and social display. When invited to send his curriculum vitae to *Who's Who*, he listed his address as Pegcroft (his cabin at Gull Lake) and his phone number as "in care of Dolly's store." On being invited by the prime minister to be chief justice, he described himself as a mere "mugwump." His pedigree hunting dog had the registered name of Just Plain Sam. In so many wonderful ways William McGillivray was "just plain Bill." He loved a tall tale and characters who, like himself, were larger than life. He had the common touch so necessary for a compassionate lawyer and judge.

The lawyers of Alberta miss him. It is fitting in every way that this book should be dedicated to his memory.

# Contents

# Preface

Researchers in all disciplines, from archaeology to zoology, may be familiar with what might be called the irrelevancy syndrome. Embarked on the pursuit of some specific objective, they come unexpectedly upon an irrelevancy that instantly displaces the original objective on the researcher's list of priorities.* That is how this book came to be written.

For almost one hundred years—it was formed in 1890—the Calgary Bar Association has been the "let-your-hair-down" fraternity of the Calgary and district legal profession. Because much of lawyers' time is spent practicing their profession vocally, they probably develop more raconteurs, wry wits, and stand-up comics than any other profession. By common consent, the outstanding raconteur of post-war Calgary was Chief Justice W.A. McGillivray, universally known as Bill McGillivray to his fellow members of the Calgary Bar Association.

McGillivray was also a history buff, and in the 1970s Calgary was on a history binge. First, there was the centenary of the arrival of the North West Mounted Police and the building of Fort Calgary. Then came the anniversaries of the incorporation of the town of Calgary, then the City of Calgary, then the arrival of the CPR. The more McGillivray thought about it, and the more involved he became with anniversary celebrations, the more convinced he became that the Calgary Bar Association should be doing something to preserve its own heritage, sacred *and* profane. As a result of McGillivray's persistent nudging, the association, in the spring of 1982, decided to proceed with the assembling of an oral history of the law south of the Bow.

The project began with a series of dinner meetings hosted by leaders of the bar at which efforts were concentrated on recalling some of the more hilarious misadventures of the profession's eminent, and not-so-eminent, practitioners—tales, for example, of hunting trip misadventures and court-room collisions. As meeting followed meeting, the same stories kept resurfacing in varying guises. Like the one about the leading barrister who doubled as a pig farmer and occasionally brought a pig to market in the back seat of his car. Once, at an Eighth Avenue traffic light the pig escaped and the barrister's appearance in court was both delayed and significantly disarranged by his long and frustrating chase after the absconding porker. And then there was the oft-repeated

*Sir Alexander Fleming's discovery of penicillin while doing research on influenza is a case in point.*

saga of the judge's hunting dog that was left unattended in the judge's office over a long weekend with outrageous consequences, both to the dog and the office furnishings.

Unhappily, the principle of client-solicitor confidentiality intruded whenever anyone was tempted to bring lawyer-client misadventures into the conversation, and this circumscribed the scope of the oral history project. Nevertheless, as one-on-one interviews with senior members of the bar took place, it became obvious that the evolution of the justice system in southern Alberta contained the stuff from which social history is made. It was a history which stretched from an era when a police magistrate could, and did, sentence offenders to a year in jail *plus a dozen lashes* for comparatively trivial offenses, to an era when the state provides the most hardened criminals with instant legal aid.

The reminiscences of the profession's senior citizenry gradually altered the focus of the oral history project, from lawyer interrelationships to the influence southern Alberta lawyers have exerted on the growth and development of Calgary and Alberta. It was a Calgary lawyer, for example, who almost single-handedly converted Eighth Avenue Calgary from a crude strip of frame shacks into a commercial rialto of brick and sandstone. It was a group of Calgary lawyers who launched the first successful oil company. Later on, Calgary lawyers and a Calgary judge devised the first comprehensive plan to regulate the production and distribution of crude oil and natural gas. It was in a Calgary police court where the first skirmish was fought in the national crusade for equal rights for women. And, it was in the Calgary court house where the conscription crisis of 1918 brought the military authority into near-violent confrontation with the civil authority.

The Calgary Bar Association was onto something a lot bigger than it knew. What was needed was a writer who could use the events surfacing in the interviews as springboards for chapters in a book that would be a significant contribution to the social history of southern Alberta. The search for an author reached to this writer and stopped. And for a curious reason.

In 1984 I was deeply involved in researching and writing *A Brand of Its Own: The 100 Year History of the Calgary Exhibition and Stampede.* In that project I had been reading the microfilm of Calgary daily newspapers, back to the year one, as it were. There, I had encountered, and frequently took time to explore, many of the very events that were discussed in the legal oral histories.

Prior to the Second World War, both Calgary newspapers paid special attention to the police beat and law courts news. Trials for serious crimes were reported in considerable detail and, when a juicy sex scandal surfaced, like the McPherson-Mattern wife swapping caper, the reportage could run to ten or twelve columns a day. So there was more than enough factual material on the public record to flesh out the bare bones of memory. I was familiar, from recent reading, with several of the events that had been identified and I had encountered other stories as well. Not only was I willing to become involved with the bar association project, I was downright eager to get on with it once the Stampede book was off to the publisher. Research was expanded far beyond interview taping to include searches through shelves of law reports and miles of newspaper microfilm, and this book is the result of that research.

For the research that produced the bulk of the raw material for this project I am indebted to the enthusiastic collaboration of Susie Sparks, the director of the Calgary Bar Association's oral history project. She not only continued on with the oral history interviews, she transcribed the tapes to make the contents more easily available. Then she arranged, and participated in, a number of re-interviews with lawyers and judges whose specialized knowledge had to be further probed. Without Susie Sparks, this project would never have got off the ground, or stayed aloft until completion.

# Chapter One

# Frontier Justice— More or Less

I n the forced draft filling of the world's empty spaces that marked the Victorian era, the North-West Territories of western Canada were unique. This was the only area where law and order were on site, firmly established and operating before the settlers started to arrive; and it was the only area known to man that had a prohibition law in force before it had any white people. So, there were no wide-open saloons serving rotgut whiskey to gun-toting ruffians who were given to settling arguments with fists and guns. South of the border, where violence was endemic, the absence of lawful authority led to reigns of terror as the authentic wild west spawned the notorious vigilante movement. In Montana alone, between 1860 and 1880, more than one hundred lives were lost to vigilante lynch mobs.

The difference in the life-styles of Alberta and Montana came about this way: in the early 1870s American whiskey traders were moving north of the border to establish posts where they traded whiskey to the Indians for their furs and hides. It was to evict these intruders that the Canadian government organized the North-West Mounted Police and dispatched them westward in 1874. To help stamp out the debauchery of the Indians, the government banned the importation, possession, or use of alcoholic beverages in the Territories. It was with the enforcement of the prohibition law that the Mounted Police were mainly engaged after they got their forts built across the western plains. Their system would have mortified latter-day civil libertarians. It was, nevertheless, admirably suited to the special needs of so sparsely settled a territory. In effect, the North-West Mounted Police were the arresting agents, prosecutors, judges, juries, and jailers, rolled into one. When a malefactor was arrested by a NWMP constable, he was turned over to a superior officer, who would lay the charge. The more serious charges were heard by the NWMP superintendent in the guise of a magistrate. Lesser charges were dealt with by a regional inspector as justice of the peace. In the latter case, a short sentence in the NWMP barracks cells usually resulted.

How could it have been otherwise? The closest civil courts were in Regina, five hundred miles away. In Macleod and Calgary, there were not even closets in town halls where prisoners could be kept. In any event, the bulk of the charges which the earliest Mounties enforced were minor-league—being drunk and disorderly, butchering a maverick steer, minor thefts and, very early in the game, prostitution and keeping bawdy houses. More serious offenses were shipped off to Regina for adjudication.

The fact that legal affairs were being adequately handled by the Mounties may explain the seeming reluctance of eastern lawyers to hang their shingles in Calgary. Or it may be that in its first half decade Calgary was the slowest growing community in the West with less than a hundred in population. But the people started drifting in in 1880 and 1881, and, by 1882, when H.Y. Bleeker arrived, a couple of hundred people were putting down roots in the Calgary area. A native of Belleville, Ontario, Bleeker had made his way to Edmonton the previous year when that locality was still prominently placed on the CPR route map. But when the railway opted definitely for the more southerly route through Calgary, Bleeker decided that the ground floor of opportunity for a young lawyer was there and not in Edmonton. He headed south and became Calgary's first lawyer in residence.

Bleeker beat James Lougheed to Calgary by several months, but it turned out to be another case of the hare and the tortoise. Lougheed settled first in Medicine Hat, which just happened to be, for the moment, the provisional headquarters for both the CPR and the Hudson's Bay Company. There, Lougheed met the regional heads of the companies and obtained retainers to represent them in Calgary when the railway reached that point. For Lougheed, these connections would provide him with a license to print money, in bills of very large denominations, without ever actually practicing much law.

Within a year of his arrival in Calgary, Lougheed had married Belle Hardisty, daughter of the chief factor of the Hudson's Bay Company and niece of Lady Strathcona of the CPR Strathconas, and was on his way to becoming the West's most successful real estate developer. He also founded the legal firm of Lougheed and McCarthy. By the time Calgary was incorporated as a town in 1884, Lougheed had also added most of Canada's largest banks, trust companies, and insurance companies to his clientele.

After Calgary's incorporation with a population of five hundred, the government of the North-West Territories decided that it had reached a stage where it could use the services of a stipendiary magistrate to take over some of the court work from the Mounted Police. It appointed Magistrate Jeremiah Travis, late of Ontario, who arrived in Calgary in September 1885 and was soon involved in turning the frontier judicial process into a travesty of a Marx Brothers movie.

Travis was the first of several no-nonsense, spare-the-rod-spoil-the-child, throw-the-book-at-them magistrates, of a type quite common in the West—magistrates who fancied themselves as cogs of the law enforcement machinery. He was a literalist who believed with religious fervor that laws meant what they said and demanded rigid enforcement. By the time of of Travis's arrival in Calgary, the debauchery of the Indians by whiskey traders had long since been solved by the North-West Mounted Police. Indeed, as the scattered settlements developed around the Mounted Police forts, the solution became part of the problem, for two particular reasons. The first was that Prohibition had become two-faced—one law for the Indians and another law for the whites. The second was an embarrassing demonstration of the soundness of one of Rudyard Kipling's observations in the days of the British Raj: "single men in barracks seldom turn into plaster saints."

The Indians were denied access to booze, and the law was enforced rigorously by the Mounties. But the whites could obtain alcoholic beverages quite easily, either by applying to the Territories for a permit to make a single purchase or by obtaining a doctor's prescription to acquire whiskey for medicinal purposes. In either case, the whiskey was purchased by mail order from vendors in Regina or Winnipeg and was shipped in one-gallon or two-gallon crockery jugs. All cases were purchases for private consumption of the buyer, and the sale of alcoholic beverages by the drink was forbidden for whites as well as Indians.

From the commissioners themselves and the regional superintendents, down to the newest arriving batch of recruits, teetotallers within the Mounted Police ranks were few and far between. When the patrolling Mounties ran rumrunners to earth, as they occasionally did, the seized contraband was carried back to their barracks for disposal. It was a rare occasion when the confiscated booze did not shrink substantially before it reached the barracks. Naturally, the shrinkage was ultimately retrieved for two- and three-days' drunk in the enlisted men's quarters. On such occasions, the wassail would spill out into the civilian community and there would be angry complaints from the leading citizens of the settlement to the commissioner in Regina about the rowdiness of the drunken Mounties. That would evoke strongly worded reprimands to the officers commanding, ordering them to set an example of sobriety in future.

To relieve the monotony of garrison life, the Mounties celebrated all national, regional, and religious holidays with booze-fired parties at the barracks to which they invited the leading citizens of the settlements. Some idea of the amount of alcohol consumed may be gained from the official record of the purchases of Inspector Deane of Regina who, in one sixteen-month period, obtained permits for fifty-six gallons of whiskey, five of gin, sixty-four gallons of beer, and nine gallons of wine. How much of these totals were for their own private use and how much, if any, went to fuel parties at the barracks was not revealed. In any event, the Mounties, privately and in public, singularly and collectively, had booze problems in the early days of western settlement, in Calgary as everywhere else.

By the time Travis became settled in Calgary's new combination town hall, police station, fire hall and jail, the citizenry and the police had worked out a reasonable modus operandi, even modus vivendi, for accommodating the Prohibition law to their emerging life style. Because the under-permit purchases moved in king-sized containers, small dose whiskey and wine consumers had little trouble keeping a supply on hand. Steadier imbibers of larger quantities—a mid-morning or lunch-time drink or two—made arrangements with the local hotel where they lunched: they brought bottles of their beverage from home and kept them under the dining room counter for private consumption or sharing with friends. The hotel owners (there were only three or four) had their own supplies, acquired with permits, for secret dispensing to regular guests. For the wandering cowboys with dust-caked throats, warm beer was sometimes available in cafes and livery stables.

If the liquor was consumed with seemly decorum, there was no trouble with the law, for the Mounties themselves frequently patronized local purveyors. It was only when drinking got out of hand and community leaders complained of rowdiness on the streets that the Mounties were moved to enforce Prohibition against Calgarians. They would then move in on the purveyors and haul them off, along with the drunks, to the barracks. There, nominal fines were assessed or ten-day's confinement in the police cells ordered. That was the Calgary compromise, until Magistrate Travis came to town.

Travis was in confrontation with the residents of Calgary almost from the moment he stepped off the train. Simon Clarke, a former Mountie, was one of pioneer Calgary's most popular hotel owners. He had been known to share his whiskey with dry-throated friends, guests, and occasional wayfaring strangers. Clarke had been elected a town councillor at the recent municipal election on a slate headed by George Murdock, the town's first mayor. The victory celebration at Clarke's hotel had got out of hand and became overly boisterous, at least in the view of the town's more sober citizens. Some days later, a couple of strangers appeared at Clarke's hotel, claiming to be government agents, and demanded access to his liquor supply. When they were unable to produce search warrants, Clarke evicted them, bodily. They returned some hours later with a couple of Mounties and search warrants, and Clarke was forcibly hauled away to jail. He was charged with being drunk and assaulting a police officer. When Clarke's case came up for trial before Travis, Mayor George Murdock and Clarke's other fellow councillors all appeared to testify to Clarke's upright character, civic consciousness, and general worthiness. Casting a baleful eye on them all, Travis sentenced Clarke to six months imprisonment at hard labour in the Mounted Police barracks!

The severity of the sentence set the town on its collective ear. Clarke's friends organized a public meeting to protest. Among the speakers was H.Y. Bleeker, who by right of precedence as the first lawyer in town had been appointed town clerk and solicitor. Travis called Bleeker before him and warned him that any further speech making by him could result in his being sent to jail with Clarke. And, when E.P. Davis, Bleeker's law partner, protested, Travis prohibited him from practising before him for two years! Furthermore Travis accused Davis of misrepresenting himself as a barrister when he was not in fact one.

All this was too much for Hugh St. Quinton Cayley, a non-practicing lawyer who had become editor of the Calgary *Herald* some weeks previously. He took pen in hand and roundly condemned the severity of the sentence imposed on Clarke. Travis promptly had Cayley arrested for contempt of court. He also fired him from his position as court clerk. Cayley was ordered to apologise to the court, publish the apology in the *Herald*, deliver twenty-five copies of the paper to the court, and pay a fine of $100, all by the following Tuesday. When Cayley defaulted, Travis increased the fine to $500, or $200 and three months in jail. Cayley joined Clarke in jail.

Everything went down hill from there. In the 1885 town election, Murdock's group had been opposed by a slate headed by James Reilly. Reilly appeared before Magistrate Travis with a petition charging vote fraud in the recent election, accusing Murdock of adding names of unqualified electors to the list. Travis promptly declared the election null and void, and declared further that Reilly and his slate were the only duly elected town council.

There was more. Travis fined each of the councillors on Murdock's slate $100 and fined Murdock $200. When Murdock refused to pay, Travis ordered the sheriff to seize Murdock's goods and sell them at auction.

In early February 1886, word came from Ottawa that the minister of justice, reacting to the flood of protests from Calgary, had rescinded Cayley's fine and ordered him released from jail. The minister of justice and later prime minister, Sir John Thompson, went farther. He ordered Judge Taylor of Winnipeg to look into the administration of justice in Calgary. Taylor recommended that Travis be replaced. He was, by C.B. Rouleau of Battleford who was quickly moved to Calgary. (He later became Mr. Justice Rouleau when the Supreme Court of the North-West Territories was established in 1887.)

The first impression that Judge Rouleau likely obtained of Calgary from all this was undoubtedly of a pioneer community of unusually sensitive and highly principled people—people with a deep commitment to natural justice, coupled with the courage to insist that justice be done. Certainly it was not every frontier village that could boast of a newspaper editor who would go to jail for a principle, nor a public that would dig deeply to finance the sending of a delegation all the way to Ottawa to protest a perceived injustice.

Within a matter of months, Judge Rouleau himself would become involved in a revelation of the nether side of human nature, of the almost bestial insensitivity of a few pioneer Calgarians. This time it was Judge Rouleau who was determined to see that justice was done and it was the general body of Calgary citizenry that was openly disdainful of justice in one of its guises. After all, the murder victim in this case was only a Cree Indian woman and what white man with a clear conscience could punish another white man for murdering an Indian?

The story began when William "Jumbo" Fisk crossed the path and, presumably, the palm of Rosalie, a Cree Indian prostitute, on a cold winter afternoon in February of 1889. Seeking shelter from the cold, the pair walked to the Turf Club, a two-storey house that had been converted into a clubroom catering to the nether reaches of Calgary society. At the Turf Club, Fisk introduced Rosalie, or Rosalie introduced Fisk, to George Kelsey who doubled as bartender and custodian of the establishment. Kelsey lived in a room above the club, and a deal was done with Kelsey for the use of his room for the rest of the afternoon.

"Jumbo" Fisk, a muscular young man in his early twenties, had come west from Ontario in 1885 as a volunteer with the troops fighting the Riel Rebellion. He had part of one hand and a couple of fingers shot away in that fighting, and after the rebellion he had settled in Calgary, where he worked at various odd jobs. In a town where everybody knew everybody else, he was well and favourably known for never having been in trouble of any kind.

Some time later that afternoon George Kelsey could hear loud groans coming from his bedroom and eventually went up to investigate. Fisk was standing by the bed with his hands and mouth covered with blood. There was some blood on the bed, and on the floor, and on his shoes. Rosalie was lying on the bed, apparently unconscious, her lower body covered with blood and with more blood around her lips and nose.

Kelsey would later testify that he asked Fisk what he had done to the woman. Fisk told him. They discussed what to do next. Kelsey advised Fisk to clean the blood off his hands and clothes and report the matter to Tom Dillabaugh, the town policeman. Fisk agreed and, after he cleaned up, the two men went downstairs and had supper, leaving the unconscious woman on the bed. Only then did Fisk go off to report to the police. When Dillabaugh arrived, he called a doctor who pronounced the woman dead. Fisk was taken into custody, along with Kelsey who was held as a material witness, and turned over to the RCMP. The post-mortem verdict was that the woman had bled to death after a hand had been forced into her vagina, punctured the peritoneum, and torn her internal organs apart.

The Calgary newspapers promptly dubbed it the Calgary "Jack the Ripper Case," after a series of mutilation-murders of prostitutes that had taken place in London the year before. There was one difference. The London murderer was never caught and in Calgary the culprit was already in custody, a fact that caused a great deal of grumbling. Were the police actually going to charge "Jumbo" Fisk with murder for killing an *Indian* girl? An *Indian prostitute* no less, who, like all prostitutes, bring whatever trouble they get into on themselves?

So widespread did the grumbling against the police become that the *Herald* and the *Tribune* took note of it and reminded the grumblers that life was just as sacred to Indians as it was to whites, that murder was murder no matter the race of the victim. The grumbling continued, nevertheless, and when the case came to trial before Mr. Justice Rouleau the following April, it took two days for the court to put a six-man jury together, such was the reluctance of the local citizens to become involved in Fisk's trial. Perhaps the best measure of the depth of public opinion in Calgary was a statement by J.R. Costigan, the crown prosecutor. He regretted, he said, that it was his duty to conduct the case against the accused whom he had known for several years as a genial, accommodating, and upright young man, but his position as crown prosecutor compelled him to take the case in hand.

In the meantime, Fisk had retained E.P. Davis to defend him. However, when his parents in Ontario heard of their son's predicament, his mother made such an emotion-charged appeal to one of the most prominent criminal lawyers of the time that, as he explained to the jury, he had come to Alberta at his own expense and without a penny of fee to defend young Fisk. He was Frank Tyrrell.

Such was the public interest in the trial that the court rented the large immigration hall near the CPR station for the occasion. The combination courtroom and council chamber in the new town hall was wholly inadequate to accommodate the crowd that wanted in on the action. A temporary judge's bench and tables for the lawyers, a makeshift dock for the accused, and chairs for the policemen, court clerks, and reporters were segregated at one end of the large hall by a hastily erected wooden railing. (Plans for a new stone court house building, which would have two court-rooms, rooms for the judges, and lockers for the lawyers, were still waiting approval in Regina.) The few chairs for the public were quickly occupied, the standing room was filled to capacity, and several score of people stood outside near the windows to watch proceedings they were too far away to hear.

At the end of the week-long trial at the end of April, and despite the overwhelming evidence against Fisk, the jury brought in a quick verdict of "not guilty." That verdict took Judge Rouleau's breath away. When he recovered, he refused to accept the jurors' decision, sent them back to reconsider the facts which he said could not sustain such a verdict. After fourteen hours, they were still unable to reach any other conclusion. Judge Rouleau dismissed them and sent Fisk back to the Mounted Police cells to await another trial at the next session in July.

Judge Rouleau's charge to the jury in the second trial left it with only two choices. They could convict Fisk of murder if they thought the crime premeditated, or they could convict him of manslaughter if an element of misadventure was involved. Here is his charge to the jury as it was summarized by the Calgary *Herald* on July 20, 1889:

### THE JUDGE'S CHARGE

The charge to the jury of His Lordship Mr. Justice Rouleau, was a clear, concise and careful review of the evidence, and impartial introduction to the jury. He cautioned them not to allow their sympathies or any external influences to in any way interfere with their coming to an honest conclusion as to the guilt or innocence of the prisoner. It made no difference whether Rosalie was white or black, an Indian or a negro. In the eyes of the law every British subject is equal. He defined at some length the difference between murder, manslaughter and justifiable homi-cide. "This case," he said, "had no parallel either in law or in medicine, and it was so horrible as to make any honest man shudder. In the first place I cannot understand how George Kelsey would allow a man and woman to go upstairs in the saloon for immoral purposes, but we know that there are people so lost to all sense of decency as to permit of almost anything. I regard it as a most unchristian and heartless act for those two men (Fisk and Kelsey) to calmly wash their hands and go to supper leaving that poor squaw upstairs suffering excruciating pain. I do not wish to say anything prejudicial, but I do regard that one act as so extraordinary, so cruel, that I cannot refrain from mentioning it. Kelsey's evidence is corroborated by the admissions of the prisoner himself. So far you have an unbroken chain of evidence that nobody else was in the room with the squaw but the prisoner. That part of the evidence referring to how the injuries were inflicted during their occupancy of the room is all circumstantial. I need not again describe to you the nature of the injuries or the manner in which the medical evidence shows they must have been inflicted. But the line of demarcation is that if you believe he inflicted the injuries maliciously you must find a verdict of murder; but if you believe he did the act with the consent of the deceased, and an accident occurred, then you must find a verdict of manslaughter. The prisoner's previous character is good, and that is something we must always favorably consider; but however kind-hearted, decent or prudent a man may be for years, if when the temptation arises to commit crime he had not the moral courage to resist, he must suffer the penalty of the law."

These are a few of the main points of His Lordship's able charge and it was agreed by all that it was a wise and impartial summary of the case.

This time the jury had little difficulty coming to a verdict that Rouleau would accept. They found him guilty of manslaughter, and Rouleau sent him to prison for fourteen years at hard labour. A couple of days later the *Herald* published this short editorial under the heading "That Other Jury":

The harsh language and unworthy insinuations which are being circulated against the men who composed the former jury in the trial of William Fisk, are entirely uncalled-for and out of place at this stage of the game. They were, as is well known, honorable men, of good standing in the community, and possessed of education and intelligence. How they arrived at the result of their deliberations is only known to themselves, but to assert that they were "fixed" is an unwarrantable and libellous imputation. Let the matter now rest as it stands. Heaven knows the whole proceedings were unsavory enough to be allowed a good deep burial.

Clearly there was nothing shallowly ephemeral about the animus Calgarians felt toward those who would punish a white man for killing an Indian girl; it was still alive and audible five months after the original arrest of "Jumbo" Fisk.

With Fisk finally gone from the scene, Calgarians turned their attention from Indians and murders to a mini-boom that was developing, as the CPR completed a branch line to Edmonton and then to Lethbridge, and turned Calgary into the main distribution point for Alberta for income traffic in goods and people. By 1888 the railway had been completed between Calgary and Montreal, connections with Edmonton and Fort Macleod were in the final planning stage, and the town was growing at the rate of a thousand people per year. But it had been able to attract less than a corporal's guard of lawyers who were arriving at the rate of about one-and-three-quarters a year. Peter McCarthy, Colin Campbell, and E.P. Davis joined Bleeker and Lougheed in 1883, and, as the 1880s waned, a baker's dozen were more or less in practice in Calgary. For most of them the living was very much on the thin side. There was work around for lawyers to do, mostly drawing up land sale agreements, registering titles, forming and unforming partnerships, and collecting delinquent accounts. But, in the main, the community was too busy with practical matters to need involvement with the legal profession.

When P.J. "Paddy" Nolan arrived from Dublin in 1889 with a brand new bachelor of laws degree and a gold medal in oratory, he was intent upon practicing law. But when he looked around at the competition for the business that was being done, he decided to postpone it. Instead he got a job on the Calgary *Herald* rewriting and expanding the telegraph copy coming into the office. He then used the income from the *Herald* job to subsidize his fledgling law practice. The plain truth was that there were simply too many lawyers for the amount of business available to them. The inevitable result was that fees dropped. Out of that concern, the Calgary Bar Association was born.

Late on the balmy afternoon of May 12, 1890, a veritable convention of lawyers gathered on the Stephen Avenue sidewalk outside the entrance to the new Clarence Building, stamped the dust from their shoes, and trooped up the stairs to the second floor office of Lougheed, McCarthy, and Beck. They were there at the invitation of McCarthy to discuss and take remedial action to restore the prosperity and professional standing of the legal profession. Item number 1: Get rid of the unlicensed real estate agents and sundry promoters who had invaded the conveyancing field and were making mincemeat of the lawyers' fee schedules. Before they got around to that, however, the assembled lawyers put their minds to drafting a declaration on which they could all agree. It read: "There being a consensus of opinion of the members of the Calgary Bar for some time past that the Bar of Calgary are sufficiently numerous to form an association for the purpose of cultivating a feeling of professional brotherhood [in order to discuss] various matters affecting the interests of the profession and to take united action thereon." The declaration was signed by Peter McCarthy Q.C., J.B. Smith Q.C., E.P. Davis, T.B. Lafferty, P.J. Nolan, A.L. Sifton, J.P.G. Jephson, J.R. Costigan, E. Cave, N.D. Beck, T.C. West, John C.F. Brown, and W.L. Bernard.

Once the declaration had been signed by everybody at the meeting, the association got down to the business of establishing a conveyancing tariff. That done, a strong resolution was adopted that any lawyer found to be undercutting the association minimal schedule should "be denied further professional courtesy." There were solemn handshakes all round to underwrite that statement. Then one dollar was collected from each member for bar association expenses, and it was agreed that a formal complaint about the mismanagement of the Land Titles Office be forwarded through Senator Lougheed to the Dominion Government.

Once in business, the Calgary Bar Association's first project was to collect and organize a law library and a collective to keep a wary eye on the professional behaviour of its members. Eight years later a regional society elected the first panel of benchers, but it would be fifteen years after the formation of the Calgary Bar Association before the Alberta Law Society would be chartered by the first session of the Alberta legislature.

Perhaps the most important development of that decade for the bar was the discovery by the Territories' politicians that the appointment of justices of the peace was an admirable vehicle for making political mileage. For one thing, it did not cost the government anything, because the appointees depended for their emoluments of office on the fees they could collect from their customers for minor court hearings, witnessing documents, performing marriages, and so forth. Because there were few lawyers in residence in the villages then beginning to take root along the railway lines, there were all kinds of lay justices, ranging from school teachers and farmers to merchants and station agents. In Calgary in the nineties, the competition between the justices to hear by-laws and other law infractions eventually got out of hand.

Once, when two justices of the peace tried to occupy the same bench at the same time to hear the same case, one justice threw the other justice's chair off the bench into the courtroom. There were also charges of magistrates trying cases while drunk, or that they neglected to turn the fines they collected into the government. All this caused the Calgary *Herald* to complain that the appointees were third-rate men, that they should all be fired and a fresh start made with non-patronage appointments.

This was the state of affairs when Superintendent G.E. Sanders assumed command of District E of the NWMP at the confluence of the Bow and the Elbow in 1896. With time out for service in the South African War, from which he emerged with the rank of colonel, Sanders held sway in "The Barracks" on Sixth Street East for the next ten years. Then, with Calgary doubling in population almost annually, Alberta became a province and decided Calgary needed a stipendiary civilian police magistrate. Over the next five years, a couple of appointees failed to give satisfaction, and on December 4, 1911, Colonel Sanders was appointed to that post.

He was welcomed to the bench in the Calgary police station by the *crème de la crème* of the Calgary legal profession, headed by Crown Prosecutor James Short, P.J. Nolan, A.A. McGillivray, and at least twenty other lawyers. Nolan, in his welcoming address, said that the lawyers would much have preferred the office to be filled by one of their own, but Colonel Sanders' quarter of a century service with the Mounted Police gave him the kind of experience that would compensate for his lack of formal legal training. He congratulated Sanders on his appointment and expressed the confidence of the profession that he would fill the office with distinction.

Behind the welcome to Sanders was the undisputed fact that Calgary's growing pains were becoming excruciating. Its burgeoning population, including its population of whores, brothel operators, drunks, brawlers, petty thieves, gamblers, and footpads, was bursting all its seams. It had reached a point where petty offenders were frequently floated out of town because there was no more room in the jail cells.

Consider such statistics as these: In the five years 1907 to 1911 inclusive, Calgary's population rose from roughly fifteen thousand to forty-five thousand. During the same period the number of theft charges laid by the Calgary police rose from 6 to 311, assault cases increased from 23 to 194, bawdy house charges from 30 to 185, vagrancy from 4 to 323, and drunkenness from 483 to 1,895. Such statistics normally set up a clamor for more vigorous law enforcement and the making of examples of transgressors caught in the toils of the law. Calgary was no exception.

So the time was ripe for just such a grim-visaged, no-nonsense Draconian as Colonel Sanders, the only monocled cadi in Canadian judicial history and spiritual heir of Jeremiah Travis. That he affected the monocle on the bench to enhance the grimness of his visage, as many suspected, was untrue. He had picked up the affectation early in his Mounted Police career. By the time he reached Calgary the monocle was a permanent attachment. Once, on a service club safari to Seattle, his appearance so enchanted some of the American brothers that they spread the rumor that he was a member of the British aristocracy only slightly removed from royalty. In later years on the bench, occasional startling testimony would pop the monocle into his lap. But most of the time the eyepiece remained as rigidly attached as if it had been riveted to his right eyebrow.

Sanders, moreover, did not need a monocle to establish himself as another no-nonsense, law-and-order, spare-the-rod-and-spoil-the-child zealot. He had done so in spades during his long tenure at the Barracks. In the twenty-two years he would preside in the city police court, there would be no softening of attitude, with but an odd exception. Sanders would melt occasionally where drunks were concerned. Once, in a rare rush of leniency to the head, he turned a dozen drunks loose as a gesture to mark the King's birthday. Few such lapses into sentimentality ever occurred when the hapless prisoner in the dock was a starving woman shoplifter or youthful first offender. An enthusiastic supporter of the Boy Scouts, he was particularly harsh with young men who found themselves in the toils of the police for the first time. His jail sentences were frequently accompanied by animadversions on the folly of the soft-headed coddling of young offenders that prevented them from learning the stern lesson of life—that the tree of crime bears bitter fruit and the wages of sin are painful retribution.

On the other hand, Sanders had only admiration for physical prowess sportingly demonstrated. Thus a couple of bully-boys who beat each other to a pulp in a bout of back-alley fisticuffs might encounter Sanders in an understanding mood, if the fight had been fair and square with only fists used. Then a suspended sentence was by no means uncommon. A case in point was that of the Irishman who exploded in a rage at a drinking companion who had called him an Irish son-of-a-bitch.

"But what," Sanders asked, "made you react so violently to mere words?"

"Wouldn't you get mad if somebody called you an Irish son-of-a-bitch?" the prisoner asked.

Sanders, who was born in British Columbia and had acquired the broadest British accent west of the Saskatchewan border, replied that he was not Irish.

The accused persisted. "But suppose somebody called you the kind of son-of-a-bitch you are?"

Sanders' leniency with brawlers did not extend to those who violated the marquis of Queensberry rules and particularly those who engaged in gang fights. A group of nine young men once turned up in the dock charged with beating up a tenth member of the drinking group and stealing seven dollars from him. The assault had taken place in the lane behind an Eighth Avenue hotel. After the assault, the assaultee staggered out to the front street, located a policeman who whistled up the paddy wagon, and the nine were carted off to jail. Sanders acquitted three of the nine and convicted the other six. The sentence—nine months in jail at hard labour and fifteen lashes, half to be administered ten days after beginning the sentence and the other half ten days before they were due to be released at the end of their sentence.

The lash, which was used throughout western Canada until 1960, was a fearsome torture weapon. Known familiarly as "the cat-o'-nine-tails" it was made of nine leather thongs about two-feet long attached to a foot-long wooden handle. For inflicting the lash, the prisoner usually was shackled by his wrists to a tall pole, with his toes barely touching the ground. While a doctor supervised and the jail warden looked on, the chief guard reared back and laid the cat-o'-nine-tails across the prisoner's bare back. Five strokes of the lash was usually enough to lay his back open from neck to waist in a hamburger-like mess that would take a couple of weeks to heal.

Corporal punishment, in one form or another, was quite popular with Calgary police magistrates from the first days of the court. During the regime of Magistrate Crispin Smith at the turn of the century, the magistrate himself used to inflict the punishment. In August 1903, for example, the parents of four boys who had been caught stealing hauled their offspring before the magistrate and asked him to inflict the thrashing. He was willing to oblige. A couple of days later the police brought in a small boy whom they charged with wantonly embarking on a window-smashing spree. Smith sentenced the boy to be whipped and carried out the sentence himself.

Until Mrs. Alice Jamieson was appointed juvenile court commissioner in January 1914 to take over responsibility for under-eighteen-year-olds juvenile offenders of all ages were tried in adult courts and served their sentences in adult jails. That their age seemed to have little influence on their sentence can be seen from the Harold Boardman case.

Boardman had just passed his eighteenth birthday in March 1914, when he was arrested and charged with assaulting Mary Jeffy, seventeen, and stealing her purse. Four days later he appeared before Magistrate Sanders and pleaded guilty. A parade of witnesses characterized him as a model of Christian probity. He was a regular attendant at the Sunday School of Central Methodist Church and played the violin in the Central Methodist orchestra. He had never been in trouble with the law and until being recently laid off was a steady worker in the employ of the CPR Ogden shops. Taking cognizance of his spotless record, Sanders said he would impose the lightest sentence possible. He then sentenced young Boardman to six months in the Lethbridge jail at hard labour, with twenty strokes of the lash, ten six weeks after sentence had begun and the other ten six weeks before he was to be released.

The severity of the sentence shocked the community. The *Herald* protested its severity and wondered, if six months at hard labour and twenty lashes was Sanders' idea of a light sentence, what would constitute a heavy sentence? The sentence was appealed, and Mr. Justice Walsh granted the appeal to the extent that he suspended the imposition of the lash. Not, incidentally, because of the severity of the punishment, but because of errors of omission and commission committed by Sanders in the way in which he had passed the sentence.

Sanders was quite free with the lash, as the above sentences surely indicate. He probably established a record of some kind when he got his hand on a rapist whose victim had been a seven-year-old girl. The sentence: one year in jail and thirty lashes, fifteen applied in six months and the other fifteen ten days before the prisoner was due for release.

To his place on the police court bench in 1911, Colonel Sanders brought as gaudy an array of racial prejudices as would be found in a day's march but were common coin of the western Canadian scene during his twenty-two years of service. During that double decade the following *obiter dicta* surfaced during his sentencing:

ITEM: The Calgary Galician settlement was overrun with blackguards, eager to sabotage the efforts of the police to obtain evidence against one of their number, so that he was forced to allow the guilty to go free.

ITEM: The rising Calgary crime rate was linked directly to the immigration of criminal elements from countries less respectful of the law than Canada. Statistics proved most committers of serious crime in western Canada came from the United States.

ITEM: Black Americans were an undesirable lot and there were "too many saucy niggers" parading Calgary streets living off the avails of prostitution.

ITEM: Jews could not be trusted to tell the truth under oath.

ITEM: Chinatown was infested with gambling dens, opium dens, and every kind of vice, which meant the police must keep them under surveillance to prevent white women from being spirited away into lives of degradation.

Before Sanders' appointment, an impression was abroad in Calgary that the police department had become discouraged by the leniency with which the magistrate treated law breakers. So the police had eased up on arrests. With the monocled colonel throwing the book at the law breakers, the Calgary police court docket was soon filled to capacity. Indeed, in order to keep up with the increased flow, Sanders' court ran from early morning until late in the evening. Within a year he persuaded the government to appoint a second magistrate, W.R. Davidson, to lend a hand when the docket became too heavy for Sanders to get through in a normal working day.

One explanation for the increasingly heavy docket was the increased emphasis on the enforcement of the Lord's Day Act. Originally passed in 1888, it had been re-enacted in 1906 with the strong support of the Protestant churches, the moral reform movement, and the trades unions as an adjunct to the One Days Rest in Seven Act. It stipulated that no man could carry on his ordinary business, occupation, or calling on Sunday. In 1912 the Calgary police launched a crackdown on Sunday violators.

One of the first court appearances was by an employee of a client of R.B. Bennett, who, though he was nearing the peak of his power in Calgary legal circles, was not above pleading a case in court. Bennett's case, which he argued with great vigor and at length, concerned the sale of a cigar in a local hotel. City detectives kept the newsstand in the hotel under surveillance, and, when a guest bellied up to the counter and purchased a cigar, the detectives pounced. The clerk was charged with "carrying on his ordinary business, profession, or calling on Sunday."

Bennett ridiculed the charge. If his client had simply ordered the waiter serving his dinner in the hotel dining room to bring him a cigar to finish off his meal, there would have been no charge. Moreover, the "ordinary business, occupation, or calling" being carried on on Sunday was not that of the clerk, W.H. Fairley, who made the sale, but of Charles Taprell, who owned the hotel and the cigar stand. He was the one who should have been charged.

In the course of his defense Bennett had, with his usual arrogance, cast an aspersion or two on Sanders' lack of legal training. When Sanders announced his findings, he said sarcastically, "I don't know how a supreme court justice would interpret this law, but as a police magistrate I have a duty to take an ordinary common sense view of the law. My common sense view is that the accused who was employed at the cigar stand was carrying on his ordinary calling of selling cigars. The penalty is twenty dollars and costs."

Sanders also had to come to a "common sense" decision later about whether the sale of an ice cream cone on Sunday by a restaurant broke the law. Expert testimony was produced to show that ice cream was a nutritious food and was frequently served with meals as a dessert. But this particular ice cream had been purchased by the cone and not by the dish. Sanders found that, as it was sold as a refreshment and not as a food, the sale broke the law. Again the penalty was twenty dollars and costs.

The importance of these cases lay in another *obiter dicta* of Sanders in passing sentence. To wit: "As far as I know it is the intention of the authorities to have this law strictly enforced from now on. The police will do their part and those who infringe the law are warned that they will be dealt with accordingly in this court!"

This was only one of the many warnings that Sanders issued to lawbreakers in a way that demonstrated beyond any shadow of doubt that he, like the other magistrates, viewed himself as being a vital cog in the law-enforcement machinery of the country and not as an impartial arbiter. That the justice system, as it was then, took the same view is demonstrated by a simple fact: the justices of the peace and country magistrates served without remuneration except for what they could exact from convicted persons by way of court costs. It cost them all money to acquit.

They would have been less than human if they had not come into court with a built-in predeliction toward conviction, regardless of the nature of the case they were to adjudicate. Justice J.H. Laycraft recalled that as a young lawyer he frequently journeyed into the hinterlands to litigate before county magistrates. One such fellow was well known for the infrequency with which he acquitted, although he had been known to do so. In one particular case Laycraft was able to convince him that the law was such that he had no alternative but to acquit. He did so, but as he left the courtroom with Laycraft he put his fatherly arm around his shoulder and said, "Now son, maybe the next time *we'll* win!"

The case occurred forty-odd years after Colonel Sanders nailed his colours to the law enforcement mast in the Lord's Day Act enforcement campaign.

# Chapter Two

# Bennett's No Deal— The Collision that Recharted Canadian History

T he English playwright Nathaniel Lee put it this way three hundred years ago: "When Greeks joined Greeks, then was the tug of war!" It would be difficult to find another hoary quotation that more aptly describes the legal collision of two titans of Canadian politics, Sir James Lougheed and R.B. Bennett, in the late summer of 1922.

They came together over as inconclusive a law suit as ever came before a Canadian court, but there is no doubt that it had a most profound effect on the course of Canadian history. What, for example, would that course have been if R.B. Bennett had never become the leader of the Conservative party of Canada and ruled this country from 1930 to 1935? When, if ever, would there have been a Bank of Canada, or a Canadian Broadcasting Corporation, a Canadian Wheat Board? Certainly our history would have been different without all that was connoted by such expressions as the "Bennett Buggy," "The Bennett New Deal," and even "Iron-heel Bennett." It was the Lougheed-Bennett confrontation that made all this possible. Without it, R.B. Bennett would have been an obscure footnote in the history of Alberta, never mind the history of Canada.

The Lougheed-Bennett association began in 1897 when Sir James Lougheed invited the twenty-seven-year-old graduate of the Dalhousie Law School to become his partner in Calgary. The invitation was issued only after Lougheed had thoroughly canvassed the field, for he had the most lucrative practice in Calgary and wanted the best he could get for a partner. The financial arrangements that brought Bennett to Calgary were these: he would receive 20 per cent of the net income of the partnership up to $3,750 and 30 per cent of the net earnings above that figure. These percentages were each increased by 5 per cent the following year. Thereafter until 1905, earnings were split evenly between the two.

Lougheed had also become deeply involved in the politics of the Territories, ran for the Northwest Territories Council and was elected, and then, in 1889, was named to the Canadian Senate by Prime Minister Sir John A. Macdonald. He was also, in the same year, appointed a Queen's counsel by the governor general, Lord Stanley. He was also, at thirty-five, one of the richest men in frontier Calgary, thanks to his original speculation in Calgary building lots.

The twenty-five-year partnership of Lougheed and Bennett was an impersonal, arms-length relationship. They were both Conservatives with a capital C. They were both deeply interested in politics and Lougheed encouraged Bennett to seek public office, first to the Territories Assembly and then as a member of the legislature. Both were blessed with the Midas touch. Both Lougheed and Bennett were members of the original syndicate that drilled the Dingman well in Turner Valley in 1914; later Bennett became a large shareholder in Royalite Oil; and Lougheed was a substantial investor in the original gas company. Bennett was a ground floor investor in Calgary Power and the Alberta Pacific Grain Company. Both were millionaires long before they were fifty.

There similarities ended. Lougheed was the enthusiast, the booster-joiner type pioneer that Calgarians thought of first when casting about for people to head up new committees. He had a genius for making friends and a passion for becoming involved. Bennett was the cold, calculating, ruthless, thinking-machine who almost never made a friend and would have given Dale Carnegie conniption fits. Certainly one of the ablest of Canadian barristers, he dominated whatever he touched, for he combined an infallible, total recall memory with an aggressiveness to match. In his private life he was a hide-bound Methodist who neither smoked nor drank and despised those who did. Dedication to the British Empire, which would become a Bennett hallmark, even obsession, came naturally. So, naturally, was his bilious reaction to such simple pleasures of life as dancing, card playing, participation in sports of any kind, but most of all, any appetite for spirituous liquors.*

The Methodist church was the centre of the Bennett family's

---

*There are reports, however, that after he went to England to live he developed a taste for Kirsch on fruit salad and crème de menthe parfaits.

life, and the Bible was one of the feeders of the young Bennett's insatiable appetite for the printed word. Bennett was always a voracious reader; he seldom sat down without a book in his hand. More than being an avid reader, he had very early in life acquired the ability to store great gobs of what he had read in his long-term memory. Bruce Hutchison once recalled an interview with Bennett during which Bennett was able to lead the conversation through the Canadian tariff, to the wars of the Caesars, to the China of the Ming dynasty, to the American Revolution, to the cavalry tactics of Oliver Cromwell, and to the problems of Quebec.

After teaching school for two years, Bennett enrolled at Dalhousie University at nineteen, graduated in law at twenty-two, and joined L.J. Tweedie (the uncle of Thomas, later Mr. Justice Tweedie, of Alberta) in practice in Chatham, New Brunswick. At the first opportunity he indulged what would develop into a passion for politics by running for the Chatham town council and being elected.

The Lougheed-Bennett partnership came into existence almost simultaneously with the launching of the great western Canada population boom. The Laurier Liberals had evicted the Conservative heirs to Sir John A. Macdonald from power in 1896 and Sir Clifford Sifton had embarked on his massive recruitment of settlers for the West. Calgary had already become well established as the wholesale centre for Alberta and eastern British Columbia, and the CPR made it the headquarters for the promotion and development of its vast real estate holdings in Alberta. It was not long before Calgary was bursting at the seams and Lougheed was perpetuating his family names in downtown office buildings. To the original Clarence Block, named for his eldest son and which housed the partnership offices, was added the Douglas, Edgar, and Norman buildings for his other sons.

The doubling and redoubling of Calgary's population naturally brought a flood of business into the Lougheed and Bennett office. Eventually it came to occupy the entire second floor of the Clarence Block and, when this space became cramped, expanded to the third floor as well. All this would, of course, come later.

In 1900 the Clarence Block was destroyed by fire and the firm's library was a total loss. The partners had both contributed their own substantial libraries to the partnership and replacing the loss was not complete when they occupied their new office in the rebuilt Clarence Block in 1902. In that year H.A. Allison was hired to take over the routine legal work that was flowing in and to manage things when Bennett and Lougheed were otherwise engaged elsewhere. Some time later, W.H. McLaws who had been articling with the firm was taken on staff when he completed his studies. Still later, another barrister, W.H. Taylor, joined the firm.

The hiring of Allison coincided with the launching by the CPR of its massive irrigation development east of Calgary and the appointment of Bennett as solicitor for that project. Bennett became so involved in that undertaking that he eventually got office space in the Natural Resources Building and did all his CPR work on those premises. In the meantime, Lougheed had become so deeply involved in Ottawa politics and in his real estate developments in Calgary that he had little time for the practice of law. On the other hand, the extent of which R.B. Bennett dominated the Calgary legal scene midway through the great boom may be illustrated by a paragraph in a letter to Max Aitken in 1904: "The court is in session here and I am very busy. Of the 24 largest cases on the court docket in June we had one side or the other of 20, and I only lost one, which we will appeal."

By 1905 Lougheed was contributing little or nothing to the legal earnings of the partnership, so Bennett negotiated a new arrangement. Lougheed thereafter was to draw $3,000 a year from the partnership, and his son, Clarence Lougheed, was to be employed by the firm, at a salary established by Lougheed and charged against his $3,000. After deducting the $3,000, the earnings of the office were to be divided 40 percent to Bennett, 22.1 percent each to Allison and Taylor, and 15.8 percent to McLaws.

Did this mean that the Lougheed-Bennett partnership was at an end? Not at all. Lougheed still maintained his office there and the library and all the office furniture was owned by the partnership. In 1909 Taylor left the firm and a new profit-sharing arrangement was made with Allison, McLaws, and J.E.A. Macleod who had joined the group. Bennett's function, meanwhile, had diminished to that of counsel as the day-to-day operations were left largely in the hands of Allison and McLaws.

While Lougheed's long membership in the Senate entailed lengthy sojourns in Ottawa, Bennett's own closer-to-home political career was best described as fitful. He had been a member of the North West Territories Assembly from 1898 to 1900. He resigned to run for the House of Commons in the 1900 election but was defeated by Frank Oliver. He was re-elected to the Territories Assembly in 1901 and 1902 but was defeated in the first Alberta provincial election in 1905. It was then that he decided to abandon politics to concentrate all his attention on becoming wealthy enough to indulge a taste for world travel and an interest in British politics.

At the end of 1909 he was only lately back from England when the Alberta legislature was dissolved and he received an urgent appeal from Sir Robert Borden, the federal Conservative leader, to re-enter provincial politics. Bennett was unpersuaded, but while he was off in Edmonton the party organizers in Calgary nominated him, without asking his permission, for the Calgary West seat. He ran, was elected, and served until 1911.

By this time Bennett was not only solicitor for the CPR but he was vice-president of the Canadian Pacific Irrigation and Colonization Company. As such he was frequently in Montreal. On one such occasion he was visited by Borden who appealed to him to resign his seat in the legislature and run for the Conservatives in the 1911 federal election. It was a proposal with little appeal for the practical-minded Bennett. He was confident that the Conservatives would win and, in that event, the appointment of Senator Lougheed to the Borden cabinet was a foregone conclusion. That meant it would be wholly unlikely that Borden would appoint a second member of his cabinet from Calgary, indeed from the same law office in Calgary!

Bennett placed the problem squarely before Borden, who conceded it was indeed a conundrum but that it was one that was surely capable of some reasonable solution. But, Bennett did run. In his words, in a letter much later to Borden, "I returned to Calgary, accepted nomination as a supporter of your policies, resigned my lucrative position as Counsel to the Canadian Pacific Railway Company, expended a large sum of money and was elected, being the only Conservative returned from Alberta."

Unhappily for Bennett, Borden failed after the election to come up with any reasonable, or even unreasonable, solution for the consanguinity problem created by the presence of two members of a single Calgary law office in his caucus. So while Lougheed was called upon to play an increasingly important role in the Borden cabinet, Bennett was condemned to fritter away his time and talent in idleness and mounting frustration on the back-benches of Parliament. In addition to continuing as government leader in the Senate, Lougheed served as minister of the interior, minister of mines, and minister of soldiers re-establishment. Bennett had to be content with minor transitory appointments, including a junket to London with the prime minister.

If Bennett had the presence to dominate any courtroom he entered from his first appearance in Calgary, and he did, he was also the dominant figure in any legislative body to which he got elected. That was equally true of the old North West Territories Assembly, the Alberta legislature and the House of Commons. His greatest tour de force in the Alberta legislature was undoubtedly the occasion, in 1910, when he spoke for five solid hours on the Alberta Great Waterways Railway scandal and all but single-handedly drove Premier A.C. Rutherford from political life. Of Bennett's arrival in Parliament for the first time, Bruce Hutchison has written:

His legend had preceded him to Ottawa. "Bonfire Bennett" as he was called in the west for his fiery style of speech, could utter 220 words a minute, as measured by a stopwatch, never misplacing a syllable or missing a predicate. Without a note to guide him, his language flowed like a purling brook, a swelling stream and, as he gathered momentum, like a muddy spring freshet while the Hansard reporters despaired. In public or private, only sleep could interrupt that burble of elegant English.

He was also an imposing figure of a man who in his whole life never even owned an informal item of clothing. His wardrobe encompassed closets full of elegant clothing, and his favourite costume was undoubtedly a morning coat with striped trousers, grey vest, and winged collar. On his travels abroad he was travelling light when he did not have a dozen pieces of luggage along. As a politician, he dug deeply into his own pocket for his campaign expenses. On the hustings, he was a superb orator who was at his best when the going was toughest.

Bennett's commitment to his Conservative credo was his greatest political asset. Nobody ever had any doubts about where he stood. But when politics is often a compromise between the ideal and the attainable, when clashing interests have to be reconciled, stubborn adherence to principle can become an embarrassing liability. For Bennett just such a condition developed when the Borden government decided to bail out the bankrupt Canadian Northern and Grand Trunk Pacific railways and eventually created the Canadian National Railways.

Bennett, as the former counsel for the CPR, was unalterably opposed to any rescue of the competing railways. And he said so, loudly and persistently, whenever the opportunity arose in the Conservative caucus. Indeed, Bennett's mounting umbrage might have exploded him clear out of the party had the Great War not broken out. Then his fervid support of the British cause helped to paper over his opposition to the rescue of the railway promoters, and in 1916 Borden offered him the post of Alberta director of National Service which he accepted.

The appointment precipitated another crisis. This board was to undertake the national registration of Canadian manpower. To bring it off, the board proposed penalties for not registering. Borden vetoed the proposal and the national director resigned. Bennett was asked to take over and he did so, despite his own conviction that nothing less than compulsion would bring the registration off. Later, he said he should also have resigned but stayed on because he felt it was his patriotic duty to do so. He stayed as national director until the Military Service Act was passed bringing in conscription in 1917.

During the last session of Parliament, Bennett decided he was not going to run again and asked Borden to appoint him to the Senate when the session ended. Borden, according to Bennett, readily acquiesced, with the statement that Bennett had "claims to consideration which could not be disregarded or overlooked" and promised him a Senate seat. When the Union Government was formed and the national election was called in 1917, Bennett yielded the Calgary West constituency to Major D.L. Redman and returned to Calgary to await his Senate appointment. His feeling of outrage may be appreciated when on February 5, 1918, he learned from the newspapers that he had been passed over for the Senate appointment in favour of W.L. Harmer, an obscure Liberal of no previous legislative experience.

If ever R.B. Bennett could have been imagined to have had a low point in his life, the hour of his Senate unappointment must have been it. (a) He had recently returned to Calgary to find his law partnership in a shambles; (b) not only had the firm lost a lot of business through downright inattention, it had become deeply indebted to the Canadian Bank of Commerce; (c) a number of new lawyers had been hired under improvident terms; (d) Lougheed and Bennett Limited had become the guarantor of a large loan for a debtor who had skipped the country and had thus incurred a large liability to the Royal Bank. In midst of his efforts to reorganize the firm, without McLaws and L.M. Roberts, who had resigned, Bennett came down with a painful attack of erysipelas that immobilized him for weeks that stretched into months.

Then, hard upon the unappointment to the Senate, Bennett received a letter from Prime Minister Sir Robert Borden offering to submit his name for inclusion in the King's honours list of members of the new Order of the British Empire. His outrage at the offer was horrendous. His response was a four-thousand-word letter, written over a period of several weeks. If the award was to compensate for Borden's reneging on the promised Senate appointment, his answer was "thanks but no thanks!" On the other hand, if the award was being made without reference to his not having been appointed to the Senate, he would accept the offer. "The question involved," he wrote, "must be determined by you and you alone. Whatever action is taken will be equally satisfactory to me. If the recommendation is not made I will have protected my personal honor. If it is made I have not sacrificed my self respect."

Bennett's name was not among those recommended for the honour.

Meanwhile, with McLaws and Roberts gone, Bennett got the staff reorganized on the following basis: All accounts collected, whether old or new business, were to enure to the benefit of Lougheed Bennett and Company. There were undetermined obligations which might have to be the subject of mutual discussion and arrangement, some going back as far as 1913. The net earnings of the company were to be divided thusly:

| | |
|---|---|
| R.B. Bennett, KC | 20 percent |
| A.M. Sinclair, KC | 20 percent |
| J.C. Brokovski, KC | 12$^1/_2$ percent |
| Alex Hannah | 12$^1/_2$ percent |
| D.L. Redman | 12$^1/_2$ percent |
| P.D. McAlpine | 10 percent |
| P.L. Sanford | 10 percent |

That left 2$^1/_2$ percent of the earnings unallotted. The agreement also provided that the participants could draw monthly on their earnings, up to $500 a month for Bennett and Sinclair, down to $250 a month for McAlpine and Sanford. McAlpine died in April 1921, and O.H.E. Might replaced him in the agreement which was continued into 1922.

By this time Sir Robert Borden had retired as prime minister and leader of the Conservative Party and was succeeded by Honourable Arthur Meighen. Meighen came to power on July 10, 1920, and in preparation for the December 1921 election he persuaded Bennett to give federal politics one more try. In October 1921 Meighen appointed Bennett minister of justice and attorney general. It was Redman's turn to vacate the Calgary West seat in favour of Bennett. He did so and Bennett got the shock of his life from the election results.

Neither Redman nor the local Conservatives had done much politicking to keep the Calgary West seat solid and happy and, as a result, the returns on the night of the election were extraordinarily close. They were:

| | |
|---|---|
| Bennett (Conservatives) | 7,372 |
| Shaw (Labor) | 7,366 |
| Ryan (Liberals) | 1,354 |

Bennett believed, naturally, that his small margin would at least be sustained on the inevitable recount. But the overall result of the election, in which the Meighen government was defeated, was bad news for Bennett, for the defeat headed him toward another tour of duty on the back-benches of the House of Commons, and on the opposition back-benches at that. There was worse to come. In the recount, the judge discovered that a number of ballots cast for Bennett had contravened the election act by being marked with ink or coloured pencil instead of the prescribed black lead pencil. Bennett's six-vote margin of victory on the first count became a sixteen-vote margin of defeat on the second.

Naturally Bennett took the issue to the Alberta Court of Appeal, which confirmed Shaw's election. So did the Supreme

Court of Canada when Bennett eventually got there. By the spring of 1922 the disgusted Bennett had had enough of politics and he was becoming increasingly disenchanted with Calgary, whose electors he felt had betrayed him, and with the Calgary law practice and its interminable squabbling with partners. Furthermore, his faith in the future of Canada had been sadly shaken, both by the events in anti-conscriptionist Quebec and in the country's seeming drift toward the United States, and this at a time when his own deep dedication to British Imperialism was steadily increasing. Once, in an early appearance before the Privy Council in the Waterways Railway bond case, he had so impressed the court with his performance that he had received a fan letter from a justice of the Privy Council. This became one of his most prized possessions.

And there was more. Bennett's wartime experience had intensified his devotion to the British Empire. His friend Max Aitken was now a peer of the realm and, as Lord Beaverbrook, was not only a power in the British government but a dominant figure in British journalism as well. Bennett, already a multimillionaire from a series of shrewd investments in Calgary, had inherited the controlling interest in the E.B. Eddy pulp, paper, and match company. He could well afford to join Beaverbrook in the House of Lords, if such could be arranged.

Would the practice of law in London, England, not be a more fitting career for a man of his stature than spending a life in the obscurity of backwater Calgary? Bennett thought it might, but, never a man to act precipitately, he talked over with several of his associates the idea of leaving the firm and moving to London.

When word of Bennett's cogitations got to A.M. Sinclair, he immediately was seized with the idea of buying Bennett out and establishing a new partnership with Lougheed. In the background, too, lurked the figure of W.H. McLaws, who had left law for a business career and was now wanting to get back into it, and he had talked to Lougheed.

It was during this period of indecision that it became obvious to Bennett that his was not a happy legal family. Sinclair was clearly the wheelhorse of the group and had become so out of patience with some of his associates that he wired Bennett, who was absent in Ottawa, that he was going to retire from the firm. On his return to Calgary, Bennett discovered that Sinclair's main grievance was that two of the people were not doing enough business to justify their drawings from the firm. Bennett persuaded Sinclair to leave arrangements as they were until the end of 1922 when something different might be negotiated. There were also conversations between Bennett and Sinclair over the possible sale of Bennett's interest in the firm to Sinclair if he decided to leave Calgary. Sinclair clearly believed that Bennett had agreed to sell him his share of the partnership. Bennett remembered no such specific undertaking. In any event, if an actual deal was discussed, the conversation never got around to terms or conditions.

It was along about here in early June 1922, that Bennett received word that an appeal he had launched with the Privy Council had been scheduled for early hearing and he had to leave for London. Enroute he stopped over in Ottawa for several days to discuss his plans for departure from the partnership with Lougheed. Sinclair was also due in Ottawa at the same time so it was agreed that the three would discuss Bennett's sale of his interest to Sinclair when he arrived. However Sinclair did not arrive until after Bennett had to leave to catch his boat for England, and the matter, in Bennett's view, was left in abeyance until he returned from England in the fall. (After he finished with the Privy Council hearing in July he proposed to take an extended holiday in the British Isles and the Continent.)

Certainly, in Bennett's view, disposing of his interest in Lougheed and Bennett was not a matter in which time was of the essence. Prior to leaving Ottawa he wrote to Hannah, Brokovski, and Redman outlining his conversations with Lougheed about his future plans and apprising them of his intention of discussing his plans with them on his return to Calgary. It was left to Lougheed to do the same with Sinclair when he arrived in Ottawa. Bennett remembered his conversation with Lougheed as being in agreement that the interests of all the associates in Calgary should be taken into account in the changes that would result from Bennett's departure.

On the 19th of July, five weeks after the Ottawa meeting, Bennett received the following telegram from Lougheed: "Acting on Ottawa conversation Sinclair will purchase your interest as mentioned and organize new firm of myself, Sinclair, Hannah, Redman, Sanford who will assume present guarantees. Unless immediate steps taken dissolution probable. Cable reply."

When Bennett recovered from the shock he immediately replied as follows: "Cable settlement [of] important questions involving future activities clearly impossible. Must await my return."

A week later Bennett received the following reply from Lougheed: "Your cable answering mine so adds to uncertainty of firm affairs that Sinclair and Redman have served notice of dissolution on me. No other alternative now remains than dissolution, of which this is notice."

Bennett's reply was:

Hoped different termination [of] twenty-five years association and effort. Greatly hurt action taken during absence. Will hasten return to protect property and professional rights. Sincerely trust avoidance meantime [of] causes [of] possible friction with resultant deplorable bitterness. Still believe friendly settlement whole situation preferable and possible.

Far from yielding to Bennett's request for delaying negotiations until he could get back to Calgary, Lougheed responded as follows:

Answering cable 31st. You told me Ottawa break up of office threatened and nothing here further interested you. Also offered sell Sinclair your interest and requested me see and make arrangements with Sinclair and others on my arrival. Redman also had letter from you saying nothing left here for you, and you negotiating sale with Sinclair, also to make arrangements with me otherwise complete break-up. You also wrote Brokovski see me. You also informed Sanford you were withdrawing. Sinclair requiring confirmation from you to sell him your interest, but your reply so unsatisfactory Sinclair gave notice of immediate withdrawal. Sinclair made arrangements join McLaws followed by Redman. This meant complete break-up of practice founded by me, and to protect my own interests including old firms obligations, have joined partnership of above parties, otherwise I would be main victim of breakup. Old firm interest receiving every protection. Sinclair still willing to purchase your interests fair basis and hopeful you may carry out first arrangement. Present position result of your own suggestions and necessary much regret. Therefore if you consider this action unfriendly, if your withdrawal not intended, what was the object of Ottawa instructions and letters to Redman and Brokovski?

From the perspective of sixty years, several questions leap from this exchange of telegrams. Why was Sinclair in such a rush to get a deal for Bennett's interest completed? As a lawyer, how could he possibly believe that a deal had been made when no terms were agreed upon? And why did not Lougheed work out a deal with Sinclair on Bennett's behalf and cable it to Bennett for approval? Some of the answers to these questions may well have been conveyed to Bennett when he met Hannah in London for a report on Calgary developments.

Bennett's final word was contained in this telegram:

Cable argument futile. Having just seen Hannah fully appreciate incompleteness, inaccuracy and insincerity your messages. Only occasion Sinclair mentioned purchasing my half interest partnership, assets and good will we recognized impossible without your approval. Accordingly arranged conference Ottawa, failing which you stated matter must stand until my return. As no conference held, offer made, or price or terms even mentioned, advised you, replying your message, cable negotiations impossible and must await return. Your subsequent action taken without consideration my wishes during absence [on] firm business prevented friendly settlement and compels govern myself accordingly. Sailing Thursday.

Bennett sailed from Southampton on August 14. His decision to cut short his vacation, abandon all thought of taking up residence in London, and rush home to Calgary was almost the reverse of what one might have expected. To have put the Atlantic Ocean between himself and the conspirators in Calgary would have made much better sense. Besides, he would have been freed of all financial responsibility for the debts of the old partnership. He had no hostages to fortune in Calgary and the episode must surely have reinforced his conclusion that "there was nothing more for him in Calgary."

Bennett arrived back in Calgary on August 24 and discovered that the new firm had taken possession of the old firm's offices, furniture, fixtures, and files, and had had the courts appoint a receiver for the assets of Lougheed and Bennett. But if Lougheed, Sinclair, McLaws, and Redman expected him to come storming in like a wounded grizzly they were doomed to disappointment. He had spent seven days on the Atlantic and three days on the train with nothing to do but think about the depth of his resentment against the quartette for their behaviour toward him, and how best to proceed to achieve maximum recompense for the hurt and grief he had suffered. The instrument he chose would be the reply to the statement of claim they had filed for dissolution of the partnership.

But there were some preliminaries to be taken care of, the first of which was the receivership the court had appointed to receive the assets of the partnership pending dissolution. Alice Millar, Bennett's lifelong and devoted secretary, had arranged to lease an office for him on the sixth floor of the Lancaster Building. As soon as he was settled he called in Horace Howard, the trust company manager.

"Horace," Bennett said, "I hear you've been appointed receiver of all the assets of the partnership."

"That's right, R.B."

"Well then, receive! Carry out your duties! Take the assets into your possession. You're responsible. Get them under your lock and key now, everything, and at once!"

Over the next three days, the offices in the Clarence Block were stripped of every item of partnership property they contained, down to packages of paper clips. Included, of course, were all the files of all the clients of the firm. The entire caboodle was stored in the top floor of the Southam Building and remained for years to come under the watchful eye of a woman caretaker.

When the moving was finished Bennett again sent for Howard and asked if he had taken everything. Howard said he had.

"You're wrong," Bennett replied. "The brass plate—Lougheed and Bennett—is still outside. Take that down, too."

It was done immediately.

The next step was to sort out the personnel left over from the old firm and get another practice in place. Only Sinclair and Redman joined Lougheed and McLaws. Bennett, Hannah, and Sanford became the new partnership with O.H.E. Might, H.G. Nolan, and E.J. Chambers as associates.

The sense of outrage that Bennett felt at the behaviour of Lougheed and his former associates may best be illustrated by recourse to the Bennett statement of defense and counter-claim. It runs to forty pages of typescript, one paragraph of which, number 46, is twenty-four pages long. In it Bennett sets out the entire history of the partnership in infinite detail, including the texts of cable correspondence between himself and Lougheed, and trenchantly challenges the facts as adduced by the plaintiffs.

The tone of the argument may be illustrated by paragraph number 45 which might be called the preface to that non-stop paragraph, number 46.

> The Defendant [Bennett] says that the conduct of the Plaintiff [Lougheed]...in bringing this action and making an ex parte application for the appointment of a Receiver, all during the absence in England on business for his said firm, was and is wholly inconsistent with the obligation of good faith which the Plaintiff as a Knight Commander of the Most Distinguished Order of St. Michael and St. George, a member of the Privy Council of Canada, one of His Majesty's Counsel, and a senior member of the Bar of the Province of Alberta, owed to this Defendant as his partner for twenty-five years, and further says that the action was brought and subsequent proceedings for the appointment of a receiver herein was taken by collusion with the defendants McLaws, Sinclair and Redman, and at their instance and for their advantage and benefit.

Julius Caesar said it more succinctly with "et tu Brute?" but neither left any doubt about the depth of the wound that had been inflicted.

Ernest Watkins, himself a lawyer, in his biography of R.B. Bennett, published in 1963 by Kingswood House, Toronto, made the following comment on the pleadings:

> But, while lawyers, and gentlemen, may trade insults in drawing-rooms, in clubs, and even in Court, they are not supposed to do so in pleadings. Bennett knew that any judge would most certainly order paragraphs 45 and 46 of his statement of defence to be struck out if the other side applied for that, and Mr. Justice Ives did

exactly that, on Lougheed's application, later in 1923. But the defence set out in detail all that he felt. It said it more promptly than any trial could, and he can hardly have been unaware that its whole contents would be given the widest publicity once it was filed. He had been hurt, he was out to retaliate, and he did.

As for Bennett himself, all thought of abandoning Calgary in favour of a Privy Council practice in London had gone from his head as he concentrated his entire attention on putting his practice back together in Calgary.

Prior to the break-up, Lougheed Bennett had grown into the biggest legal factory west of Winnipeg and spilled across two floors in the Clarence Block on Eighth Avenue. Both Lougheed and Bennett had elegantly furnished offices with oriental rugs and imported drapes, though there were long stretches when neither was in Calgary, let alone in his office. At that time Lougheed Bennett employed the talents of a dozen lawyers, along with three or four articled students, a couple of telephone operators, fifteen secretaries, a business manager, and several clerks. And it had more than enough business to keep all of them busy. When the break came, only their secretaries went with Sinclair, McLaws, and Redman while all the rest of the partnership and the legal and clerical staff stayed with Bennett. That fact bespeaks of a side of Richard Bedford Bennett less publicized than the granite-like reputation that he acquired in later life. He engendered trust and loyalty to an extraordinary degree, among his staff and clientele alike, and he could command almost total commitment from his associates, like Alice Millar who was his secretary and confidant for more than thirty years, like Ruth Patterson who was there for fifty years, and of course Chambers, Nolan, Might, and a host of other ornaments of the bar.

Bennett never suffered fools gladly, he was a sticker for performance, and he was as formidable a courtroom performer as Alberta ever produced. But he could also frequently go out of his way to lend a hand, to give a leg up, to young lawyers on the threshold of their careers. Ben Ginsberg was fond of recalling his own experience on that score. He had arrived in Calgary as a young lawyer from South Africa and applied to a local bank for a loan with which to furnish his office. The manager accepted his application and instructed him to return the following day for a decision. The loan was then granted, and, as time passed, and Ginsberg appeared in the bank to make payments on the loan, he was puzzled by the reaction of the manager. Instead of being anxious to get his money back, the manager suggested that Ginsberg take his time about repaying the loan, perhaps use the money for something else.

This un-bank-managerish attitude puzzled Ginsberg. The

manager didn't know him from Adam, so why this leniency toward him? The manager explained that before he made the loan he had made enquiries of other lawyers about young Ginsberg, including talking to R.B. Bennett. No, Bennett did not know him, had never met him, but if he was a young lawyer borrowing money to furnish an office, Bennett would back his note, sight unseen, as he had done for other young lawyers in similar circumstances.

Bennett, moreover, was also capable of making the most quixotic of gestures on occasion. One such was his involvement in the Harvey-Scott chief justice feud, a confrontation with a lot of comic opera colouration. The trouble arose out of the reorganization of the Alberta superior courts system in 1921. Prior to the establishment of the provinces of Alberta and Saskatchewan, the North-West Territories court had been manned by seven judges. After home rule each province was allotted five judges. Four of the Territories' judges were reappointed to the Alberta court. They were A.L. Sifton, the chief justice, and David Lynch Scott, Horace Harvey, and Charles A. Stuart. Nicholas Beck was appointed to round out the five.

The five justices constituted the trial division and when an appeal was launched the group sat as court *en banc*. This arrangement prevailed for fifteen years. Then it was deemed appropriate to have a full-time Court of Appeal. Legislation bringing the change into effect became operative on September 15, 1921. Meanwhile Sifton had left the bench to return to politics and Harvey had succeeded him as chief justice in 1910. In the 1921 reorganization, Harvey remained with the trial division as chief justice while Scott became chief justice of the Court of Appeal.

Who, then, was THE chief justice of Alberta?

Faced with that question, the overwhelming majority of ordinary Albertans would have shrugged, picked one or the other, and gone about their business. But for Harvey and Scott it was the question of the ages. Each claimed the title by right of statute and/or seniority. In matters of precedence, such as who followed whom in ceremonial processions, or who sat where at formal tables, the controversy threw protocol into confusion worse confounded. Neither disputant would yield an inch, so when they marched together ceremonially they did so shoulder to shoulder, dead spit even.

To settle the question, Harvey succeeded in getting it referred to the Supreme Court of Canada. Its decision in 1922 favoured Harvey, and R.B. Bennett was so outraged by the decision that he urged Scott to appeal to the Judicial Committee of the Privy Council and volunteered to undertake the appeal at his own expense. Behind that gesture lay almost two decades of dislike which Bennett had cultivated for Chief Justice Harvey. Bennett, the Conservative Calgarian, blamed Harvey, the Liberal who had moved to Edmonton, for the Alberta government's decision to locate the University of Alberta in Edmonton. There had been a widespread belief that Calgary would get the university to balance the location of the capital in Edmonton. Like the proverbial elephant, Bennett never forgot and never forgave, particularly if forgetting and forgiving involved a betrayal of a Calgary interest.

In 1923 Bennett succeeded in persuading the Privy Council to reverse the Supreme Court of Canada Court and it unanimously awarded the title to Scott. The latter, however did not long survive to relish his victory and, when he died in 1924, Mr. Justice Harvey was appointed to succeed him as chief justice. Nevertheless, thanks to Bennett, Horace Harvey had been forced to exist as a sort of dethroned monarch for over a year until the death of his hated rival.

Justice Harvey, for his part, survived in the role of chief justice of Alberta until his death in 1949 with an undiminished animosity toward the cause of his embarrassment, and to all his heirs and assigns. Members of the Bennett firm who had occasion to appear before Justice Harvey during those years have rueful memories of the chastisement vested upon them at the hands of the chief justice.

But, to return to the Lougheed-Bennett confrontation: Bennett's action of insisting that the trust company take physical possession of all the assets of the partnership was almost fiendishly quixotic. It certainly led to legal traffic jams on both sides of the former partnership, for those assets included all the clients' files. The Lougheed-Bennett file index read like the catalogue of the top five hundred Canadian corporations. It included four chartered banks, the CPR, the Hudson's Bay Company, Imperial Oil, Alberta Pacific Grain Company, Burns and Company, and so on, and so on. In order to facilitate filing and retrieving, each file was colour-coded for the lawyer who was in charge of it. When the lawyers wanted access to their files once the trust company was in possession, it took court orders to retrieve them.

When the partnership broke up, the overwhelming majority of the clientele stayed with Bennett. There was of course a certain erosion from a practice as extensive and varied as Bennett's, but losing a client was not something Bennett accepted with equanimity. Indeed, one way to earn Bennett's undying enmity was to fall heir to, steal, or otherwise acquire one of his clients. Alex Ballachey of High River and M.M. Porter of Calgary discovered that.

During the partnership troubles, Ballachey had one of Bennett's innumerable trust company clients switch to his office. With such a plethora of trust company clients as he had, one might have assumed Bennett would hardly miss a defection of a small one to a country lawyer. Not R.B. The next time he had occasion to meet Ballachey in court, Bennett went in bristling. The case was barely open when, as Ballachey was endeavouring to present an affidavit that had not been disclosed at discovery, Bennett roared his objection and added, "Ballachey, that was a blackguardly thing to do."

"Are you calling me a blackguard?" Ballachey demanded, drawing himself up on tip-toe to reach his full five feet in height.

"If the shoe fits, Ballachey, put it on!" Bennett was replying when Ballachey hauled off and smacked him on the nose. Bennett pushed back. Judge Tweedie, who was presiding, embarrassedly called the clerk to intervene and adjourned the court until decorum could be restored.

Fisticuffs were avoided in the Porter case. It began when the manager of the Hudson's Bay store needed some urgent legal advice and in the confusion then prevailing could not extract it from the Bennett firm. So he contacted the Bay's head office in Winnipeg where the Munson Allan firm was consulted for a recommendation of an alternative law firm in Calgary. George Allan, who had used Porter previously, recommended him for the job.

It began as a minor problem, with the way a new minimum wage act might affect the Bay's Calgary operation. But it got into court and eventually Governor Sale of the Bay himself became involved. The ultimate result was that Sale became so impressed with Porter's work that he nudged the Hudson's Bay Company account out of the Bennett office into the firm of Porter, Moyer, and Naismith. As things turned out, it was a costly loss for Bennett because the Hudson's Bay Oil and Gas Company eventually grew into a life-long and extremely lucrative client for Porter. And it earned Porter the life-long enmity of R.B. Bennett, who was not long in demonstrating his feelings.

Shortly after the Hudson's Bay transfer, Porter had occasion to represent a client who was negotiating a deal with a Bennett client. When all the details were worked out, Bennett's client suggested that Porter draft the formal agreement and take it over to Bennett for his approval. Porter did so, and was forced to spend two days sitting in Bennett's outer office waiting for him to receive the agreement. Then he rejected Porter's draft out of hand and instructed one of his own staff to redraft it.

Being retained by a former Bennett client was not the only trigger to Bennett's animus, though it was something that Bennett never forgave. In his thirty-year career in the Calgary courts, he had many notable collisions with opposing counsel. One such was climaxed by A.L. Smith calling Bennett "a goddam liar!" On another Bennett was acting in a complicated law suit over the purchase of a Calgary hotel. J.E. Varley was the leading counsel for the other side and, apparently, prior to the opening of court, he and his clients had been drinking. Shortly before noon Varley was showing obvious signs of indulgence and got into a nose-to-nose shouting match with Bennett, to whom drink and drinkers themselves were equally abhorrent, and belched fumes of strong drink.

"Varley," Bennett roared, "You are nothing but a reprobate barrister!" As Varley hauled off for a physical response, the judge called for a noon adjournment, and cooler heads at the counsel table muscled the disputants out to the barristers' room. There, after much mumbling and grunting the cooling off process set in and Bennett apologized, to the astonishment of all concerned, for he was notorious for his ability to carry a grudge. Indeed, his apology was so eloquently phrased that it brought tears to Varley's eyes.

Bennett's decision to abandon his notion of abandoning Calgary and his law practice meant, of course, that he had also to recommit himself to Canadian politics, for his passion for politics was as much a part of him as his dedication to the law. Of him it could have been said that he was married to the law but politics was his mistress. After 1923 it might have been more accurate to describe those roles in reverse. As already noted he was financially able, if he so desired, to devote his life to the service of the public interest and let the law diminish into a sometimes thing.

Once he recovered his health and got his Calgary law practice back in shape, Bennett became more deeply involved than ever in the affairs of the national Conservative Party. Elected to the House of Commons in 1925, he was minister of finance and minister of the interior of Arthur Meighen's ill-starred one-day government. After the Conservative defeat in 1926, Meighen retired from the leadership of the party and Bennett was elected to succeed him at the Winnipeg convention of 1927. He then led the Conservatives to their overwhelming victory in 1930, and the rest is Canadian history.

It is Canadian history upon which the imprint of R.B. Bennett has been etched at least as deeply as that of any other prime minister. And it is one of the ironies of history that it was R.B. Bennett who took possession of the prime minister's office as the conservative of conservatives, who set the course of the Canadian nation irrevocably in the direction of welfare statehood. Indeed, the deed was done almost by accident during the first hours of Bennett's accession to power in 1930.

Canada, though no one imagined it at the time, was on a greased slide into the Great Depression when the Conservative Party defeated the Liberals of Mackenzie King in the summer of 1930. Wall Street had recovered somewhat from the crash of 1929, but the world-wide financial crisis was worsening by the hour, and unemployment, mainly in central Canada, had reached a point where almost one hundred thousand had lost their jobs. On the

Winnipeg Grain Exchange the price of wheat had dropped well under a dollar a bushel, and the terminal elevators were still full of unsold wheat from the 1929 crop.

Bennett had ridden to power on his pledge to end unemployment in Canada and restore its export market or perish in the attempt. No politician ever assumed office more confident that he had the solution for the nation's problems. His was a simple formula: increase Canada's protective tariff on all manufactured goods to a point where he would force France, Germany, and others to reduce their tariffs on Canadian wheat in return for access to the Canadian market.

While he was putting his formula to work, Bennett had Parliament appropriate $20 million to spend on public works projects to put the unemployed to work and for direct relief for the unemployed until they could be reabsorbed. Until 1930, Canada lagged behind even poor-laws England in concern for human welfare. Ours was a root-hog-or-die economy, in which no governmental agency existed to succor the destitute. Some municipalities in the West had emergency make-work jobs for seasonally unemployed heads of families who were destitute. For the others, there was private charity, centring mainly on the churches, and nothing else.

Bennett's $20 million was doled out in part to the provinces to enable agencies to be set up to feed and shelter the unemployed. It began with the issuance of food vouchers based on family size. Then, as the Depression deepened, rent vouchers were added. Then, with the coming of winter, fuel vouchers were supplied. Much later, vouchers were issued for clothing. Unintentionally, unbeknownst to anybody, the Government of Canada assumed responsibility for the care of Canada's destitute. That fact would not be given legal recognition, but, as months stretched into years, the national government continued to appropriate ever increasing funds to the provinces for the relief of the unemployed. First it went out as direct expenditures on public works, then as shared costs of direct relief, then as loans for provincial shares, then as loans to provinces to finance municipalities. The emergency legislation of R.B. Bennett's first weeks in office in 1930 broke the root-hog-or-die psychology that had prevailed for generations and laid the foundation on which the future welfare state would be erected by his successors.

It was this emergency legislation, moreover, that shielded most Canadians from the extremes of suffering experienced by the American unemployed during the final months of the Hoover administration of 1932. There was, of course, a great deal of privation in Canada outside the cities which went unassuaged by the urban relief systems. And the prime minister was made increasingly aware of this underside of Canadian poverty by the increasing stream of letters flowing into his office. They were tearful epistles from last-ditch-desperate Canadians seeking help. Soon it was taking a couple of secretaries to answer this mail, answers which frequently included small personal cheques from the prime minister.

For the prime minister, and for Canadians generally, there was also a seemingly endless litany of dreary stories from the hearings of the Stevens Price Spreads Commission—stories of examples in Canada of sweatshop working conditions and wages comparable to those existing in industrial England in the 1830s. Across Canada, as economic conditions worsened, and nothing any government tried effected any improvement, the deepening conviction that a massive government intervention in the economy was imperative spread from the colleges, the pulpits, and the union halls, to the prime minister's advisors. When President Franklin D. Roosevelt launched his New Deal, the prime minister himself sat up and paid attention. By the spring of 1935, Bennett had become a convinced interventionist and went on the national radio to announce his own New Deal.

In addition to measures to scale down farm mortgages and some criminal code amendments, Bennett's New Deal included a number of laws based on League of Nations treaty items. These included a national minimum wage law, a national limitation on hours of labour, a national unemployment insurance scheme, to all of which Canada had officially subscribed. The judicial committee of the Privy Council had recently agreed that the Canadian government could regulate and control radio broadcasting and aeronautics by reason of its adherence to international treaties concerning these activities. Bennett relied on these precedents to sustain the constitutionality of his New Deal.

However, instead of giving the New Deal legislation royal assent after it had passed through Parliament, the governor general referred it to the Supreme Court of Canada for an opinion of its conformity with the Canadian constitution. The Supreme Court, by majority decision, held much of the legislation to be *ultra vires*. An appeal was taken to the Judicial Committee of the Privy Council in London. It decided in the spring of 1937 that most of the New Deal was *ultra vires*.

Canadian reaction to the Privy Council decision focussed attention on the BNA Act as it has seldom been focussed before.

Bora Laskin wrote, "[The Privy Council's] performance in those cases is surely a monument to judicial rigidity and to a complacence which admits to no respectable explanation."

Prof. F.R. Scott wrote, "The decision of the Judicial Committee on Mr. Bennett's New Deal statutes will have grave and far reaching consequences. It is probably not too much to say that they have created for Canadians a constitutional situation scarcely less critical than that which led to Confederation itself."

The *Canadian Forum* wrote: "The decisions are the most important, from every point of view, that have ever been rendered by that body for Canada since Confederation. The results are nothing short of disastrous."

The *Round Table Quarterly* wrote:

> The Privy Council...destroyed once and for all the hope that social and economic change in the Dominion might be directed along national lines by the use of existing constitutional powers.... It became clear that the Canadian people would either have to trust for their salvation to economic forces over which they can exercise little government control, or else have to undertake the exceedingly difficult task of changing the constitution in order that the Dominion Parliament can be an efficient instrument for carrying through a positive national policy.

A consensus quickly developed that appeals to the Privy Council had to be abolished and that some method had to be devised of amending the constitution. Unhappily, before anything much could be done, World War Two intervened and it was not until 1949 that appeals to the Privy Council were abolished. It would take more than thirty additional years before an amending formula for the BNA Act could be agreed upon.

And all this happened the way it did because Sandy Sinclair suddenly, in mid-summer of 1922, developed an insatiable appetite to acquire R.B. Bennett's equity in the Lougheed and Bennett law partnership.

# Chapter Three

# Chief Justice Harvey's War with the Army

L aymen, becoming embroiled with the Canadian courts system for the first time, are frequently baffled by the behaviour of barristers in and out of court. During a court hearing, opposing counsel may appear to be at such loggerheads that they may come to blows at any moment. Then court adjourns, the lawyers disrobe and go off to lunch, arm in arm, as if nothing had happened. Lunch over, they return to the courtroom in the same spirit of camaraderie, until the session resumes. Then they are back at each other like a couple of Kilkenny cats. Is it all simple play-acting? Or is the camaraderie itself only a false front, covering deep-seated animosities?

Or, per corollary, are mercurial changes in judicial moods mere play-acting, or do some of the things that happen in courtrooms, or in jury rooms, move judges to emotions too deep for tears? Do judges ever allow real or fancied injustice done to intrude on their consciences or disturb their slumbers in their lives beyond the courtroom? Or do they erase from their emotions whatever has transpired in their courtrooms, including the sometimes perversity of jury decisions, when they close the door behind them?

There are two cases from the life and times of the Honourable Horace Harvey, sometimes chief justice of Alberta, which can be used to argue the judicial question either way. Horace Harvey was an ornament to the Alberta bench for longer than any other judge in Alberta history, maybe even longer than any other judge in Canadian history. He was on the bench during the great Alberta land boom and Calgary's first population explosion, and his term encompassed the First World War, the Great Depression, and the Second World War, a total of forty-four years.

Born in Ontario in 1863, Harvey practiced law in Toronto after graduation from the University of Toronto and in 1896 moved to Calgary. After serving as registrar of land titles for southern Alberta he was named deputy attorney-general for the North West Territories in 1900 and moved to Regina. In 1904 he was appointed puisne judge of the Supreme Court of the North West Territories. When Alberta achieved provincial status in 1905 he was named to the Supreme Court of Alberta and was appointed chief justice in 1910. In 1921 when the court system was reorganized, he was chief justice of the Trial Division, and in 1924 was appointed chief justice of the Court of Appeal.

An austere man of spartan tastes, he neither smoked nor drank; he had no interest in, nor talent for, small talk. He had, however, developed a passion for bridge, which he played nightly if other players were available at the Braemer Lodge, his residence for many years. If he had a weakness, it was one he shared with R.B. Bennett—an insatiable appetite for chocolates, which he consumed by the box whenever he was working on a written judgment. In composing such judgments, he was meticulous in his study of the case law involved. He had the shortest fuse of any judge with lawyers who came before him ill-prepared, or who had neglected to pay sufficient obeisance to a previous Horace Harvey judgment when quoting precedents.

The first of the famous Harvey cases was the Carbon murder trial, which was the sensation of the central Alberta coal fields in the early 1920s. John Coward and John Gallagher were owners of small coal mines in the vicinity of Carbon, forty miles northeast of Calgary and the same distance west of Drumheller. Sometime before the murder, the men had joined forces and were in the process of amalgamating their interests with those of another miner. After supper on September 28, 1921, Gallagher left his house with Coward to drive to Carbon in Coward's car. Enroute they called on a miner who lived on Gallagher's mine property. After the meeting, Gallagher changed his mind about going to Carbon. Instead he rode a short distance on the running board of the car, dropped off, and took a shortcut back to his home, a quarter of a mile away.

At three o'clock the following morning, Coward's wife discovered his dead body in his car near the intersection of the road to Carbon and the road from Gallagher's mine. He had been shot three times. The lights of the car were still burning and Coward's body was still warm.

Gallagher was charged with murder and, with A.A. McGillivray prosecuting and A.M. Sinclair defending, he was found guilty by jury in January and sentenced by Mr. Justice Simmons to hang on April 15, 1922. The verdict was appealed and the Alberta Court of Appeal awarded Gallagher a new trial.

Between the first and second trials the main witness against

Gallagher died in a mine accident after coming into possession, mysteriously, of a large sum of money. Gallagher took the stand, vigorously pleaded his innocence, and was acquitted. Chief Justice Harvey, who presided at the second trial, said the verdict of acquittal was the only possible one they could have come to on the evidence. But he added quietly that Gallagher, and Gallagher alone, knew of his guilt or innocence.

Two years later Gallagher was again in court before Mr. Justice Harvey on a charge of arson in connection with the burning of some buildings on his mine in order to collect the insurance. Gallagher, it developed, had been under great financial pressure in trying to pay his legal costs for two murder trials. He was convicted of arson and sentenced by Chief Justice Harvey to *life imprisonment*. A sentence of unprecedent severity for arson in Alberta, surely. But it was a leniency-tinged sentence for murder, imposed by a chief justice convinced it had been done, even though the evidence before him had been insufficient to bring a conviction.

Another famous Harvey case was a Canadian cause célèbre that occurred in Calgary four years before the Carbon murder trials, in July of 1918. However, it is necessary to set the stage for it in some considerable detail.

In July of 1918 the final German offensive of the First World War was reaching its bloody crescendo. The German army had crossed the Marne for the second time, briefly, and shells from "Big Bertha," the most awesome giant of a gun ever invented in wartime, were falling on the outskirts of Paris. In the three months this battle had been raging, upwards of three hundred thousand casualties had been suffered by the combined combatants. Included in those armies were one hundred thousand Canadians then fighting as a unit within the British Expeditionary Forces in France. The arrival of the Americans was beginning to turn the tide, but the need for Canadian reinforcements was critical, and had been for three months.

Canada went into that war not as a self-governing member of the British Commonwealth but as a Dominion of the British Empire which went to war when Britain went to war. It was a country a cut above a Crown Colony, but not that large a cut; a fact attested to by a series of post-confederation treaties negotiated by Britain with the United States that adversely affected Canadian interest. It was attested to further by a cable which David Lloyd George, British prime minister, sent to the governor general, *not* to the prime minister of Canada, on March 31, 1918:

> I have been inspired during the past week with the constant news of the dauntless courage with which the Dominion troops had withstood the desperate assault of vastly more numerous

German forces. This battle shows that the Empire had reason to be proud of all its sons. Our armies cannot have too many of these splendid men. As already announced we propose to ask Parliament to authorize immediate measures for reaching fresh troops.

I would also urge the Government of Canada to reinforce its heroic troops in the fullest possible manner with the smallest possible delay. The struggle is only in its opening stages and it is our business to see that our armies get the maximum measure of support that we can give them. Let no one think that what even the remotest of our Dominions can do will be too late. Before this campaign is finished the last man may count.

One of the least productive measures taken by Lloyd George himself soon after dispatching that cable was to announce Home Rule for Ireland, along with conscription of the Irish into the British army. That was the prelude to the ultimate establishment of the Republic of Ireland.

At that time, Canada already had two conscription laws on the statute books and it was with these laws that Chief Justice Harvey became entangled. Indeed there were three laws involved. The first piece of legislation was the Militia Act of 1906. It provided, by section 10, that "all male inhabitants of Canada of the age of 18 years and upwards and under 60, not exempt or disqualified by law, shall be liable to service in the Militia; provided the Governor General may require all the male inhabitants of Canada to serve in the case of a levee en masse."

By section 69 the act provided that "the Governor in Council may place the Militia, or any part thereof on active service anywhere in Canada and also beyond Canada for the defence thereof, at any time when it appears advisable to do by reason of emergency."

The second piece of legislation was the War Measures Act of 1914 which provided that "the Governor General in Council shall have power to do and authorize such acts and things, and to make from time to time such orders and regulations, as he may by reason of the existence of real or apprehended war, invasion or insurrection deem necessary or advisable for the security, defence, peace, order and welfare of Canada."

Although the Militia Act provided for compulsory service, enlistment in the armed forces during the first three years of the war was on a voluntary basis. The social pressure placed on young Canadians naturally increased with the progress of the war, and over three hundred thousand enlisted and were sent overseas during those first three years. The high casualty tolls—forty thousand killed and one hundred thousand wounded—retarded recruiting which failed to bring in the reinforcements required by the battalions in the field of action.

Prime Minister Robert Borden visited Britain and the battlefronts in the early spring of 1917. He returned to Canada convinced that the country must immediately adopt conscription in order to supply the reinforcements now so desperately needed in France. But how should the government proceed? By the Militia Act? Or by the passage of a separate statute? Under the Militia Act, the recruits to be taken in at each draft would be selected by lot, a process which the government apparently did not favour. Instead it opted for a new law, the Military Service Act of 1917, which provided for a number of exemptions so that the field from which the recruits were drawn was much narrower than the "everybody" of the Militia Act.

There were health exceptions and occupation exceptions. Tribunals were set up to pass on the qualifications of all who applied for exemption. Among those exempted were farmers as long as they remained in that occupation. In many cases, the adult sons of farmers were exempt if they could demonstrate their labour was needed on their parents' farm.

The conscription proposal split the country on racial lines. The French-Canadians in Quebec, Ontario, and New Brunswick, who were at best lukewarm to the whole idea of participation in a British war, were unalterably opposed. English-speaking Canada was generally in favour of conscription on principle but until 1917 backed away from adopting it because of Quebec opposition. But even outside Quebec, support for conscription was far from unanimous. To bring it in with the least possible strain on national unity, the Borden Conservatives invited the Liberals into a coalition government which would go to the country in a national election. The English-speaking Liberals deserted Sir Wilfrid Laurier and the Quebeckers, and a Union government in favour of conscription was formed. It swept the country outside Quebec in the general election of December 1917.

However, by October 1917 the government had its conscription machinery in place. It had conducted a national registration and had the names and addresses of most of the male population between eighteen and sixty on file. Its appeals tribunals were hard at work categorizing the population and issuing identity cards which all men were forced by law to carry on their persons and produce on request by special police or others authorized to demand them. Unhappily, by the spring of 1918, the conscripting drive had produced fewer than twenty thousand recruits, less than twenty percent of the required reinforcements. And even those figures are overly favourable. Those twenty thousand conscripts were months away from becoming fighting soldiers who could be thrown into the fray. As the coming of spring intensified the fierceness of the fighting in France, the calls for reinforcements became more insistent.

From one side of the country to the other, the newspaper front-pages were monopolized by the war news. And while the papers, in Calgary as elsewhere, put the best gloss they could on the news, emphasizing Allied gains and German defeats and casualties, the truth was that the armies of both sides were being decimated on the killing fields of Flanders. But the Germans, reinforced with troops freed from the Russian front, threw more than two hundred divisions into the greatest offensive of the war in March 1918 in an attempt to destroy the British and French before the full force of American troops entered the fray.

To beef up reinforcements, the government took several actions. Thousands of prospective soldiers had been deferred for flat feet and other minor physical disabilities. These were all to be called into service and put at non-combatant jobs in the army. In addition an anti-loafing order in council was passed making it an offense punishable by a fine of $100 for any male over sixteen or under sixty not to be gainfully employed in Canada.

On April 20, another order in council was passed abolishing the exemptions granted to twenty- to twenty-two-year-old farmers under the conscription law. That order also lowered to nineteen the age at which young men became liable for military service. That enactment set off a near insurrection among farmers from one side of the country to the other. In a little over a week, more than five thousand Ontario farmers had organized a march on Ottawa to protest the action. In Quebec, uncounted more thousands went into hiding to avoid the draft, as they had been avoiding the recruiting officers and blandishments of their leaders since the war started.

Conscription had already triggered a minor civil war in Quebec. Acts of vandalism against the recruiting offices in Quebec City and Montreal had occurred from time to time. On the evening of March 28, 1918, in Quebec City, a full-scale riot erupted around the recruiting offices. The offices were smashed, filing cabinets full of documents were burned in the streets, buildings were set afire, and when the troops were called out they were peppered by missiles from the housetops. More troops were called in from neighboring camps. These were fired upon and exchanged fire with the rioters. Five soldiers were wounded, four civilians were killed, and fifty-eight were arrested. Still the rioting continued until, on April 4, habeas corpus was suspended and the city was placed under martial law.

Nothing like the Quebec insurrection occurred anywhere else in Canada and certainly not in Alberta. Like the rest of English-speaking Canada, it had given overwhelming support to the Union Government party which brought the Conservatives and Liberals together to bring in conscription. Nevertheless there was a sizeable minority of Albertans, mainly farmers, who viewed the whole conscription issue with a jaundiced eye.

From the second year of the war, great emphasis had been placed on the production of food for Britain by Canadian farmers. Many of the farmers of Ontario in particular and to a lesser extent in Alberta were of solid British stock. To them Britain's war was their war and they participated to the hilt both in the armed services and in food production. As the war continued, and as the German submarine offensive sent more and more food ships to the bottom of the Atlantic, the need for increased Canadian food production intensified. As it did, the notion grew among Alberta farmers that Canada had its priorities all backwards. Instead of concentrating on providing soldiers for the British army, it should be raising even greater quantities of food for the British people and supplying equipment and supplies for the armies in the field. That made better sense than allowing skilled farmers to rush into the army and off to France. Indeed in the early years of the war, a sizeable proportion of the recruits were young farmers' sons. They had joined up in such numbers that a shortage of farm labour developed and became more acute with each passing month.

Some Alberta farm organizations, notably the Non-Partisans League, openly opposed conscription because it would further exacerbate the farm labour shortage. In the 1917 general election it had nominated four candidates to run on an anti-conscriptionist ticket. While all four were soundly beaten, they nevertheless polled respectable numbers of votes. Other organizations such as the United Farmers of Alberta strongly supported a maximum war effort, including conscription, but also strongly urged that farmers and farm labourers be exempted because of the critical shortage of farm labour and the need for increased food production of all kinds. Taking cognizance of this opposition, the Union Government had placed special advertisements in Alberta newspapers on the eve of the December 1917 election, emphasizing that the farmers and farm labour would be exempt from military service.

On the battlefield, the Germans had thrown more than 100,000 men and one thousand artillery pieces into its drive on Paris, and on April 13 Field Marshal Sir Douglas Haig issued his famous "stand and die" orders to the British Army which, of course, included the Canadian troops. By this time the overseas army of Canadians had reached 364,700 men.

Faced with the political pressure that the agricultural revolt was creating, the government temporized, but not much. Because the farmers were in the middle of spring planting, the date for induction into the armed services was put off until July 1. Then from time to time the newspapers carried dispatches from Ottawa that the exemptions for western farmers might be continued until after harvest. But in the meantime the special Dominion police were reinforced and mounted a national campaign to pick up the non-farm defaulters, of whom there were supposed to be thousands. In that connection, a special appeal was made to the citizenry to keep an eye open for defaulters they knew and to turn them in to the authorities.

The extent to which the public responded was never revealed, but throughout that spring and summer the newspapers seldom had an edition go to press without a report of defaulters being arrested and turned over to the military. (One day the police in Lethbridge hit the jackpot when they picked up half a dozen young Americans, who seemingly had crossed the border into Alberta to escape being drafted into the American army. Given the choice of enlisting in the Canadian Army or being deported, they opted for the Canadian Army.)

That is the background to Harvey's war with the army. Now, in Calgary the First Alberta Depot Battalion, under Lieutenant Colonel Philip Moore, was established in a barracks in Victoria Park. It was the manning pool to which the conscripts were taken to be inducted into the army. Once they were processed they were assigned to the main army camp at Sarcee pending transfer to permanent units.

To the Victoria Park barracks, on a bright afternoon in early June 1918, came a young Calgary area farmer to report for service under the April 20 order in council. His name was Norman Earl Lewis, and while he was being processed by the army, his angry father went looking for a lawyer to investigate the possibility of getting his son released. He found R.B. Bennett. For just about everybody in Canada—the federal government, the army, the judiciary and the newspapers—the fat was about to hit the fire.

Bennett, intellectually, was a conscriptionist. As director of national registration he had quarrelled with Prime Minister Borden because this registration had not been made compulsory on all Canadians. But as director of mobilization he had become acutely aware of the desperate labour shortages that were developing on the farms and in some war industries. He had supported conscription in the 1917 general election, but with the general assurances that the government was giving, namely, that farmers would be exempt. Such assurances previously were given when the provisions for civilian appeal boards were written into the conscription law when it was debated in the House of Commons. In Bennett's view, such fundamental provisions of the law, which Parliament had insisted upon, could not be repealed by order in council, particularly when Parliament was in session. As a matter of principle, the government should have gone back to Parliament for approval before making such a fundamental change to the law. The Lewis case was more, much more, than a case Bennett as a lawyer would accept for a fee. This was the kind of case that got his gastric juices flowing and boiling.

Bennett's original pleading of the case is a revealing insight into the kind of public surliness that became so prevalent during the last months of the First World War. Instead of filing suit in the name of the son, it was launched by his father. This made the claim defective, so Bennett had to amend it in the name of the son. The reason he had used the father's name, he said, was to prevent abuse of the son by the military for trying to avoid service. He knew of other cases of conscripts who sought to avoid service and were physically beaten in the army. In addition, he mentioned he had had several personal experiences with the arrogance and abusiveness of military authority.

The argument that Bennett advanced before the Supreme Court of Alberta was roughly this: The War Measures Act of 1914 contained no provision for conscription because that was already provided for in the Militia Act of 1906. There was no provision in the War Measures Act that gave the cabinet power to change existing laws. The Military Service Act of 1917 had been enacted by Parliament and it contained a number of qualifications and exemptions established by Parliament. These provisions could only be amended or repealed by an act of Parliament, and not by a mere order in council when Parliament was in session. He argued that the repeal was illegal even though it had been approved as a resolution of Parliament almost immediately. The hearing of June 21 and 22, 1918, was before Chief Justice Horace Harvey and justices Hyndman, Stuart, Beck, and Simmons. James M. Muir, appeared for the minister of justice.

The court got down to the consideration of the Lewis case almost immediately and a week later announced its verdict. It voted four to one to declare the order in council *ultra vires*, that the exemptions in question could only be extinguished by an act of Parliament. The minority of one, holding that the order in council was perfectly in order and dismissing the application for habeas corpus, was Chief Justice Horace Harvey. Assuming that the federal government would submit the Alberta judgment to the Supreme Court of Canada for a final ruling, application of the Alberta ruling was to be held in abeyance for two weeks.

The judgment was handed down on Friday, June 28, on the eve of the Dominion Day holiday, which fell on Monday. Sometime between Friday and Tuesday, the Alberta decision was transmitted to the minister of justice, Honourable J.C. Doherty, and, presumably, to the army's judge-advocate general in Ottawa. On Wednesday the solicitor general's department issued the following statement:

> The government has had under consideration the case of Norman Earl Lewis, one of the younger men whose exemptions were withdrawn under the regulations sanctioned by the order-in-

council of April 20 last, and who, having been in consequence, ordered to report for military duty was recently ordered to be discharged by the supreme court of Alberta for reasons given in a judgment rendered by Beck, Stewart, Hyndman and Simmons, J.J. Chief Justice Harvey dissenting.

These regulations were deliberately sanctioned by the governor-in-houses of Parliament, upon the recital of a condition still continuing that 'There is an important and urgent need for reinforcements for the Canadian Expeditionary Force and the necessity of these reinforcements admits of no delay', and the regulations were approved as required by resolutions of the Senate and the House of Commons.

The government is advised that it had adequate authority under the War Measures Act, 1914, for the passing of the regulations and that the opinions pronounced by the majority of the judges of the supreme court of Alberta are erroneous. Consequently, an appeal will be asserted to the Supreme Court of Canada and prosecuted with the utmost expedition.

Meanwhile the government will proceed as heretofore in the execution of the powers conferred by the regulations, and the judgment pronounced by the Alberta court will not be permitted to affect the custody or moving of the troops authorized by the regulations.

The Alberta Supreme Court ruling, though it was reported at length in the newspapers, created little stir among the general public at first in Calgary, perhaps because the city was in the throes of gearing up for the annual Calgary Exhibition. But lawyers read newspapers, and very shortly other lawyers were following R.B. Bennett's example and appearing in court seeking writs of habeas corpus on behalf of clients who were being processed into soldiers under the April 20 order in council. In Quebec, the military authorities willingly brought the men into court, but there too the decision on the application was postponed, and the men were held by the military, until the final decision was to be rendered by the Supreme Court of Canada. In Calgary, relatives of other inductees retained lawyers to apply to writs of habeas corpus on their behalf. First in line was J.E. Varley on behalf of one Chester Norton. Then came Leo H. Miller with no less than eleven clients. The number ran up to twenty from there.

One problem for the lawyers was on whom to serve the writ. Colonel George Macdonald was commandant of Military District 13, while Lieutenant Colonel Phillip Moore was in charge of the Victoria Park establishment. When the Calgary sheriff went to Victoria Park to serve Colonel Moore with a summons to appear before the court, he was barred access to the premises and was told Colonel Moore was not there. A journey to the Sarcee headquarters yielded the same information.

Inevitably the fourteen-days' grace period elapsed, and the

court reconvened on Wednesday morning to have Lieutenant Colonel Moore bring in his conscripts. Instead of Lieutenant Colonel Moore, it was Major J.M. Carson, the assistant judge advocate general, who appeared to present another order in council to the court. It had been issued on July 5, and instructed all military commanders to ignore all orders from civilian courts and proceed with matters in hand. The order-in-council read:

P.C. 1697.
At the Government House, Ottawa.
Present His Excellency the Governor-in-Council:

Whereas, in the case of one Norman Earl Lewis, the Supreme Court of the Province of Alberta, appelate division, decided on the 20th day of June that the order-in-council of the 20th of April, 1918, P.C. 919, have not the force of law and that consequently all exemptions cancelled by the order-in-council of the same day, P.C. 962, remain in full force and effect.

And, whereas, the acting minister of militia and defence represents that the military conditions make it imperatively necessary that the principle of this judgment should not be permitted to have effect, and that it is impossible to suspend the operation of the order-in-council pending an appeal if the exigencies of the military situation are to be met.

Therefore, His Excellency the Gov.-General, on recommendation of the acting-prime minister, is pleased to order and direct and doth hereby order and direct, that men whose exemptions were cancelled pursuant to the provisions of the order-in-council of 20th April, 1918, above referred to, be dealt with in all respects as provided for the said order-in-council, notwithstanding the judgment and notwithstanding any judgment, or any order that may be made by any court, and that instructions be sent accordingly to the general and other officers commanding military districts in Canada.

(Signed) F.K. BENNETT,
Asst. Clerk of the Privy Council.

In tendering the document, Major Carson told the court that the military authorities considered the habeas corpus situation anything but patriotic and very distressing to the morale of the entire army. He called attention to an order in council passed in connection with national registration stipulating that no habeas corpus proceeding should be allowed to interfere with the prosecution of violators of the regulations.

Instead of calling an end to the entire proceeding pending the result of the appeal to the Supreme Court, as Major Carson requested, the court adjourned until two o'clock to enable Lieutenant Colonel Moore to appear. When the court reconvened, Major Carson explained in response to questions from the chief justice that Lieutenant Colonel Moore had been ordered by the adjutant-general not to appear. Neither were any of the conscripts, and Major Carson was unable to tell the court whether or not any of them, other than Lewis, were still being held in the province. Lewis, he said, was still in Alberta.

Speaking for the court, the chief justice said that it had a duty to uphold the law in Alberta, and when J.E. Varley asked the court to issue a writ of attachment to bring Lieutenant Colonel Moore before the court, the court adjourned to consider the request. The request was then granted and the writ was issued. Again execution of the writ was delayed for a last minute compromise appeal to Ottawa.

If proceedings in Calgary were stayed pending the decision of the Supreme Court, would Ottawa agree that the conscripts would not be shipped out of Alberta in the interval? Ottawa's reply was that the military situation in France was so desperate that no delay in shipping the reinforcements to the war front was possible.

As Chief Justice Harvey and justices Stuart and Beck went off to consider their next move, it was apparent that Calgary had become the site of the most serious confrontation between civil law and the military in Canadian history. The court house was jammed to overflowing with lawyers, army personnel and curious spectators. And, like spectators everywhere, they were tending to take sides vociferously, and the *Herald* considered the situation serious enough to appeal for calm on all sides.

For the first time in weeks the proceedings at the Calgary Court House drove the war out of the newspaper headlines. The Calgary *Herald* trumpeted the case with an eight-column black headline across page one: CRISIS IN HABEAS CORPUS CASE.

Beneath the veneer of unity and amity on the surface, four years of war had desperately strained and over-stressed the body politic. Racial and nationality prejudice and animosity were rampant. The woods were full of critical, self-righteous, super patriots eager to scrutinize the war effort of everybody else. And there were still those who allowed the war to impact them as lightly as possible, the "slackers" and "corner-cutters." And there were the second generation Canadians with German, Ukrainian, and even Scandinavian names whose patriotism was instinctively impugned by the Anglo-Saxons. There were representatives of them all on the list of draftees that were involved in the litigation.

In a word, the atmosphere in Calgary, where the Court of Appeal was considering its course of action, was explosive. But the court came to the only decision it could come to. It voted unanimously to enforce the law as it interpreted the law. On Friday afternoon, July 12, 1918, Chief Justice Harvey took his place on the bench to read their final judgment which was:

This court is the highest court of this province. It is duly and legally constituted for the purpose of protecting the legal rights of all persons who may come before it. It has all the powers, substantive and incidental, of all the common law courts of England. Those courts grew up and acquired their powers not merely by legislation but through exercise for centuries. During these centuries those powers were exercised in times of turmoil and in times of stress as well as in times of peace and quiet, and more than once in the past, although happily not in recent years, these courts have had to exercise those powers in the face of hostile opposition and even as against hostile force. It would be surprising then, if machinery did not exist for such emergency. Such machinery does exist.

The chief justice went on to point out that, in order to enforce its orders, it could call on the assistance of all the able-bodied men within its jurisdiction. If it did they were duty bound to assist and those to whom the order was directed were bound to obey. He called the situation which now confronted the court the most astounding in the twentieth century.

An order had been issued to Lieutenant Colonel Moore to bring the conscripts into court. The order was disobeyed. When a writ of attachment was made, the sheriff was met with armed military resistance, with the approval of the Canadian government. The Government of Canada was thereby set in defiance of the highest court in the Province of Alberta.

The choice facing the court was horrendous. If it backed down it would be telling the citizenry they had no rights that the military was bound to respect or the court to uphold. In doing so the members of the court would be violating their own oaths of office. But suppose the sheriff organized a posse, stormed the barracks, and carried off Lieutenant Colonel Moore bodily to the court and then to jail for contempt of court. That would still leave Lewis and the other conscripts in the hands of the army. Here a new complication had arisen. A number of the conscripts named in the suits had already been removed from the province by the military, so they were beyond the jurisdiction of the court.

The federal government had already said that the Alberta ruling would be appealed to the Supreme Court of Canada immediately. Ergo, the course of justice would be served by the sheriff taking custody of the conscripts and holding them pending the Supreme Court decision. The Alberta court would be quite willing to grant a stay of proceedings if the Dominion undertook to guarantee the safety of the applicants.

The minister of justice ordered his representatives in Calgary to refuse consent to any condition attached to the stay of proceedings. What then? The chief justice ruled the court had no alternative but to order the sheriff to proceed, by force if necessary, to take the applicants into his custody. He therefore ordered Sheriff Graham to proceed immediately to the Sarcee military camp and seize the conscripts.

Consternation swept the courtroom from all sides. Major Carson arose immediately and made an impassioned plea for the court to withhold or delay action until somebody could go personally to Ottawa in an effort to find a way around the impasse. He volunteered to go himself or suggested that Colonel Macdonald might go. On one point the chief justice was adamant: he was prepared to hold off, but only on condition that the men were delivered to the custody of the sheriff while the journey was being made. To the suggestion that any effort by the sheriff to obtain custody of the men would yield to violence, Chief Justice Harvey countered that violence would occur only if the military defied the law of the land and used force against the sheriff.

Ultimately, into the breech stepped H.P.O. Savery, who had been sitting in the courtroom with Frank Freeze, the acting mayor. He asked to address the court on behalf of the mayor and, in an emotionally charged speech, suggested that the execution of the writ be delayed until later that evening or even until Saturday. Then perhaps there could be a meeting between the civilian authority, the mayor, and the military authority at the city hall to see if there were any areas of compromise that had not been explored.

The chief justice liked that idea. He said the action by Sheriff Graham could be held off until noon Saturday to give the civic authorities a chance to work something out. The court adjourned, the justices went home for supper, and the lawyers, military officers, the acting mayor, and several aldermen reassembled at the city hall.

Late on Friday night Colonel Macdonald came up with a face-saving compromise that got everybody off the hook. It was his authority to assemble the units in Calgary for shipment to eastern training bases or embarkation points. He was forbidden by explicit instructions from his superiors to take orders from the Alberta Supreme Court. But he could undertake, without disobeying his superiors, to give Sheriff Graham twenty-four hours notice in writing before he approved any of the listed men for shipment out of the province. When the compromise was referred to the chief justice he acquiesced in the decision and called off the sheriff.

Nobody ever spelled it out, but the unspoken understanding was that, in the hiatus between the Friday compromise and the decision of the Supreme Court of Canada, Colonel Macdonald would not find it necessary to include the half dozen litigating draftees still left in Calgary in making up a draft of recruits for the east.

In any event, Colonel Macdonald gave his personal assurance

to the chief justice that he would honour the compromise. Macdonald notified Ottawa of his action. Honourable C.J. Doherty, minister of justice, Honourable Martin Burrell, acting minister of militia, and Colonel O.M. Biggar, judge-advocate general, spent Saturday morning confronting the new situation which Macdonald's compromise had created. They agreed to respect the understanding. For its part, the Court of Appeal dropped its action against Lieutenant Colonel Moore and retired from the scene to await the decision of the Supreme Court of Canada.

Paradoxically, after its short life as a Canadian cause célèbre, the Lewis case never did get to the Supreme Court of Canada. Instead the federal government chose to use an Ontario case for the test of the legality of its April 20 order in council. It involved a twenty-two-year-old farmer named George Edwin Grey who had habeas corpus proceedings on identical grounds used in the Lewis case. The Supreme Court, by a vote of four to two, in effect overturned the Alberta decision by holding, as Chief Justice Harvey had held, that the April 20 order in council was valid.

And this brings us back to the beginning. Chief Justice Harvey was noted as one of the stiffest-necked and stiffest-minded judges ever to sit on an Alberta bench. It was clear from the judgment he wrote that he was utterly convinced that the government was legally justified in the way it had proceeded. But he had been unable to carry a single one of his colleagues with his reasoning. Nevertheless when the court became involved in the endless controversy arising from the habeas corpus proceedings, he was the one who had to lead the court's defense of its position. He was propelled into defending a case he did not believe in, a case indeed, in which he was sure the Supreme Court of Canada would vindicate his judgment and repudiate that of his colleagues.

Given all that, there was nothing in the mien of the chief justice, or in any of his comments from the bench over the course of the litigation, that gave the slightest hint of his not being wholeheartedly committed to the position he was taking.

But by saying all this, is the whole affair being subjected to a serious misinterpretation? From the first order on the military to release young Lewis, the issue was not the legality of the April 20 order in council. The Alberta Court of Appeal, highest court to that point in Canada, had decided by four to one that the order in council was invalid. Until that decision was overturned by a superior court that was the law of the land. The issue was the transcendence of the civil law which the military authority was required to obey. As the chief justice pointed out, as he tried to explain that point to counsel for the government, it was fundamentally the disregard and disrespect for the law on the part of the German general staff that led to the war in Europe.

How Chief Justice Harvey felt deep down about having to so vigorously carry forward all the results that flowed from a verdict from which he dissented is, of course, lost to history. We can never know whether he stomped the court house corridors inveighing against the stupidity of his associates in coming to the decision that precipitated the crisis. Or, did he indulge in a few "I-told-you-so's" when the Supreme Court reversed them? Whatever. What we do know is that Harvey tried time and time again to find a way out of the dilemma. He backed off, he hesitated, he delayed. But when Chief Justice Harvey came to his point of no return, he crossed the Rubicon and ordered the sheriff to proceed to the Sarcee camp and take the men into custody.

In the confrontation between the civil and military authority, it was the military that backed down, that found the compromise. On the other hand, it was no ignominious surrender for the military either. Fifteen of the twenty-odd men involved, it was later revealed, had already been shipped east. Keeping the other half dozen sequestered in Calgary for a week or so was surely no big deal. The army did not release them or even transfer them to the custody of the Calgary sheriff. Above all, the army demonstrated that in times of war the doctrine of habeas corpus is an uncertain shield of the rights of the citizen.

Here, for the record, is Chief Justice Harvey's judgment:

> It is hereby declared that the powers of the Governor in Council shall extend to all matters coming within the classes of subjects hereinafter enumerated, that is to say:
>
> "(a) censorship and the control and suppression of publications, writings, maps, plans, photographs, communications and means of communications;
>
> "(b) arrest, detention, exclusion and deportation;
>
> "(c) control of the harbours, ports and territorial waters of Canada and the movements of vessels;
>
> "(d) transportation by land, air, or water and the control of the transport of persons and things;
>
> "(e) trading, exportation, importation, production and manufacture;
>
> "(f) appropriation, control, forfeiture and disposition of property and of the use thereof.
>
> "2. All orders and regulations made under this section shall have the force of law, and shall be enforced in such manner and by such courts, officers and authorities as the Governor in Council may prescribe, and may be varied, excluded or revoked by any subsequent order or regulation; but if any order or regulation is varied, extended or revoked, neither the previous operation thereof nor anything duly done thereunder, shall be affected thereby, nor shall any right, privilege, obligation or liability acquired, accrued, accruing or

*Sir James Lougheed, Calgary, c. the 1890s.* Glenbow Archives, NA-3232-7

*Lady Lougheed, Calgary, c. the 1920s or early 1930s.* Glenbow Archives, NA-3232-5

*Judge Jeremiah Travis, c. late 1890s, in a sketch by R. Randolph Bruce.* Glenbow Archives, NA-2240-1

Patrick (Paddy) J. Nolan, K.C., in front of the original Ranchmen's Club, Calgary, c. the early 1900s. Glenbow Archives, NA-2520-57

Gilbert E. Sanders, Calgary. Glenbow Archives, NA-1266-1

Calgary's first town council. From left to right: front row—Mayor George Murdoch, Treasurer C. Sparrow, Clerk T.T.A. Boys. Back row—Councillor S.J. Hogg, Assessor J. Campbell, Solicitor H. Bleeker, Councillor Dr. N.J. Lindsay, Councillor J.H. Millward, Councillor S.J. Clarke, Chief J.S. Ingram, Collector J.S. Douglas, and Councillor I.S. Freeze. Glenbow Archives, NA-644-30

*The Hon. James A. Lougheed,*
*K.C., Calgary, c. 1913.* Glenbow
Archives, NA-3737-1

*"Beaulieu," the residence of Senator James Lougheed in Calgary.*
Glenbow Archives, NA-4441-2

*Richard B. Bennett, c. 1911.*
Glenbow Archives, NA-1351-4

*John Edward Annan Macleod,*
*Calgary, c. 1915.* Glenbow
Archives, NA-4150-2

*J.C. Brokovski, and Chinese cook
and houseboy Wing Lee, 1915.*
Glenbow Archives, NA-3186-1

*The front sitting room in the Lougheed home, Calgary, c. the 1920s.*
Glenbow Archives, NA 3232-8

*The stage of the Sherman Grand Theatre in Calgary, 1933–1934.*
*The lowest box was owned by the Lougheed family in perpetuity,*
*and was used until 1952.* Glenbow Archives, NA-4560-3

*Judge Nicholas Dominic Beck, Alberta Supreme Court, Edmonton, 1921.* Glenbow Archives, NA-200-5

*Judge David Lynch Scott, Chief Justice of Alberta, 1921–1924.* Glenbow Archives, NA-1560-2

*The Clarence Block in Calgary, which housed the law offices of Lougheed and Bennett, c. the 1890s.* Glenbow Archives, NA-64-3

*R. B. Bennett's return to Calgary after leading the Conservatives to power and becoming prime minister, 1930.* Glenbow Archives, NB-16-180

*Stephen Avenue in Calgary, 1892. The Lougheed block, which housed the law offices of M.C. Bernard and W.L. Bernard is on the far left.* Glenbow Archives, NA-1702-7

occurred thereunder be affected by such variation, extension or revocation."

## POWERS OF COURT

The Court's officers, in carrying out the decrees of the court, have the legal right and authority to call upon all able-bodied men within their jurisdiction to assist in the execution of the court's orders, and it is not merely the right but the duty of everyone so called to furnish assistance, and what he does in giving such assistance is legal and justifiable, while any opposition to the court's officer and those assisting is illegal and punishable, no matter from whom it comes. This court is now confronted by a situation which is most astounding, arising, as it does in this twentieth century. Orders have been issued out of court directed to one Lieutenant-Colonel Moore, a military officer; which orders have been disobeyed. An order for a writ of attachment against the said Lieut.-Col. Moore has been granted and a writ issued, and the sheriff has been met by armed military resistance in his effort to execute the writ. Counsel for the military authorities of Canada has appeared before us and stated that Lieutenant-Colonel Moore has disobeyed the orders of the court and is prepared to use force to resist arrest under the direct orders of the highest military officer in Canada, and it appears that these orders have been issued with the approval of the executive government of Canada. This seems to me that the military authorities and the executive government of Canada have set at defiance the highest court in this province.

## CIRCUMSTANCES OF CASE

The disturbances out of which this situation arises are due to a decision of the court given two weeks ago in re Lewis, 1918, 2 W.W.R. 657, in which it was held by a majority that a certain Canadian order-in-council was invalid and that the applicant in that case was entitled to be discharged from military custody and control. The court stayed the issuance of the order in that case for two weeks pending the consideration of whether an appeal would be taken. Since that decision several other persons, about twenty in all, claiming to be in the same position as Lewis, have applied by habeas corpus proceedings for their discharge. It is the refusal to obey an order directed to the said Lieut.-Col. Moore to produce the applicants so that if so entitled they may be discharged that has caused the writ of attachment to issue against him for his contempt in such refusal.

## NEW ORDER-IN-COUNCIL

Since the issue of the order which has been disobeyed, counsel for the military authorities has produced to us what purports to be an order-in-council passed by the governor-general on the 5th inst. which after reciting the judgment in re Lewis and the orders-in-council orders and directs "that men whose exemptions were cancelled pursuant to the provisions of the orders-in-council of the 20th of April, 1918, above referred to, be dealt with in all respects as provided by the said orders-in-council notwithstanding the judgment and notwithstanding any judgment or any order that may be made by any court and that instructions be sent accordingly to the general and other officers commanding military districts in Canada."

It is apparent that if as was held in re Lewis the governor-in-general had not authority to cancel the exemptions by order-in-council this order-in-council can have no greater effect than the earlier ones and that it, therefore can be deemed only a notice that the decisions of the courts of Canada are to be ignored and treated with contempt and that the military authorities are to be so instructed.

## TWO COURSES OPEN

Upon this situation two courses are open to this court. It can either abdicate its authority and functions and advise applicants to it for a redress of their wrongs and the protection of their legal rights that it is powerless, which, of course, means there is no power except that of force which can protect their rights, the consequence of which could scarcely mean anything less than anarchy, or it may decide to continue to perform the duties with which it is entrusted for the purpose of guarding the rights of the subject and not prove false to the oath of office which each member took when he "solemnly and sincerely promised and swore that he would duly and faithfully and to the best of his skill and knowledge exercise the powers and trusts reposed in him as a judge of the said court."

## ONLY ONE ANSWER

There can be only one answer to the question, which way will this court act? It will continue to perform its duties as it sees them, and will endeavour, in so far as lies in its power, to furnish protection to persons who apply to it to be permitted to exercise their legal rights.

It is apparent that the refusal of Lieut.-Col. Moore and the order against him are only incidents in this application and that the substance of the application is to obtain the release of the applicants. If the person ordered to produce them will not do so then unless the court is to confess impotence it must send someone to obtain and produce them. It is apparent that putting Lieut.-Col. Moore in jail would be of no service to the applicants unless it served to cause him to do what he was ordered to do and it is for that purpose primarily and not because anything he has done has offended the dignity of the court that a writ of attachment was issued against him. But if he were in jail under the writ it would still be necessary to obtain the applicants and have them brought before the court in order that they might be discharged if so entitled. The evidence before the court shows that they are so entitled if the decision in re Lewis be right and so long as it remains unreversed it must be deemed to be the proper expression of the law in this province. It is admitted by counsel for the military authorities that he has been informed that some of the applicants have been removed by the military authorities since the applications were launched in defiance of an order of the court that they should not be so removed.

This is confirmed by counsel for the applicants.

## NO JURISDICTION

This court can now exercise no jurisdiction in respect of these applicants, although in due time it may possibly be able to punish these persons who disobeyed its orders. It is stated that the decision in re Lewis will be reviewed by the Supreme Court of Canada very promptly and under such circumstances it would be right and proper to allow the application to stand until after such review but from what has been said it is apparent that then it may be too late to protect any of the applicants who may be removed from its jurisdiction. The order should, therefore, go directing the sheriff to obtain the persons of the applicants or such of them as may be within the jurisdiction of the court and to bring them before the court and that then they be discharged from military custody and control without further order. They will then be in the province where they can be obtained if it is held that they are subject to military duty.

In deciding to pursue its proper functions, this court is not unmindful of the fact which the minister of justice desires to press on us, that the need of Canada for soldiers is very great and urgent, but it is apparent that to allow such a consideration to be our guiding principle would be to substitute expediency for law as the basis of judicial decision.

It is also apparent to us that, without doubt, there is enough might, though not right, behind the military authorities to prevent the court's officers from performing their duty, and even to destroy both the members of the court and its officers, but while the court remains it must endeavor to perform its duty as it sees it.

The court has shown every desire to do nothing that might hinder the military and executive officers, so far as could be done consistently, with its duty to the applying to it for a redress grievances, but has met with little success. After the application had been ignored and the other disobeyed, counsel for the minister of justice yesterday, in the person of Mr. Muir, appeared for the first time when the court was about to deal finally with the applications, and formally apply for a stay of all proceedings. The court intimated that it would be quite ready to grant the stay if the orders were obeyed and proper provisions made for the protection of the applicants in the event of the decision in re Lewis being sustained, and adjourned further consideration until this morning. This morning, no word having been received from the minister of justice, at Mr. Muir's request a further adjournment was made to this afternoon at 4 p.m. and now after more than twenty-four hours Mr. Muir states that he had just received instructions from the minister of justice to refuse consent to any conditions.

Under these circumstances there seems no other proper course than to make the order as above mentioned.

(signed) HORACE HARVEY
July 12, 1918    Chief Justice

# Chapter Four

# McKinley Cameron, the All-Purpose, All-Around All-Star

The Calgary, the southern Alberta, to which the soldiers came home at the end of the First World War, was a far cry, a world removed, from the Calgary and southern Alberta they left in 1914. They had left at the end of the greatest population growth the city, and the country, had ever seen—a fifteen-year boom in which the population had doubled and redoubled and redoubled. In the process it had stimulated the greatest of all building booms and orgies of real estate speculation, in every aspect of which the legal profession was involved. There was not a law office in town that was not overflowing with work—with land titles to be transferred, companies to be incorporated, agreements to be signed, leases to be drafted, sales to be formalized. And with armies of unattached males taking their fun where they found it, in the downtown street corner bars and in the conveniently located brothels—there was work aplenty for all the barristers in the city police courts and provincial law courts.

Of all of this, nothing survived the war. Gone was the army of risk-takers, promoters, and speculators and gone, too, the seemingly endless flow of investment capital. Gone was the optimistic atmosphere of the immigration years, replaced by despondency, social discord, and an economic malaise that would blight the land and the people for a generation.

The Calgary that would put its money where its mouth was in support of any civic undertaking was replaced by a Calgary that would not be found dead passing a money by-law of any kind. Sunk without a trace went the construction trade, if anything greater than converting stables into garages was involved. For the legal profession, office routine had a lot more to do with mortgage foreclosures, bill collecting, debtor pursuing, and restructuring of agreements for sale than it had to do with anything else.

Though the post-war depression was attributed to the Great War and its after-effects, the legal business recession really began in 1912 with the drying up of mortgage money. That was a shattering blow to business of all kinds in southern Alberta. The war simply put the finishing touches to a well-begun process. Curiously, one wartime development had the effect of mitigating the impact of the Depression on the legal profession, at least for those who were able to convert solicitor skills for barrister skills. That development was Prohibition.

Alberta, along with the rest of Canada except Quebec, outlawed the production, distribution, and consumption of beverage alcohol. Alberta voted for prohibition in 1916, and in 1917 the federal government adopted national prohibition and outlawed the shipment of alcoholic beverages between provinces. But mere expression of the public will did by no means eradicate a public taste for alcohol that had survived from the beginning of recorded history. Not when the drafted laws contained loopholes which the thirsty quickly discovered. Breweries were permitted to brew two percent "temperance" beer and the bars were permitted to sell it. But temperance beer was only diluted regular beer and, any way, a vast quantity of undiluted beer surreptitiously found its way to the saloons. Whiskey was allowed to be prescribed by doctors and dispensed by druggists for medical reasons. It was not long before the druggists were doubling as liquor vendors. And out in the country, particularly in the "foreign" settlements, barnyard distilleries sprang up to provide moonshine for the thirsty. Prohibition provided the governments with additional laws to be enforced and the enforcement became grist for the lawyers' mill. During the more or less bone dry years of 1917–1919 it never developed into a bonanza but defending or prosecuting liquor offenders created a steady enough income to pay the rent and keep the landlords happy.

All this changed substantially for the better from the barristers' viewpoint in 1920 when the ukase against interprovincial shipments of beverage alcohol was lifted just as the United States prohibition law came into effect. The first development was the establishment of mail-order stores in Saskatchewan, Alberta and British Columbia from which out-of-province residents could have liquor shipped to them by mail. The second was the establishment of strings of liquor agencies in the prairie town adjacent to the border to sell liquor for export to the United States rumrunners. There was, of course, considerable spillage from these export houses into the domestic trade. Consequently, with the arrival of the 1920s, illegal access to booze brought increased enforcement which in turn increased the traffic through the police courts and business for the barristers.

Then, as if the enforcement agencies did not have enough trouble, their lives were further complicated by the decision of British Columbia, in 1920, to substitute a government retail liquor monopoly for Prohibition and set up government liquor stores throughout the province. From these stores rumrunners could obtain supplies to market in the United States. Resident Alberta bootleggers could obtain supplies and refills from the same sources.

It was the British Columbia development that led to one of Alberta's most notorious murder cases, a case which fatally blemished the reputation of a Calgary lawyer who, by common consent of his peers, was one of the ablest barristers of his times. He was McKinley Cameron, chief defense counsel in the Picariello-Lassandro murder trial of 1922.

With the repeal of Prohibition, the illicit liquor traffic as a source of income for criminal lawyers rapidly diminished in importance. Then, as the post-Prohibition era passed into the depression era, malefactors with the wherewithal to hire lawyers of any kind became endangered species. One of those caught up in the transition was J. McKinley Cameron.

Cameron, unlike McGillivray and Sinclair, practiced alone and confined himself strictly to criminal law. It was said of him that he had committed the entire Canadian criminal code to memory, subsection by alphabetized subsection, that he had certain memory recesses in which he kept track of the precedent establishing cases of the Supreme Court of Canada and the Privy Council. He did not suffer adverse decisions of lower courts in silence and was before the Alberta Court of Appeal more often than any other barrister between 1912 and 1932. And he was involved in a number of landmark decisions, of which more anon.

Cameron was a classmate of McGillivray's at Dalhousie University law school. After graduation he practiced in Nova Scotia for some years as counsel for the Mine Workers' Union in its struggles for recognition by the mine owners. In 1909 he joined the immigrant trek to the West and settled in Calgary. He began practice with the firm of Stewart, Tweedie, and Charman, but in 1914 left the firm to practice on his own and was alone until his death in 1943 at the age of sixty-three. Though he acquired a fine home in Mount Royal and directorships of McDougal-Segur and other pioneer oil companies, he rubbed shoulders easier with miners than with bank managers or ornaments of the bar. Indeed he delighted in deflating the pompous establishment of the bar with his unorthodox style.

In appearance, Cameron was the antithesis of the public's perception of an eminent King's Counsel, if that perception was related to the appearance of an R.B. Bennett, or an A.A. McGillivray. They came to work in striped trousers, morning coats, grey vests, and winged collars, the very personification of unbending formality.

Cameron was the personification of irreverent informality. He was never seen in pants that matched his coat. In the winter he never wore shoes, only rubbers over heavy lumberjack sox. Though he owned a fine home on Prospect Avenue he preferred on occasion to sleep in the loft of his garage with his hunting dogs. When he took his dogs for a walk through Mount Royal he risked being mistaken for a prowler by the watchmen who patrolled the district. He was never one to allow awe of the judiciary to vitiate his irreverent approach to life. Cameron was inches short of average height, and he spoke with a thin, squeaky voice that contrasted sharply with the deep bass tones most barristers of the era affected. But if his courtroom batting average and the size of his practice were any criterion, he was the ranking criminal lawyer of his times. Cameron and Prohibition came together once in one infamous murder trail, the Picariello-Lassandra case.

The Picariello-Lassandro case was one of the few authentic cases of rumrunner violence in Alberta during Prohibition. By 1921, running whiskey across the wide open Montana border from Alberta and British Columbia had become a lucrative trade that was dominated in the main by Americans. They, after all, were more familiar with the routines and the veniality of the American customs patrollers and, most important of all, they had their contraband pre-sold before they bought it. It was, nevertheless a trade in which southern Albertans frequently took part. One such was Emileo Picariello, the owner of the Alberta Hotel in Blairmore.

Little factual material exists about his operation but it is known that by 1922 he owned six McLaughlin six-cylinder touring cars, each capable of moving a couple of dozen cases of Scotch or rye at high speed over Alberta's gravelled highways. It was perfectly legal in 1920 for Picariello to load up one of his cars at Fernie, British Columbia, with booze consigned to any one of a half dozen American border points. But once interprovincial shipment became illegal following the October, 1920, plebiscite which restored Prohibition in Alberta, a legal gray area developed. Under federal law, booze could still be shipped from Fernie, to Sweetgrass, Montana, but it could not be shipped legally into Alberta which was the only way to get from Fernie to Sweetgrass. And because Alberta authorities believed a lot of booze from the export trade was being diverted into illicit markets in Alberta, it tried to shut off the traffic.

In an effort to combat the illicit traffic through the Crowsnest Pass into Alberta, the Alberta government stationed a detachment of its newly established Provincial Police in Coleman to set up roadblocks and check-points to catch Albertans bringing back booze from British Columbia. In particular, the detachment was charged with stopping the commercial rumrunners. As a result, an elaborate game of hide and seek developed along the highway.

The main route through the Crowsnest Pass ran down the main streets of Coleman, Blairmore, Bellevue, and Frank. When a village policeman in Bellevue, Alberta, spotted a suspicious-looking car speeding west toward Fernie, a phone call to Coleman could alert the Alberta Provincial Police and they would set up a trap to catch the rumrunner after he loaded up in Fernie and was heading home to Alberta. Or if the police in Coleman saw a liquor runner speeding eastward through town, they could notify the police at Blairmore in time for them to set up a roadblock there.

In theory, the police should have been able to shut down the liquor traffic because there were few side roads or trails until well east of the pass. But the people running booze also had their friends watching police movements and it became a relatively simple matter to slip through when the sadly undermanned police force was otherwise engaged or was off-duty. Then, too, the runners frequently moved in pairs. The first car, which carried no liquor, would act as a scout. If it encountered a police check-point it could warn the trailing, loaded car in time for it to reverse direction and head back to the safety of the Alberta–British Columbia border. So the entire exercise degenerated into an elaborate charade, with few arrests being made and fewer convictions registered.

This was the background of the events that unfolded on the afternoon of September 21, 1922. Emileo Picariello and his son Steve, twenty-one, had been identified heading for Fernie in two cars. A roadblock had been set up just west of Blairmore to catch them coming back. However, the elder Picariello, driving the empty pilot car, spotted the police in time to signal his son, who wheeled his car full of booze around and headed back to Fernie as fast as the car would go, while the elder Picariello blocked the road to impede the chase by the roadblockers. The frustrated police at Blairmore phoned the police at Coleman, five miles to the west, and, as young Picariello raced through that town, Constable Steve Lawson tried to stop him by firing a couple of shots in the air. When that failed, Lawson commandeered a car and gave chase, got within a couple of hundred feet of his quarry and fired another shot. It struck Steve Picariello in the hand but he kept going and Lawson was forced to give up the chase when his car blew a tire. Steve made it safely back to Fernie.

The elder Picariello went home to his hotel in Blairmore, where the report of the gun play at Coleman drifted back in a garbled version. He only knew that his son had been shot, not how badly, and he was reported to have said, within the hearing of several witnesses, that if the police had killed his son he would wipe out "every God damned policeman in the Pass." Back in Coleman, Constable Lawson finished his shift and went home to the barracks, literally a small house on a side street, and had supper with his wife and five children.

Sitting in his car in front of his hotel in Blairmore in the gathering dusk, Picariello decided he was going over to Coleman to, as his friend Florence Lassandro was later to tell the police, "get Lawson." Lassandro decided she was going with him but he objected. There was an argument and eventually Picariello acquiesced and Lassandro then "went in and got [her] gun." (The woman was later to tell the police that she wanted to accompany Picariello because she was "fond of Steve." That was as close as the record ever got to identifying her relationship with the Picariellos.)

It was approximately 7:00 P.M. when Picariello and Lassandro drew up in front of the police-barracks-cum-Dawson-home in Coleman. On the seat between them were two hand guns. One was a .32 calibre revolver and the other was a .38 calibre. Picariello had been issued permits for both. Constable Lawson by now had shed his police tunic and was in his undershirt fitting a handle to an axe when his wife called him to the front door where she said a man wanted to see him.

Lawson went out to the car. There he stood, with his arms folded, with one foot on the running board for five minutes or so talking with Picariello. Then he was seen standing on the running board wrestling with Picariello with his arms firmly wrapped around the driver's neck. Then two shots were fired, one shattered the speedometer glass and the other went through the windshield. Then two more shots were fired and Lawson fell mortally wounded in the street with a bullet in his back.

The car then turned across a vacant lot in front of the police barracks and drove off. Lawson's fifteen-year-old and six-year-old daughters had witnessed the shooting from the corner of the house. Mrs. Lawson, emerged at their screams, saw her husband lying in the street, and ran to him while a neighbour ran for the doctor. The reports of the first shots had attracted the attention of several bystanders to the shooting and all were able to recall events as witnesses at the subsequent trial.

Who was Emileo Picariello? He was an Italian immigrant who had settled in the Crowsnest Pass in the great immigration wave prior to the First World War. He was only one of the thousands of settlers from Italy and central Europe who found employment in the coal mines of Lethbridge and the Crowsnest Pass area. It was to this heavy admixture of "foreigners" in southern Alberta that the pronounced "wet" vote was attributed in the first and second

Prohibition plebiscites. And it was the same population mix that was blamed for an abundance of homebrew and bootlegging during Prohibition.

From the pre-war operation of an ice cream and peanut stand, Picariello had acquired ownership of the Alberta Hotel in Blairmore during Prohibition. During that period he had several brushes with the law for bootlegging and was reputed to have become a man of considerable wealth. He was also reputed to carry large sums of money with him, particularly when travelling from Blairmore to Fernie on liquor-buying trips. One of Alberta's widely circulated legends is that it was Picariello that the Gassof gang was looking for when they committed the famous train robbery near Sentinel in August 1920. Picariello was supposed to have been on that train enroute to Cranbrook, British Columbia with a wad of money to buy a carload of whiskey. If he was aboard he eluded the gunmen for they only got four hundred dollars and a collection of watches from the other passengers for their trouble. It was this robbery that led later to the shoot-out at the Bellevue cafe in which two policemen and a train robber were killed. But that's another story.

By 1920 Picariello was one of the Crowsnest Pass area's most prominent citizens. At Christmas time he dispensed packages filled with fruit, candy, and other goodies to the poor of the area, and entertained the children of Blairmore and Coleman at special motion picture shows. He was elected an alderman of Blairmore. Somewhere along the way, he picked up two nicknames. One was "Emperor Pic" and the other "The Bottle King." Both were widely used in the reportage of the Lawson murder.

As the story of September 21, 1922, unfolded it appeared that Picariello, unaware of the real extent of his son's injuries, had gone to the police barracks either to get even with Lawson for shooting his son or to persuade Lawson to accompany him to Fernie to bring his son home to Blairmore. In any event, Picariello and Lassandro drove from Blairmore to Coleman and up and down the front street, apparently looking for Lawson. When they failed to locate him, they drove to the police barracks.

The idea that the pair had come to Coleman to shoot Lawson was hardly strengthened by subsequent events. They were sitting in the car, both armed, as Lawson walked towards them. If Picariello had come to Coleman to "get" Lawson, Lawson, unarmed in his undershirt, made a target he could not have missed. Instead of shooting, they talked for five to ten minutes. One scenario was that Lawson refused to go to Fernie with them and that Picariello then picked up his gun and pointed it at Lawson to persuade him to change his mind. At that point Lawson leaped onto the running board and got a bear-hug around Picariello's neck and tried to wrestle the gun away from him. That was when the gun went off, hitting the speedometer and the windshield. Then Lassandro fired her gun, hitting Lawson in the back while his daughters watched.

After returning to Blairmore, Picariello did not return to his hotel but hid out for the night and the next morning took off onto the mountain above the town. Lassandro spent the night with a woman friend. Lawson died within a matter of minutes and a posse was formed to search for Picariello and Lassandro. He was located the following day and surrendered to police officers. His only words were "How is my son?" and "How is Constable Lawson?" When informed that his son suffered only a superficial wound and that Lawson was dead, he said nothing. Lassandro was picked up by other policemen and a joint charge of murder was laid.

The Lawson murder was a sensational interest-arouser all over Alberta for it touched several of Alberta's most sensitive spots. Both the accused were "foreigners," and "foreigners" suitably adjectivized was a dirty word in western Canada from the outbreak of the First World War. For example anti-German prejudice was so rampant in Calgary that a German-owned restaurant and a German-owned hotel were wrecked by rampaging mobs. It was not long before antipathy toward Germans was extended to all "foreigners." Nor did the Russian Revolution abroad or industrial strife in the coal mines at home do anything to reduce the prejudice.

In the 1916 and 1920 Prohibition plebiscites, the wet votes were concentrated in the "foreign" areas, and when the enforcement agencies raided illegal stills the operators were usually people with foreign names. So the impression spread that "foreigners" were lawbreakers in general and Prohibition lawbreakers in particular. So the accused were not only "foreigners," they were lawbreakers and bootleggers into the bargain. Before the trial, press coverage of the murder (with side excursions into the bootlegging history of the area) was so extensive that when a motion was made to move the trial from Lethbridge to Calgary, it was quickly granted.

It is doubtful that Calgarians were any less aware of the details of the murder than residents of the deep southern part of the province. Indeed, Calgary newspaper reportage was so extensive on the eve of the trial that Mr. Justice Walsh, who presided, criticized it as being in contempt of court. And so great was the public interest in the case that Judge Walsh on several occasions had to order the corridors outside the courtroom cleared of noisy crowds to permit the hearing to proceed.

In the interval, between the preliminary hearing and the trial, attention was kept focussed on the story by the search that was conducted by Picariello's lawyers for a suitable counsel to conduct the defense when the case came to trial. One story reported that J.E. Gillies of Blairmore, who had handled Picariello's legal affairs, had approached one of Canada's outstanding barristers, R.A. Bonner of Winnipeg. Unable to retain Bonner, Gillies was trying, the newspapers reported, to obtain the services of McKinley Cameron or Macleod Sinclair of Calgary. The search went on during October until the government announced that it had appointed A.A. McGillivray and Sam Helman of Calgary to prosecute the case. Gillies' search for a leader for the defense team ended in mid-November when Cameron was finally persuaded to take the case. A third member of the team was S. Herchmer of Cranbrook.

When the trial opened on November 27, John E. Brownlee, the attorney general of Alberta, appeared personally to lay the murder charge against the accused. Moreover, Brownlee remained in court for the entire five-day trial. It was the first time in Alberta history that any attorney general had taken such action. And unless they were utter dolts, the jurymen must have been persuaded by his presence that the Government of Alberta was certainly going all out to send Picariello and Lassandro to the gallows. They heard the testimony of more than thirty witnesses, a surprising half dozen of whom were actual witnesses to the shooting or identified the man and woman at the scene of the shooting. The defence called no witnesses and neither accused took the stand. Mr. Justice Walsh completed his charge to the jury shortly before four o'clock on Saturday, December 2, and the jury retired. After a supper adjournment, the court resumed at 8:00 P.M., and the jury found both accused guilty of murder as charged. Mr. Justice Walsh said he agreed they had come to the only possible verdict and sentenced Picariello and Lassandro to be hanged on February 21, 1923. They were shipped off that night to Edmonton and the Fort Saskatchewan penitentiary.

McKinley Cameron found thirty-three points in Judge Walsh's conduct of the trial and in his address to the jury on which to base an appeal. The Alberta Court of Appeal by a vote of four to one, found none of them of sufficient consequence to interfere with the jury's verdict. Mr. Justice Beck, however, dissented and, after a lengthy dissertation on the law governing manslaughter, said he would quash the conviction and order a new trial.

The Beck dissent enabled Cameron to carry his appeal to the Supreme Court of Canada. The execution was postponed pending that hearing. On April 11, the Supreme Court dismissed the appeal. The Supreme Court judgment left the fate of Picariello and Lassandro up to Prime Minister W.L. Mackenzie King and the federal Cabinet, which was bombarded with petitions and letters urging that the sentence of Lassandro be commuted to life imprisonment. The spectacle of a woman being hanged was just too much for many Canadians to contemplate. Two letters were also received urging the government to stand firm and allow the law to take its course. One was from the Lawson family in Coleman. The other was from Magistrate Emily Murphy in Edmonton. On May 2, 1923, Picariello and Lassandro were hanged.

When the Picariello-Lassandro case went to the jury that December afternoon, there could hardly have been a literate Albertan extant who would not have bet the family farm on a conviction of murder being registered. Constable Lawson had been gunned down on the street in front of his home while his daughters watched in horror. He was murdered in full view of several other witnesses. The male accused was a convicted Italian bootlegger at a time when the prejudice against all foreigners and bootleggers ran deep in the heart of the Alberta Bible Belt. The female accused was the girlfriend of his son, and the suspected mistress of Picariello himself. Constable Lawson was Scottish-born, a recently returned, decorated, war hero. And all six of the jurors were certifiable, pure-blooded Anglo-Saxons.

If ever there was a copper-rivetted, open and shut case, that was it. Yet when Cameron lost the case he never had a chance to win, he became the enduring target for a second-guessing chorus of criticism from his brother barristers. The question of whether the circumstances that prevailed in front of Lawson's house could have reduced the charge from murder to manslaughter was raised, but Cameron, inexplicably, had said that he disowned a defense on that ground. Cameron, seemingly, rested his case on the argument that Lawson's wrestling with Picariello made the shooting an act of self-defense. Some argued one way, some the other.

Where there was general agreement, however, was that Cameron had made a fatal mistake in not insisting that the two accused be tried separately. The argument here was double pronged: (a) Picariello was in a strangle-hold by Lawson when Lassandro fired the shot that killed him. It was highly unlikely that any jury would have convicted him of murder in face of that fact. (b) While Lassandro had pulled the trigger on the gun that killed Lawson, it could have been argued that this was a hysterical act of a frightened woman; and the most such a woman could ever be convicted of was manslaughter. In any event, no woman had ever been hanged in Alberta and at the time it was highly unlikely that any woman would ever be hanged in Alberta.

To the buzz of criticism of both his strategy and tactics, Cameron turned a deaf ear. But it was something that would not go away and no matter the success he later achieved, the Picariello-Lassandro case remained McKinley Cameron's albatross. It was not until many years later that Cameron volunteered the explanation in a conversation with a friend and neighbour M.M. Porter, later Mr. Justice Porter. "Trying them separately was what I

wanted to do as soon as I became involved in the defence,"
Cameron told Porter, "but Picariello would not stand for it. He said
it was he who got Florence Lassandro into the mess, and he was not
going to save himself by letting her be convicted, even of
manslaughter." Faced with such a hopeless cause, Porter said that
Cameron's only hope was to try to create as much confusion as he
could in the minds of the jurors, to remove all reasonable doubt, in
the hope that they would bring in a lesser verdict.

An Alberta *Tale of Two Cities* surely—Coleman and Blairmore—with Emileo Picariello assuming the role of Sidney Carton
in a real-life enactment of, "It is a far, far better thing that I do,
than I have ever done; a far better rest that I go to, than I have ever
known." An Alberta *Tale of Two Cities*, but with this difference:
One, the Scarlet Pimpernel, was a well-bred English figment of
Charles Dickens' imagination. The other was a real-life, illiterate
Italian immigrant placing honour above life itself.

The murder of Constable Lawson and the Picariello-Lassandro
trial added to the mounting disenchantment of Calgarians with
Prohibition. Adding impetus to the changing mood was the fact
that British Columbia was earning a million dollars a year profit
from its liquor stores, a king's ransom in the eyes of the cash-
starved provincial government. The following November the
people of Alberta went into the liquor business. On May 10, 1924,
the first government liquor stores opened for business in Calgary.
That opening put the kibosh on the practice of criminal law as a
viable professional specialty until legal aid was adopted in 1970.

Devoting oneself to the defense of criminals was never a short
cut to affluence in Calgary, and it was only during the Prohibition
era that those in that field could count on clients sufficiently
solvent to make their defense a rewarding activity. As with everything else, the names of some exceptions will come to mind—
A.A. McGillivray and A.M. Sinclair, for example. McGillivray
was reputed to have pocketed a fifty thousand dollar fee for
participation in the successful defense of Harry Bronfman in
1930, and he made a similar sum from the failed defense of I.W.C.
Solloway in the same year. Both McGillivray and Sinclair,
however, coupled civil with criminal practice and each was a
member of a leading law firm. McGillivray was the senior
member of McGillivray, Helman, Mahaffy, and Smith; while
Sinclair was counsel in Lougheed, Sinclair, McLaws, and Redman.

Those who kept their hands in such bread-and-butter aspects
of a law practice as registering mortgages, arranging leases, partnership agreements, incorporations, marriage separations, insurance claims, oil well drilling leases, and so on, survived the end of
Prohibition. Those who did not were reduced to a hand-to-mouth
existence on the miniscule fees they could extract from burglars,
brawlers, sneak thieves, and brothel operators.

It was not that the Prohibition era was a gravy train for the Calgary coterie of defense attorneys. Bootlegging there was, but it was by no means as widespread as latter-day myth-makers have contended. Over the stretch of six years, the Calgary courts might have handled fifteen or twenty liquor violations a month, many of them coupled with disorderly conduct, prostitution, and gambling. Prostitutes and gamblers could always find money for lawyers' fees. So could the farmers who tried their hands at converting washtubs and copper kettles into bootleg stills. And every now and then a wayward freight car full of booze would be seized, or a king-sized moonshine operation be stumbled upon. In those cases, the owners could be assessed a substantial fee by their defenders.

At one law society meeting Cameron spoke from the back of the room in response to a motion that would appoint a public relations man to oversee the image of the local legal profession. "Waal, now," Cameron drawled, "you fellows know that I don't know much about the law. I make my living keeping the crooks out of jail and the hookers on the street. But I do know something about public relations men. Many of my clients keep them on retainers. *My* clients call them pimps."

He had somewhere acquired a life-long aversion for the gowning codes of his profession, to say nothing of the dress codes of ordinary society. No suit of Cameron clothes had ever known a pressing iron or been touched by a dry cleaner's art. But there was nothing unkept about the Cameron mind, or unprepossessing about the Cameron courtroom presence before a jury, nor was he ever less than meticulous in his preparation for jury trials.

An essential part of Cameron's preparation for the defense of a client in a jury trial was the fine-tooth combing of the jury list. Because of the province's sparse population in the beginning, which would have made the gathering of a twelve-man jury difficult in many communities, Alberta juries were composed of six good men and true. Over the years, Cameron had put together a card index of southern Albertans eligible to serve or who had served on juries. When he was defending a case at some country point, he would always arrive in town several days before the trial to ferret out everything he could about as many men on the jury list as possible. By cataloguing salient facts about a juror's mind bent, personality, marital status, and other important facets, he would be able to decide whether he wanted such a person on the jury. As the names were called in the selection process, he could challenge the ones he did not want and they would step aside.

In the mid-1920s, Cameron was retained to defend a Lethbridge woman on a murder charge. This madam of a well-known Lethbridge brothel had conked a customer with a whiskey bottle with unseemly force during a drunken brawl in her house. The murder charge resulted and her Lethbridge solicitor retained Cameron to conduct the defense. As the jury selection proceeded, Cameron was well satisfied with those who were filling up the box. Several men he had wanted on because he felt they would be sympathetic to his client's plea of self-defense were there. And several who might have been less sympathetic had been asked to step down. When the last place on the panel was being filled, Cameron discovered to his chagrin that the prospective juror was a Mormon farmer from the Raymond area, but he had already exhausted his challenges. The Mormon took the final place.

By general reputation and common consent, the Mormons were Alberta's most straight-laced minority. They did not drink. They did not smoke, and they lived by the strict regimen of their church which interdicted most worldly pleasures. With a Mormon on the jury, Cameron felt that his prostitute-client had at least two strikes against her before the trial even began. The lawyer's challenge was to find a way during the trial to prevent two strikes evolving into three.

He apparently succeeded because, when the jury eventually returned, his client was acquitted on the grounds that the customer had been killed in self-defense. But the wait for the decision had been interminable. The case had closed around four o'clock in the afternoon and it was not until three o'clock the next morning that a verdict was reached. Cameron and J.V.H. Milvain, who at the time was an articled student in the Virtue office and was assigned to shepherd Cameron around during his stay in Lethbridge, walked back to his room in the Lethbridge Union Hotel. They agreed that the five jurors must have had a terrible time getting the Mormon to vote for acquittal.

At the hotel elevator they encountered the Mormon juror who was also staying at the hotel. They exchanged greetings and small talk about the length of the jury's deliberations. Then in a lull in the conversation, Cameron said, "I've got a bottle of Scotch in my room, would you care to come in for a nightcap?" To which, to Milvain's amazement, the Mormon replied, "I most certainly would because it was an exhausting time I've had these last twelve hours!"

Cameron got his second shock when after the second drink the juror revealed that he had been for acquittal from the beginning and the other five jurors had all voted for conviction on the first ballot! It had taken *him* almost twelve hours to change *their* collective minds!

There are Mormons and there are Mormons, just as there are Presbyterians and Presbyterians, Jews and Jews, and there are times when nothing can be as perverse as the verdict juries arrive at, or fail to arrive at, even with a meticulous selection from a well-worked on list.

Scrawny, unkempt, squeaky-voiced as he was, Cameron nevertheless was nobody to take lightly in a court room, as judges like Frank Ford quickly discovered. Judge Frank Ford was a stickler for form and was far from slow to anger, but when he was losing patience with counsel it was reflected in the rising colour of his face. From just above his collar he would redden to the top of his head, and then he would explode. It happened during the brokers' trials that followed the Wall Street crash in 1929, while Cameron was cross-examining a witness.

The witness was a chartered accountant and the evidence being given was complicated and abstruse; Cameron led him back and forth over his testimony until Ford angrily intervened: "Mr. Cameron, it seems to me that this is something that has been covered not once but *many* times!"

Cameron's response was to turn his attention silently to the papers scattered on the table before him. The books and papers that were exhibits in the case had been piled at one end of the counsel's table. Cameron's chair was at the other end of the table at the other side of the courtroom. Slowly and carefully, he gathered up all his papers into a neat pile, then he lifted them and made his way slowly to his seat.

Only then did he look at Mr. Justice Ford. "M'Lord", he said, "I have been practicing in these courts for the last forty years and when I undertake a line of cross-examination, I generally know what I am doing. But if you want me to stop, I'll stop."

Cameron knew that if Ford stopped him he would have a perfect case for a new trial. Ford, fully aware of the fact, said, "Very well, Mr. Cameron, go on."

So Cameron very slowly and carefully picked up his papers again and made his way back to the far end of the table. He then spread them out as they had been before, searched out, and picked up the particular sheet he wanted and returned his attention to the witness.

"Mr. Richardson, at the moment we were interrupted I was asking you—," he repeated the question and went on as if nothing had happened. The courtroom was electrified at the spectacle of this insignificant little man putting one of His Majesty's judges in his place.

There was, of course, no dividend in provoking a judge to anger and most counsel of the day were sensitized to Ford's quick fuse and backed off when they saw his colour rising. Others, with cases of borderline merit, did just the opposite. They would persist in provoking him further and further so they could take the case to appeal and win a new trial by showing judicial prejudice against them. Then faced with the additional costs of another trial, the disputants might become more amenable to amicable settlements.

In his own appearances before the Court of Appeal, Cameron

probably lost more cases than he won, for some of his arguments were far out in left field. During the Prohibition era the favoured sources of supply for middle-class Calgarians were not the grubby retailers of the outpourings from illicit stills, the bootleggers. Instead, it was the ordinary neighborhood drug store that supplied the booze. Throughout the whole Prohibition era doctors were permitted to prescribe whiskey to their patients for its alleged medicinal value. Most doctors confined their prescribing to their own patients. Others simply signed prescriptions by the pad and left them with a favoured pharmacist. In those cases, the pharmacists scribbled a patient's name on a prescription when he came in from the street for a bottle.

Because the drug stores were required to close at 10:00 P.M. by a City of Calgary by-law, late-nighters out on the town frequently missed that closing hour when they ran out of whiskey, so there was a temptation for pharmacists to ignore the closing hour. When they did, they were raided and fined. In 1919 one pharmacist thought he had discovered a loophole. He closed his store at 10:00 P.M. and put out the lights. At 10:05 P.M. he re-reopened for business. He was ultimately charged and convicted of violating the city by-law. Cameron, representing the druggist, appealed the conviction on the grounds that the bylaw did not contain the words "and after" following the specified closing time of 10:00 P.M. The appeal court dismissed the appeal, with Justice Charles Stuart commenting, "No one but a lawyer, I mean a person trained in legal technicalities, such as a judge or a lawyer, would ever think of imputing such a meaning to the bylaw."

Cameron was indeed a great one for technicalities. Very seldom did he ever carry a case to appeal on a single point of law. Usually, he would have four or five separate points, counting on the scattershot technique of winning on one if the other points failed. His style was best described by Mr. Justice Walsh in the following comment:

This appeal upon four of the five grounds presented to us in support of it, affords an excellent illustration of a class of cases with which the time of this Court is, in my opinion, too often wasted. The appellant has been convicted of a criminal offence. The object of his appeal is to free himself from the conviction and relieve himself from the punishment imposed upon him under it. The question of his guilt or innocence of this offence is not in any sense involved in any of these four grounds. The question of the justice or injustice of this conviction, because of any of the things complained of in them, is not made a matter of argument before us for there is no contention that any of them prejudiced in the slightest degree the fairness of his trial. *What is before us is as large and varied a collection of technicalities as an ingenious counsel by a vigorous but careful application of a legal fine tooth comb to the proceedings in the Court below has been able to get together out of them* (author's italics). These things have drifted into the trial of this man and simply because they are there and not because of any harm that they have done to him or anyone else it is urged that he must go unpunished of the offence of which he has been adjudged guilty.

The 10:00 P.M. closing case was as trivial a case as ever got before the Court of Appeal. But two years earlier, in another seemingly trivial appeal, Cameron was involved in what was truly a landmark decision in the field of women's rights, a decision, incidentally, which preceded the famous Persons case by more than a decade. This was the case of Lizzie Cyr who was convicted of vagrancy by Magistrate Alice Jamieson in the Calgary Police Court and sentenced to six months at hard labour in the Lethbridge jail.

The widow of one of the CPR's western executives, Mrs. Jamieson was appointed police magistrate in Calgary in December 1916. A Calgary resident since 1902, she was one of the founders of the Local Council of Women and was concluding her sixth term as president of that organization at the time of her appointment. In that capacity, she had led several delegations of southern Alberta women to Edmonton to press for such social reforms as a Dower Act and votes for women. Her appointment as police magistrate came two years after she had been appointed the first child and family court magistrate in Calgary. She was Calgary police magistrate until the Alberta government abolished the position as an economy measure during the depression.

Alice Jamieson in Calgary and Emily Murphy in Edmonton were appointed police magistrates under the Act Respecting Police Magistrates and Justices of the Peace, 1906. Never one to let any judge inhibit him, let alone the leading Calgary feminist of her time, McKinley Cameron challenged Magistrate Jamieson's conviction of Lizzie Cyr on the grounds that, as the Act appointing the woman did not specifically authorize the appointment of women to the positions, the appointments were illegal under British Common Law as it existed in 1870 when the Dominion of Canada was established.

While women had indeed held many public offices in England from the time of the first Queen Elizabeth onward, many were hereditary, and in most of the other cases, the appointing statute specifically qualified the women for the post. As late as 1889, the British courts adhered to the position that by the Common Law of England, women were not in general deemed capable of exercising public function. It was upon this point that Cameron based his case which was argued before the Appellate Court of Alberta.

In rendering the unanimous judgment of this court, which

came barely a year after the women of Alberta obtained the franchise for the first time, Judge Charles Stuart wrote:

> The courts of this Province are not in every case to be held strictly bound by the decisions of the English courts as to the state of the common law of England in 1870. We are at liberty to take cognizance of the different conditions here, not merely different physical conditions, but the general conditions of our public affairs and the general attitude of the community in regard to the particular matters in question. I therefore hold that at this time in our presently existing conditions there is at common law, no legal disqualification for holding public office in the government of the country arising from any distinction of sex. And in so doing I am strongly of the opinion that we are returning to the more enlightened and liberal view of the Middle Ages in England and passing over the narrower and more hardened view which possibly, by the middle of the Nineteenth Century, had gained ascendance in England.

It would be twelve years before the Privy Council in London would catch up with the views of Mr. Justice Stuart and define Canadian women as "persons" eligible for appointment to the Canadian Senate and, per corollary, to all other positions of government.

Judge Stuart's decision in the Cyr case came just a year after he wrote the majority decision of the Appeal Court on another of McKinley Cameron's cases. This time Cameron was on the winning side. It was a case of sedition which pinpointed the height to which wartime hysteria had soared in western Canada during the First World War.

It so happened that Calgary was one of the centres of anti-German discrimination that swept Alberta during the First World War. One reason may have been that the Germans constituted a minority of perhaps three thousand in the city's population. Prior to the war they had been welcomed as highly-esteemed settlers. As the news from the war fronts went from bad to worse to awful, that status also dropped sharply as Anglo-Saxon Canadians tended to identify the local Germans with the Germans killing Canadians with poison gas.

On the other hand, the Germans, along with more than a few recent immigrants from the United States, found little justification for Canadians to be fighting in a European war on the other side of the globe. And if the Germans maintained certain gut loyalties for the homeland they had so recently departed, British Canadians became more British than the British.

Unfortunately, all Germans were tarred with the same brush and, when it came to discrimination, "German" was very loosely defined. Thus the Prussia-born but German-hating Polish Canadians, were defined as "Germans" for the purpose of firing them off the city payroll. Also fired at the same time was the city hall telephone operator who was the daughter of a German-born Calgarian who had served with the British army in the South African War.

In such an atmosphere, super-patriotic Calgarians had their antennas stretched far out to catch what they deemed to be the unpatriotic mouthings of their neighbors. When they did, they reported the utterances to the police which resulted in the laying of charges of sedition and worse. Which brings us to the story of Arthur F. Trainor.

Trainor was a resident of the town of Strathmore, thirty miles east of Calgary and was shopping in the local drug store when word reached the town of the sinking of the *Lusitania* by German submarines in May 1915. Edward Lambert, the pharmacist, was sitting at his desk when his wife came in with the news that the liner had been sunk with a great loss of life. Trainor's reaction was to laugh and say, "Good, good, so they got her at last!" Among Mr. Lambert, Mrs. Lambert, and Joyce Pearcy, who ran the government telephone switchboard in the store, there was some disagreement about Trainor's exact words. At his trial he denied having laughed or having said "good, good." In any event, an argument broke out between Trainor and Lambert, and it quickly developed that Trainor had grave doubts about the nobility of the British cause. In his view, "war was war" and, as "the British were killing German women and children through their food blockade, the Germans had a right to retaliate by sinking British ships." Trainor was charged with "uttering seditious words with intent to raise disaffection amongst His Majesty's subjects or to promote feelings of ill-will or hostility between different classes of His Majesty's subjects."

The pertinent section of Judge Stuart's decision (concurred in by Judge Beck with dissent by Judge Walsh):

> I think it is about time that the distinction between entertaining disloyal and unpatriotic sentiments and giving utterance to them in a chance expression, on the one hand, and the crime of uttering seditious words, on the other, should be adverted to. There was a long struggle in British legal history to establish the righteous principle that to convict of treason you must prove some overt act. So with sedition, it is not the disloyalty of the heart that the law forbids. Neither is it the utterance of a word or two which merely reveal the existence of such disloyalty that the law can punish under the name of sedition. It is the utterance of words which are expressive of an intention 'to bring into hatred or contempt, or to excite disaffection against the person of His Majesty or the government and constitution of the country, to excite people to attempt otherwise than by lawful means the

alteration of any matter in the state by law established, to raise discontent and disaffection among His Majesty's subjects.' These are the words of the English draft code and the Commissioners said it was as near a definition of the law as they could make.

What the Accused said here amounted in my opinion, first, to the utterance of two words of satisfaction or delight i.e., 'That's good', at the news of the sinking of the Lusitania, second, to an argument that that act was justified because England was killing women and children by trying to starve Germany, i.e. by the blockade. This latter was uttered after Lambert had started the argument owing to the use of the first expression. I can find nothing in his words which was intended as a condemnation of England for applying the blockade with the consequences mentioned. What he was saying was that 'war was war' that any means at all were justified.

For myself I imagine the purpose of the blockade is to prevent food supplies from reaching Germany and I think if that results in killing women and children in Germany it is perfectly justifiable and proper. I cannot find that the accused denied that. Rather I think he approved of it. The gist of the complaint against him is that having been led by Lambert into a discussion of what is and what is not justifiable in carrying on war he used words which indicated that he thought Germany was justified in sinking the Lusitania. Now, I detest such an opinion as strongly as any one, but my present duty is to decide the law, not express my moral or patriotic sentiments.

For myself I am unable to see how the expression of such views, mistaken and detestable though they are, upon the proper limitations of the laws of war was calculated, or expressive of an intention, either to promote feelings of ill-will and hostility between different classes of His Majesty's subjects or to incite disaffection against His Majesty's Government. With regard to the first, I think what the rule means is certain broad general classes of people, e.g. French Canadians and English Canadians, Catholics and Protestants, foreign born subjects and natural born subjects and other such that could be mentioned. I do not think it means merely stirring up hatred and hostility against the person who utters the words.

Then, were the words calculated or intended to create disaffection and discontent among His Majesty's subjects? I am bound to say that I cannot understand how a declaration of an opinion in an argument in a country store that Germany was justified, as a measure of war, in sinking the Lusitania, detestable though the opinion is in the hearts of all of us, can be said to have been calculated or expressive of an intention, to stir up discontent or disaffection among His Majesty's subjects. It is of course running counter to the opinion of everyone who has any moral instinct at all, but why should the expression of an erroneous and even detestable opinion on the proper limits of civilized warfare be calculated, or expressive of an intention, to raise discontent and disaffection?

In deciding the law of sedition I do not think we should merely say 'This fellow is evidently a German sympathizer so we will clap him in jail'. We must show that he has broken the law, as properly interpreted, before we can do that.

So also with regard to the expression of joy over the sinking of the Lusitania. I am clearly of opinion that the words were neither calculated in themselves nor expressive of an intention to promote feelings of ill-will and hostility between different classes of His Majesty's subjects. Certainly we cannot take the accused as himself constituting a whole class of His Majesty's subjects and I am unable to conceive how the words could possibly be calculated or expressive of an intention to stir up ill-will or hostility between any two classes of people. Then, were they calculated or expressive of an intention to arouse discontent and disaffection? After giving the matter my best, and, I hope, most dispassionate consideration, I find myself unable to say that they were.

*Crankshaw* in his notes to *The Criminal Code* mentions only four cases, between 1795 and the present time, of prosecution for seditious words, and they were all cases of public meetings and addresses. He says after speaking at length of seditious libel 'with regard to *seditious words* they have *on some few occasions*, been made the subject of prosecution.' *There have been more prosecutions for seditious words in Alberta in the past two years than in all the history of England for over a hundred years and England has had numerous and critical wars in that time*. The Napoleonic crisis occurred during that period. I do not wish to say anything which would repress the patriotic zeal of our public officials, but we all have great confidence in the stability and safety of our institutions and of the certain victory of our cause. *In the circumstances, I think something is due to the dignity of the law and that the Courts should not, unless in cases of gravity and danger, be asked to spend their time scrutinizing with undue particularity the foolish talk of men in bar rooms and shops or a word or two evidently blurted out there impulsively and with no apparent deliberate purpose*. (Authors italics)

Typical of the state of affairs that Justice Stuart was deploring was the case of *Rex* v. *Cohen*. George Cohen operated a second-hand furniture store in Riverside, across the street from a grocery store operated by one Wiggins. On April 28, 1915, Wiggins crossed the street to the cigar stand in the local poolroom to get some tobacco. Lolling against the stand was Cohen reading a report in a newspaper of the defeat of the Canadians at the battle of Langemarck. Cohen, who claimed to have been a member of the officer's corps of the German army before coming to Canada, was exulting in the German victory. When Wiggins objected, he said, "You are slaves, you have to do what King George and Kitchener tell you." As Canadians had no business in the war, he said, they deserved anything they got including poison gas. The argument went on from there. Nobody but Wiggins heard anything that Cohen said. Save for a couple of pool players, the room was empty. Nevertheless, on the basis of Wiggins' testimony Cohen was convicted of "seditious intent," and the conviction was confirmed by justices Scott, Stuart, and Beck on appeal.

Mr. Justice Stuart's judgment six months later, in the Trainor case went, of course, to the very heart of the problem of safeguarding freedom of speech in wartime. It was a problem that would arise again and again in extreme form in the United States following that country's entry into the war and the enactment of Espionage Acts of 1917 and 1918. In the United States Supreme Court decision of 1919, written by Justice Oliver Wendell Holmes, it said: "The question in every case is whether the words used are used in such circumstances and are of such nature as to create a clear and present danger that will bring about the substantive evils that Congress has a right to prevent."

The "clear and present danger" argument which justices Holmes and Brandeis were to use again and again in the years that followed assured them a prominent place in the pantheon of American civil libertarians. Judge Stuart's enunciation of the same principle in different words for the Alberta Court of Appeal two years before were written on the wind.

But, it is important to emphasize, if it had not been for McKinley Cameron, Justice Charles Stuart would never have had the opportunity of writing his own "clear and present danger" judgment. And it was McKinley Cameron's automatic response to a lower court conviction that gave Stuart the opportunity to pioneer the way for women's liberation.

# Chapter Five

# The Poet Laureate of the Calgary Bar— Carried Out but Never Carried In

There may be arguments over which was the most exciting trial in the annals of the Calgary bar; whether for example, the Picariello-Lassandro murder case or the conscription confrontation of 1918 had better claim to the title. But there can never be a question as to the dullest trial in Calgary, perhaps even Canadian, history. This had to be the bakeries combine conspiracy trial of 1950–1951. The crowning irony is that this gold standard of monumental tedium was also the swan song of the career of one of the brightest, truly Renaissance men of the southern Alberta Bar. He was Stewart Blanchard, the agent of the attorney general, and the man who led the prosecution force that carried the case to its successful conclusion.

The bakeries conspiracy case derived from the article of faith of democratic governments that free enterprisers are not to be trusted. Businessmen may extol the virtues of price competition as the only measure of value. They may become downright boisterous in their contention that price competition benefits the consumers and that they worship competition. But, the government believes, if left to their own devices, if no one is watching, few businessmen can resist the temptation to join forces to fix prices, divide up markets and generally combine to put it to the consumers. So, believing this, Canada has had legislation on the books to combat combinations in restraint of trade and price fixing since 1889. (The United States had since 1890.)

One of the problems of the post-war government in Canada was that during the Second World War it had been forced to moth ball its Combines Investigation Act. There developed in wartime such a shortage of everything and an overweaning demand for everything that the free-enterprisers' beloved law of supply and demand had to be repealed. Business firms, indeed, were encouraged by the Wartime Prices and Trade Board to combine their efforts to "rationalize" production and distribution. That meant dividing up market areas between previous competitors, and, most of all, it meant fixing prices. Once the war was over, the government had to reconvert the Canadian economy to the *status quo ante*. In short, it had to persuade the free enterprisers to unlearn everything they had learned about price fixing during five years of war and return to competing with each other for markets, and with prices. By 1947 the officials of the combines branch were becoming suspicious that too many businesses were dragging their feet. It launched an investigation of the bakery business in western Canada.

A special investigator, H. Carl Goldenberg of Montreal, in 1948 recommended that McGavins Limited, Canadian Bakeries Limited, and Weston Bread and Cake (Canada) Limited be prosecuted for combining in restraint of trade in violation of the Combines Investigation Act. The three companies dominated the bakery business in Winnipeg, Calgary, Edmonton, and Vancouver. Eventually the government accepted Goldenberg's advice, and on January 23, 1950, Stewart Blanchard, the Calgary agent for the attorney general of Alberta, laid the charges before Magistrate G.H. Rose in city police court. Magistrate Rose issued summonses against the companies.

As the battle lines were drawn, the government appointed A.L. Smith to assist Blanchard. Harry Nolan of Calgary, S. Bruce Smith of Edmonton, and C.W. Brazier of Vancouver appeared for Canadian Bakeries, McGavins, and Westons, respectively.

In the preliminary investigation of the companies, the authorities carted away truck loads of documents, statements, intercompany correspondence, and intra-company memoranda. After the preliminary winnowing by the combines branch, this material had to be re-sorted, collated, and catalogued for presentation to the court. Only then could a preliminary hearing be held. The hearing lasted for thirteen days before Magistrate Rose and concluded on April 5, 1950. When the trial itself opened before Mr. Justice Boyd McBride, on May 8, it set off what was undoubtedly a Canadian record for technical objections and enforced adjournments. The defense counsel objected to the way the charges were laid, to the charges themselves, to the right of Blanchard to lay the charges. They demanded specific details of charges and adjournments to assess the material.

It was small wonder that the hearing dragged itself out to a Canadian record of ninety-nine days, stretched across twenty-four weeks, during which 636 exhibits were marked for presentation and forty Crown witnesses were called to testify. The sheer volume of the material presented by itself would have made for a lengthy trial. But the time frame was at least doubled by the fact that Mr. Justice Boyd McBride was presiding. Not the least obtuse of Alberta's trial judges, Judge McBride was noted for keeping voluminous notes, audibly scratched with an old-fashioned steel pen. More noted for an inordinate interest in the lascivious details of divorce action adultery than for his knowledge of corporate derring-do, Judge McBride contributed in no small way to the elongation of proceedings. But in the end, after thinking about it for three months, Judge McBride found the companies guilty as charged and fined them ten thousand dollars apiece.

In a real sense, Stewart Blanchard was as much out of his element at the bakery combine trial as Judge McBride. A consummate actor, Blanchard had a special talent for recognizing a potentially dramatic courtroom situation, and of playing it for all it was worth. Endless involvement with corporate financial statements and corporate minutes and correspondence was not Blanchard's piece of cake. A dyed-in-grease-paint theatre buff and founder of the Medicine Hat Little Theatre movement, Blanchard was hopelessly involved with documentation in this trial. To keep the courtroom from being buried in a blizzard of paper, a truck load of filing cabinets was whistled up and stacked at the rear of the courtroom. The services of L.J. Laycraft, later Mr. Justice Laycraft, were retained as filing cabinet custodian responsible for ferreting out the appropriate file whenever it was called for by the cross-examining barristers. It was Blanchard's job to examine or cross-examine witnesses interminably over the contents of the filing cabinets. It would have been painful enough a process for any ordinary practitioner, never mind a man of Blanchard's background. Moreover, at the time of the trial, Blanchard was suffering from a severe circulatory trauma in his lower legs. It was an affliction that would result, soon afterward, in the amputation of both legs. (Because of his physical disability, Blanchard was regularly granted the privilege of conducting his proceedings while sitting at the counsel table. He just as regularly declined the favour and insisted upon standing.)

Stewart Blanchard was born in Winnipeg in 1885 into a family that could afford to ship him off to Upper Canada College and McGill University for his education. Then, when he returned to Winnipeg and was called to the bar in 1908 he was appointed assistant city solicitor, a post he held until 1912 when he was lured to Medicine Hat by Lorne Laidlaw.

These were truly Winnipeg's vintage years. Not only was it savouring the greatest commercial, industrial, and population boom in Canadian history, it was undergoing a cultural explosion of sorts as well. Winnipeggers had had access to live theatre and opera from the late 1880s when the Winnipeg Theatre was built. Then with the onset of the population influx with the turn of the century, the Orpheum and Pantages theatres brought additional live theatre facilities to the city. The icing on the cake was provided with the opening of the super-magnificent Walker Theatre in 1908. With its plush seats, crystal chandeliers, silk-brocaded boxes, and lavishly gilded decor it was unexcelled in Canada—or in New York or London for that matter.

Winnipeg became a port of call for the grand opera, light opera, and dramatic companies then touring the main centres of North America. Gilbert and Sullivan were then at the peak of their popularity and the D'Oyly Carte Opera Company brought its full repertoire to the Walker stage. Between grand opera and light opera there was the cream of the New York and London dramatic stage to be savoured: everything from Dracula to Peter Pan, and even Ben Hur—complete with chariot races. Everybody who was anybody on the world stage was in and out of Winnipeg in those days. Martin-Harvey, Forbes Robertson, Pavlova, Mrs. Fiske, the Gish Sisters, Sarah Bernhardt, De Wolfe Hopper, Francis X. Bushman—all trod the Winnipeg boards enroute from Minneapolis to Vancouver.

This was the environment in which Stewart Blanchard grew up, an environment highly conducive to turning young law students into stage-struck thespians. In Blanchard's case it was an incurable addiction to Gilbert and Sullivan's eminently memorable, singable, and whistleable tunes and ditties. But it was even deeper than that. Blanchard became a devotee of the stage in all its aspects—acting, directing, producing, and playwriting. The depth of his interest may be measured by the fact that in later life he thought nothing of making a train trip to Winnipeg from Calgary to catch a performance of the Royal Winnipeg Ballet.

Medicine Hat, the city to which Blanchard moved in 1912, had a population just over six thousand and was then much too small to attract the kind of theatrical fare on which Blanchard had feasted in Winnipeg. But it did have an opera house, a fact that kept diverting Blanchard's attention from the main chance—getting his law practice established. If a professional theatre was impossible, why not an amateur theatre? Why not a Medicine Hat amateur light opera company? Why not, indeed?

Like as not, the clients of Blanchard's fledging legal practice, as interviews were being wound up, would be greeted by this question: "By the way, what would you think of organizing a light opera company in Medicine Hat to put on some Gilbert and Sullivan?" Surprisingly enough, he got enough affirmative responses to encourage him to keep asking.

Incredibly, within a year of his arrival, he not only had the society organized but had a cast of twenty rehearsing for its first production, *Pirates of Penzance*, which had a two-evening run in March 1914. Blanchard was the first president of the society, chairman of its executive committee, and producer of the show. In December 1914, it staged *The Mikado* and this time Blanchard could not resist also taking a part in the production. He was Ko-Ko.

The following March 1915, when he staged *The Chimes of Normandy* Blanchard stayed out of the production. But when the company returned to Gilbert and Sullivan in *The Gondoliers*, he played the part of the Duke of Plaza-Toro. In 1919, in the production of *San Toy*, he cast himself in the role of Li. Thereafter for the rest of the society's life in the 1920s Blanchard was active in its operation.

But the light opera society could not itself fill Blanchard's passion for theatre. He was active in amateur theatrical productions and wrote as well as produced one-act plays. And then, in 1930, he became the first president of the Medicine Hat Little Theatre Company and remained active in its operation until he moved to Calgary in 1937.

While the light opera company languished during the depression, the little theatre movement, thanks to the Dominion drama festivals, became quite active. In the first Alberta regional festival in 1930, Blanchard's Medicine Hat company won first prize. The little theatre provided Blanchard with an outlet for his play-writing talent; several of his one-act plays were performed there. None of the texts of these dramaturgical efforts survive but what does, fortunately, is a piece of his epic poetry from the 1920s.

The 1920s were the winding-down years of ethnic humour. The minstrel shows were dying out, but black-faced comedians were still seen on the vaudeville circuits, along with caricature Irishmen and Scots. Jew-Irishman-Scotsman jokes lightened the tone of after-dinner speeches. Dialect jokes were being told everywhere and were most popular, indeed, within the ethnic groups themselves. It took a Scot to tell a Scottish joke, a Jew to tell a Jewish joke, and an Italian to tell an Italian joke. And they did, because only they could give a dialect joke the authentic touch that made it work.

Blanchard was a master of dialect humour and his classic piece of Scottish humour, recited in a deep Scot's accent, was *McGregor's Lament*. Here it is:

The crops were a failure roun' Medicine Hat
An' a frown on the broo' o' McGregor there sat
He'd ploughed an' he'd harrowed, an' cared for his stock
But the grain withered up an' he lost half his flock.

So when August was waning an' frost filled the air
McGregor was fuming an' tearing his hair,
"Got dammit an' take it, the son o' a butch
I am thinking this luck is a hell o' a touch."

Wi' quaint heilan currse worrds he cursed up an' doon,
Then hitched up his Fordie an' drove into toon.

Arrived in the City, oor ill-tempered frien'
Sought solace an' drins wi' some lads that he kenned
An' quickly the clouds were a' wafted away
An' McGregor was singing wi' spirits fu' gay.

He sang in the tenor; he sang in the base
Tho' the notes that he took were aft sait oot o' place
Till at last wi' a hoot, oot they started tae seek
The hotel de Patsy, just over the creek.

In amorous pastimes the nicht quickly passed,
To the Club oor friends were returning at last
An' sae sick looked the party frae whuskey an' beer
That tae Mac's fertile brain there was born an idea.

Since farmin's a failure an' youth will be fules
What wi' ruining their stomachs an' abusin' their tules
I'll fix a wee place where for a moderate fee
A man can rest quiet an' get over a spree.

Sae back to the farm went McGregor fu' lick
Tae make preparations tae take care for the sick
He dismanteled his mirror and hung in its place
A Douche bag wi' frills o' the best Brussels lace.

He had bottles o' poisons, syringes an' pills
O' a nature tae cure a' unearthreall ills.
An' when a' was finished in elegant style
He awaited his patients wi' satisfied smile.

But just when his joy at his scheme was complete
A shiver passed thru him frae his crown ta his feet
The smile frae his face seemed tae wither an' shrink
As a burning sensation he felt in his dink.

"Good faix, hoot awa' mon, what de'ils work's this"
said McGregor as he lifted his kiltie tae piss
"Mon crackie, Got dammit, noo isn't this hell
The very first patient I've git is masel'!"

Over the years *McGregor's Lament* became one of the most recited poems in southern Alberta. Percy Gayner, who had been Blanchard's co-conspirator in the organization of the Medicine Hat opera, had been involved with "The Dumbells," a group of soldier entertainers who toured Canada after the First World War. He moved to Lethbridge late in the 1920s and became involved in the insurance business. Gayner was in great demand as an after-dinner speaker at service clubs and lodge celebrations all over the south country. His tour de force was always the recitation of *McGregor's Lament*. By the time Blanchard reached Calgary in 1937, his classic had already gone the rounds many times. But no bar association dinner was considered complete without *McGregor's Lament* being recalled sometime during the program.

With the completion of the bakery combine case, Stewart Blanchard decided there had to be an easier way of making a living. The $3,000 retainer that went with the job had been very much worth having in the Depression of 1939. But the $5,200 that went with a particular appointment in the oil-boom year of 1951, was not. Blanchard had been appointed agent for the attorney general in Calgary when A.L. Smith resigned to enter politics in 1939. Smith, who had held the appointment under both the UFA and Social Credit governments for over twenty years, had been receiving a stipend of $4,500. That retainer was cut to $3,000 when Blanchard took over but was raised to $4,500 when the wartime wages ceilings were abolished in 1946. By the date of his retirement in February of 1952 the stipend was up to $5,200 and when L.A. Justason, Blanchard's partner for the previous four years, was appointed in 1952 it was raised to $6,000.

Instead of retiring from the legal practice as well as from the government agency after the amputation of his legs, Blanchard acquired a wheel chair and went back into practice as head of the firm of Blanchard, Iredale, Holland, and McDill.

He was, however, forced to forego the high jinx of bar association ceremonial dinners where his presence was sorely missed. Shortly before his death in 1959, a group of his fellow lawyers, headed by L.A. Justason, determined to get him to a particular bar association dinner. They approached him with the offer to carry him into the Palliser Hotel for the occasion.

"The hell with that," said Blanchard, "I've been carried out of those dinners too often in my lifetime ever to be carried *into* one!"

# Chapter Six

# I.W.C. Solloway—
# From Hero to Bum
# in a Month and a Half

He who sells what isn't his'n
Must buy it back, or go to pris'n.

Whether I.W.C. Solloway ever heard of that ancient adage of the Chicago wheat pit is lost to history. Certainly he had sold what wasn't his'n to the tune of millions of shares of Canadian oil and mining stock. But if he had been faced with the quotation he might well have replied, "Don't look at me! I never sold a share I did not buy back! And usually at a very substantial profit! But, anyway, that quotation has no relevance to me because despite the fact that I bought back every share I ever sold short, I still went to jail!"

Solloway might also have pointed out that during his Marco Polo-ish journey through the Canadian courts, our legal system made mincemeat of the principle that no person can be placed in jeopardy twice for the same, or substantially the same, cause. The principle was later defined by Mr. Justice Rand in *Cullen* v. *The King*:

> The reasons underlying that principle are grounded in deep social instincts. It is the supreme invasion of the rights of an individual to subject him by the physical power of the community to a test which may mean the loss of his liberty or his life; and there is a basic repugnance against the repeated exercise of that power on the same facts unless for strong reasons of public policy (1) (1949), 94 C.C.C. 337 S.C.C. p. 347.

The saga of I.W.C. Solloway began in Toronto in February 1926, when Solloway and his partner, Harvey Mills, opened the

office of the newly formed mining stockbrokerage firm of Solloway, Mills, and Company. It ended in June 1930, when Solloway
closed the twenty-five offices the company operated across
Canada, laid off his one thousand five hundred employees and
retired from the brokerage business. The demise was triggered by
the decision on January 10, 1930, by Premier J.E. Brownlee of
Alberta, to prosecute Solloway and Mills personally on five
charges of conspiracy. Soon after, prosecutions on the same
grounds were launched in Toronto and Vancouver.

Although the Wall Street crash of October 1929 had shaken the
financial markets of the world almost three months before, the
real depression was still a couple of years away. Nevertheless, the
Solloway and Mills prosecution might well be described as a major
unemployment relief project for the Alberta, British Columbia,
and Ontario legal professions. Premier Brownlee reached out into
the private sector for three of the outstanding criminal lawyers of
the province to conduct case for the prosecution. Heading his
team was A.L. Smith, McKinley Cameron, A.M. Sinclair. J.J.
Frawley, from the attorney general's department, rounded out the
team. Hardly less imposing was the defense team of A.A. McGillivray and Sam Helman of Calgary, H.H. Parlee of Edmonton, and
W.B. Farris, a celebrated member of the Vancouver Bar.

There was an interesting juxtapositioning of lawyers to be
noted in the assembling of these groups. Smith, Cameron, and
Sinclair were all better known as defense counsel than prosecutors. McGillivray, on the other hand, had headed the prosecuting
teams in the Picariello and the Carbon murder cases.

The charge against Solloway and Mills was, in street jargon,
that they had been running a string of "bucket shops" across
Canada; that they had "gone short" on stocks their customers
were buying, charging their customers commission for purchases
made through stock exchanges when in fact, purchases had not
been made. The charges were laid under the common law and the
criminal code. The common law charge read:

> Isaac W.C. Solloway, of Toronto, Ontario, between the first day of
> May 1928 and the 31st day of December, 1929, at Calgary, in the
> Province of Alberta, did by diverse subtle means and devices, and
> by deceit, falsehood and other fraudulent means, conspire with
> Harvey M. Mills, Harold Hendrickson, L.L. Masson and diverse
> other persons to injure and civil wrong do to members of the
> public frequenting the establishment of the Solloway Mills Co.
> Ltd., in the City of Calgary for the purpose of purchasing stocks,
> contrary to the peace of our Sovereign Lord the King, his Crown
> and dignity.

It was curiously appropriate that the indictment of Solloway
and Mills should be couched in such archaic language because that

word "archaic" perfectly described the state of Canadian resources financing in the 1920s, as well as the regulatory machinery that was in place to protect the interests of the investors. During the 1920s a feverish interest had been stirred up in the development of gold, silver, and base metal prospects in Quebec, Ontario, Manitoba, and British Columbia, and in the petroleum and natural gas resources of Alberta. But in all areas, far too great a proportion of the money raised from the public was siphoned away by the promoters before it reached the resources being developed. Laws to prevent such depredation were non-existent. The only law that protected Canadian investors was the unwritten law of *caveat emptor*, let the buyer beware.

Though oil was discovered in Turner Valley in 1914, oil company promotion did not really get into high gear until after the Royalite Number 4 well blew in and caught fire in 1924. By that time, the mining company promotion technique had been fine-tuned to the functional perfection of a three-step waltz.

The first step was to acquire a group of mining claims in the most recently discovered "hot" prospecting area of the north for a few thousand dollars in cash and shares in a company to be formed. That company would have a capitalization of three million shares of which one million would go to the promoters for the property. A block of one million shares would then be offered to the public at thirty cents a share, fifteen cents net to the company and fifteen cents commission to the promoters. High-pressure salesmen would then dust off their "sucker lists" and start selling.

Once a few thousand shares were sold, the stock would be listed on the Standard Stock and Mining Exchange of Toronto. Then the promoters would start trading the shares amongst themselves. This feverish activity in the stock, coupled with the rumours of favourable strikes on or near the property, would bring the public into the market and the price of the shares would move steadily higher. As this happened, the promoters would feed their vendor shares into the market. When the public demand eased, or when the promoters had liquidated their holdings, the volume of trading would diminish and the price of the stock would sink back, usually to a point below what it had been when the churning started.

The wonder is that such a system, based on the sandbagging of the gullible by the larcenous, saw the actual development of oil, gold, silver, and base metal production in Canada. Indeed, some of the successful developments began as outright promotions and came to fruition only after going through several reorganizations. But it was the existence of the successes—Royalite Oil in Alberta, and Lake Shore, Wright Hargraves, and Dome Mines in Ontario—

that provided the glow that attracted the unwary moths to the promotional flame.

Essentially, this was how the mining industries of Ontario, Quebec, and British Columbia were developed in the 1920s. It was a system with two near-fatal flaws: (1) It diverted far too great a proportion of the money the public invested into the hands of the brokers instead of into the mining property development; and (2) it delayed unconscionably the time it took to bring a prospect into production. It was not uncommon for a mining prospect to be reorganized and refinanced half a dozen times before the first ton of ore was mined. With each reorganization the value of the publicly held shares was drastically reduced.

And this, roughly, was the way the oil wells of Turner Valley were financed in the 1920s. The stock salesmen would mount a promotional campaign and sell enough stock to put a drilling crew to work. It would go on working as long as the stock kept selling. When the promoters ran out of money, drilling stopped until more stock could be sold.

This then was the way Canada's national resources were being financed in 1926 when I.W.C. Solloway emerged from the north woods of Ontario to get into the mining stockbrokerage business in Toronto. Things were quite brisk in the mining market that summer, and Solloway and Mills were soon doing a thriving business on the Standard Stock and Mining Exchange. There was, they discovered, an important difference between the mining shares traded on the mining exchange and the shares of corporations traded on the Montreal and Toronto stock exchanges. And the difference profoundly affected the volume of business a brokerage firm could expect to do.

The bulk of the trading in the shares of Canadian industrial and commercial companies was done by customers trading on margin. They could deposit a quarter or a third of the value of the shares they wanted to buy and the brokers would borrow the balance on "call loans" from the chartered banks. If the price of the stock held by an investor rose, he might use his "paper profits" to purchase additional shares on margin with additional money borrowed by the broker from the bank.

The arithmetic worked like this: the investor put up $1,000 and bought 1,000 shares of VBN Company at $3 a share on 30 per cent margin. If the stock market price of VBN rose to $4 a share, the investor's equity in the transaction would rise from $1,000 to $2,000. With that much equity the investor could increase his holdings of VBN Company to 1,650 shares on a 30 per cent margin, and the broker would borrow the difference from the banks. That was what was happening on the stock markets of the world in the 1920s. As a result of margin trading, the volume of stocks traded in Toronto, Montreal, and New York doubled and redoubled as the prices pushed ever higher during the 1920s.

The refusal of the banks to lend money to brokers on the security of mining shares prevented margin trading from developing on the Standard Stock and Mining Exchange—until Solloway came into the picture. The attitude of the chartered banks was, of course, eminently sensible. The fluctuations in prices of mining shares were so violent that the value of the securities pledged as collateral for loans could disappear almost overnight on the receipt of bad news from the property. Moreover there was no way for the banks to determine whether the share values listed on the exchange were the result of genuine public demand for the shares, or the result of promoters churning up a market without much public participation.

It was only after Solloway and the other mining stockbrokers developed their own gimmick that margin trading in mining stock equalled, and soon far exceeded, that in industrial shares. The mining brokers could not, of course, afford to finance their customers' purchases of shares on margin. But they could and did go into the stock exchange and sell an equal number of shares to the number the customer had bought on margin. If they had simply taken the customer's margin money and credited him with one hundred shares of stock on their books, that would have been "bucketing" and was against the law. But by putting both buy and sell orders through a stock exchange, they thought they had found a way around the law. They had not, of course, because it is illegal to do something indirectly that is illegal to do directly.

To embroider their disguise further, the brokers like Solloway adopted a rather elaborate charade. All brokerage houses employed personnel called "floor traders" who worked on the trading floor of the stock exchanges. Orders received from customers in the brokerage offices were telephoned to these employees to execute. In addition, the brokers also employed independent brokers who traded on the floor of the exchanges. They were known as "jitney" brokers because they earned a very small fee for executing trades on behalf of the member brokers.

While the main-office order clerk was phoning an order to the floor trader to buy one hundred shares of Moose Lake Mines, the manager of the company's trading department would phone an order to the "jitney" broker to sell one hundred shares of Moose Lake Mines. Sometimes the trade would be completed between the "jitney" broker and the floor trader. At other times, other traders would be involved in both sides of the transaction. It did not matter much one way or the other; the "wash sale" had been put through the stock exchange.

At first glance, it might be assumed that Solloway and the other brokers who were taking the short side of their customers' orders, opened themselves to great risk in a rising market, and the markets were indeed rising in 1927, 1928, and 1929. The price of any number of shares increased from around two to six or seven dollars during 1928–1929. If the purchasers of these shares at the bottom had elected to sell them at the top and spend the profits on a car, a house, or even a suit of clothes, it would represent a dead loss to the broker who had sold the stock at the bottom and would have to buy it back at the top. That risk was more apparent than real because the margin speculators seldom sold their shares at a profit and got out of the market.

In addition to the seemingly universal conviction among buyers of stock on margin that whatever went up would go higher, there was a second factor in the market working for the mining brokers. Most of the brokers, and Solloway Mills most of all, acted as share wholesalers for mining and oil companies which were multiplying like weeds. The brokers advanced large sums to the companies in return for blocks of stock which they then pressed their clients to buy at higher prices.

I.W.C. Solloway made his first trip to western Canada in 1927 and was delighted with what he found. Winnipeg was populated largely by people who were forever rushing, lemming-like, into the grain exchange futures market whenever rising wheat prices became front-page news. No matter how often they got burned by collapsing prices, they always came back for more.

In Calgary, he could open his hotel room window and when the wind was right inhale the acrid fumes from the gas flares burning in Turner Valley, thirty-five miles away. Calgary, moreover, was full of his kind of people, people who for almost fifteen years had been taking small fliers in the oil stock being peddled by promoters of Turner Valley oil companies. In a matter of weeks he had added Calgary to his list of western cities in which he would open a brokerage office and install private telegraph connections to Toronto and its soon-to-be-boiling mining and oil stock markets. Early in 1928 Solloway Mills leased the ground floor of the old Albertan building at 229 Eighth Avenue West. Carpenters were whistled up and in a trice there was a new centre of gravity for Calgary's business and professional community, the fanciest brokerage office in the West.

Up a short flight of steps from the street level, the premises encompassed an area thirty feet by eighty. Along the east wall, for a distance of fifty feet, a raised platform thirty inches high and three feet wide was erected. The wall above the platform for the same distance was covered with green hardboard on which narrow vertical lines were drawn three inches apart. This was the quotation board at which a couple of teen-age employees, racing back and forth along the platform, transcribed the stock market quotations coming in by telegraph from the Toronto, Montreal, and

New York exchanges. On another section of the board, grain prices were chalked up as they came in from the Winnipeg and Chicago futures markets.

It was a perfect location, within five minutes' walk of every important office in town. Diagonally across the street was the Lancaster building which housed a dozen oil company offices and most of the town's important law offices, including Bennett, Hannah, and Sanford; Smith, Egbert, and Smith; and McGillivray, Helman, and Mahaffey. By this time the Turner Valley oil development had overrun the city to this extent: every adult Calgarian who had twenty-five or fifty dollars to spare had invested it in Turner Valley oil stock and had several certificates stashed away in bureau drawers for 50, 100 or 200 shares of thirty-five- or forty-cents oil stock. That included all the doctors, merchants, civil servants, politicians, farmers, and stockmen. And it was a puny and unprepossessing legal firm that did not have at least half a dozen oil company official seals in storage in its office.

Thanks to the time difference between Toronto and Calgary, no other development of the 1920s has profoundly changed Calgary mores as the opening of the Solloway Mills brokerage office. Everybody who was anybody in Calgary business and professions turned up to give the place the once-over. It was not long before the quotation board developed the same fascination for Calgarians that video game machines would have for their grand-children fifty years later. It began with early risers discovering that the board came to life at 7:00 A.M. in summer. Soon most of the comfortable oak chairs in the board room were filled to capacity and all the standing room in front of the board was occupied, and stayed that way for most of the morning, as the board-makers whizzed back and forth like monkeys on sticks, in frenzies of quotation changing. In the end, medical and dental appointments became difficult to obtain before noon, and busi-ness was done between trips to the brokerage offices for hourly quotation checks.

Other Toronto brokerage firms were going through similar expansion out west, and it was not long before Stobie Forlong and Company duplicated the Solloway-type board room at 115 Eighth Avenue, and Shannon and Company added a third, next to the Palace Theatre. And with the proliferation of brokers, there came a vast expansion in the sheer numbers of people "in the market." Neighbours tipped neighbours and bridge partners tipped bridge opponents about what was "good" in the market. Many of these first time investors were somewhat lacking in sophistication and had a meat-and-potatoes approach to buying oil stock on margin. For them, Mill City which was quoted at sixty cents was a more attractive buy than MacLeod which was quoted at $3.00 or United which was selling for $1.25.

The impact that Solloway had on the oil business in Turner

Valley was even more important than the changes he wrought in Calgary. Until he came into the picture, public participation in the financing of Turner Valley companies had never much exceeded the small-bore, ribbon-clerk stage. Everybody was into oils stock, but at the small lot. The result was that it took forever to get a well drilled to completion because being underfinanced was the universal lot of the wildcatters.

Solloway changed all that. He purchased gobs of oil company treasury stock and paid cash for it. A typical deal was the one he made with A.H. Mayland, a rancher turned oilman who founded the company bearing his name. He paid Mayland $500,000 for 500,000 shares of Mayland stock. Then, having sold it, came back for another $200,000 worth. Solloway's financing enabled Mayland to complete the drilling of several wells and build a refinery to process his production. Several other companies also were assisted in bringing their operations to successful conclusion by the financing supplied by Solloway.

The year 1928 brought thousands of new prairie investors into the stock market. But by the end of 1928, while the public interest in the stock market remained high, the mining and oil stockbrokers had about completed the harvest of available speculators and speculative cash. So while there was a lot of trading, there was a noticeable slowing down of the onward and upward thrusts of oil stock prices. That was true even though a number of Alberta-based companies had listed their shares on the Standard Stock and Mining Exchange in Toronto.

As the oil stock market seemed to be drifting aimlessly in the early winter of 1929, Calgary oilmen pondered how to reactivate public excitement. The consensus was that what the market needed was either a speculator discovery in Turner Valley, or the completion of a really *big* deal of some kind. They got what they wanted—first, a spectacular discovery. News broke over the weekend of February 9 that Home Oil Number 1 blew into production in Turner Valley at the rate of seven hundred barrels a day. The success doubled the price of Home Oil stock overnight, from $3.50 on Friday to $7.00 a share on Monday. Within a couple of weeks it had doubled again and in the process carried most of the stocks on the Calgary Exchange to new record highs. Then came the big deal!

Fred Green, President of United Oils; R.A. Brown, superintendent of Calgary's Electrical System and United Oils Director; and James Lowery, president of Home Oil, cooked up the legendary million dollar deal with Solloway. Solloway would buy fifty thousand shares of Home Oil treasury stock at $20 a share and Home would use the million dollars to buy a quarter-section lease United Oils owned, offsetting the Home Number 1 to the east. The directors of the two companies concluded the deal on March

9, but news was withheld from the public until March 19, presumably to allow all the directors to tip off their friends to get into the market before the news broke. (Laws to restrict the trading activities of insiders were still two generations in the future. The right of insiders to take advantage of inside information to make a quick buck on their company stock was universally regarded as a fringe benefit of company directors and managers.)

Naturally, rumours of "the big deal" spread rapidly, and, on March 15, Home Oil stock reached twenty-nine dollars per share and United touched seventeen dollars after having traded for two dollars a month before. So frantic did the clamour for oil shares become in Calgary on March 15 that the Calgary Stock Exchange had to shut down for a day to enable the staff to get caught up with their paperwork. Solloway, incidentally, then employed 115 paper-pushers, spread over four floors of his Calgary headquarters.

Ironically, neither Lowery's announcement of the details of the big deal or United's announcement of a four dollar cash dividend could sustain the power of the market advance. For the speculators in Alberta oil stocks, the party was over on March 15, 1929. There was still time for each and every one of them to get out of the market with up to and beyond ten-fold increases in their invested capital. Instead, they waited, and waited, and waited; and the market drifted, and drifted, and drifted, lower, and lower, and lower. A week before the Wall Street crash, Home was down to $14, Royalite was down to $80 from its March high of $180. All the other oil stocks were down proportionately. Black Thursday finished the job of bringing the oil shares back to reality as companies like Calgary and Edmonton Corporation, Dalhousie, Mayland, A.P. Con were off 80 per cent from their March highs.

For ordinary shareholders who had bought their oil shares for cash and stashed them away under mattresses, the stock market crash was no big deal. Their shares were still worth more than they had paid for them a year before. Indeed, Home Oil at $12 and Mayland at $3 were well above the level of the previous year. It was the people who had bought on margin and had used their increased equities to buy more as the market rose, who were victimized by the crash, and not only by the crash: Many had been sold out before Black Thursday when they could not meet calls for additional margins as the market drifted lower in late summer.

It so happened in the inevitable post mortems on the disaster that Calgarians and Albertans fell victims to the Cleopatra syndrome and blamed the bad news on the messenger. In this case, the messenger was the Calgary Stock Exchange. It was widely believed, and voiced in letters to the *Western Oil Examiner*, that if it had not been for the exchange there would have been no crash. Coupled with the search for scapegoats was a great deal of self-flagellation. "I was going to sell! I came in here two weeks before the crash to take my profits and get out! And I ran into Joe Blow and he had a tip that Home was headed for at least thirty dollars on the next rise! So instead of selling out I bought some more! Two goddam weeks before the crash I bought more!"

The brokerage offices emptied as with a bomb scare. When the margin traders met on the street they no longer bragged about the paper profits they were accumulating. Instead they commiserated with each other over the speed at which they had been sold out before they could put up more margin. John Windsor's case was legend. A Calgary produce dealer, he had run nine hundred dollars into thirty thousand dollars in Solloway Mills in a little over a year. When the market collapsed, the brokers called him for more margin; he could not provide it so they told him they were closing out his account. If the close out had taken place at the price level that existed when the margin call was made, Windsor would still have been seven thousand dollars to the good. But by the time the brokers sold all Windsor's stock, the prices had fallen so far so quickly that he had lost the seven thousand dollars and owed the brokers an additional forty-five hundred dollars.

In less extreme form, John Windsor's story was the story of hundreds of customers of Calgary brokers who, instead of having profits sitting in brokerage accounts, now had substantial debits on the brokerage books, representing the difference between what their stock brought on the falling market and the margins they had on deposit.

Naturally the cataclysmic drop in stock prices had to be somebody's fault. Some of the first targets the victims selected for their brickbats were the government agencies that were supposed to be regulating the securities business and protecting the speculators from themselves. Naturally, too, the rumblings of discontent reached the ears of the government, probably in the first instance from around its own cabinet table. In any event, soon after the crash, auditors were sent to examine the books of the Calgary Stock Exchange as well as those of all the Calgary brokers.

Around the first of December 1929, agents for the Alberta attorney general appeared in the Calgary office of Solloway Mills to obtain access to certain books and records under the Security Frauds Prevention Act. The office manager turned over the records and advised Solloway in Toronto of the event. When told of the raid, Solloway consulted his Toronto solicitors who advised him he should retain counsel in Calgary, just in case. They recommended A.A. McGillivray, who happened to be in Toronto at the time on his way to Ottawa. McGillivray had an appointment to meet Alberta Premier Brownlee in Ottawa and agreed on behalf of Solloway to talk to the premier and find out what was going on. The explanation came back that the attorney general was embarked on a broad investigation of the stock exchange and the brokerage business.

Nothing further happened until January. On New Year's Eve Solloway returned to Calgary enroute to a large banquet of the Aero Club of Edmonton at which he was to be guest of honour. The occasion for the celebration was the successful completion of the first airmail service between Edmonton and Aklavik in the high Arctic. Solloway was president of Commercial Airways which had made the four thousand-mile round trip. Charles Becker, president of the Aero Club presided at the banquet, flanked on one side at the head table by Premier Brownlee and on the other by Solloway. Other guests included the mayor of Edmonton, and aviation leaders C.H. "Punch" Dickens and W.R. "Wop" May. As one of the key speakers, Premier Brownlee was high in his praise of Solloway for his leadership in providing the pioneer flying facilities that connected Edmonton with the North.

Prior to his departure for Edmonton, Solloway had spent two days going over the books and records of the company with the government auditors, explaining the various transactions that had perked their interest. There was an agreement between the parties that Solloway would spend as much time with them as they desired and return to Calgary any time they wished to consult with him further. On January 6, McGillivray again talked to Brownlee about the investigation and was told it was still proceeding. Solloway left for Vancouver on January 7. On January 10, a warrant was issued for Solloway's arrest and an officer of the British Columbia government appeared at his hotel suite late in the afternoon to advise him of the fact. He was detained under surveillance at his hotel. At the same time, Harvey Mills was arrested in Toronto.

When McGillivray heard of the government's action he blew his top and accused the premier of bad faith in ordering the arrest without notice to counsel. In McGillivray's case, it was the unkindest cut of all. McGillivray was an old friend of Brownlee's and the relationship between the two had been close when Brownlee was attorney general before becoming premier. It was Brownlee who appointed McGillivray crown prosecutor in the Picariello case and the Carbon murder case. If an explanation for Brownlee's precipitous action was ever forthcoming to McGillivray, it never reached the public prints. By the time McGillivray made his protest, Commissioner W.C. Bryan of the Alberta Provincial Police was enroute to Vancouver to bring Solloway back to Calgary in chains, figuratively if not literally.

Solloway and Mills were arraigned and released on bail, and the investigation proceeded. In addition to the previously quoted charge under the common law, there were others. To wit: 1. Conspiracy to affect the market price of stocks; 2. Conspiracy to defraud the public under the Criminal Code; 3. Conspiracy to commit an indictable offense—gambling in stocks commonly known as bucketing.

The effect of the Solloway Mills arrests was that of a pebble being dropped into a pool and creating a waterspout. The attorney generals of Manitoba, Ontario, and British Columbia rushed into investigations of their own exchanges and mining and oil stockbrokers. On January 30, warrants were issued in Toronto for the arrest not only of Solloway and Mills, but for the partners of ten Toronto brokerage firms, including five of the largest firms in Canada. These included D.S. Patterson and Company; Homer L. Gilverson and Company; Stobie, Forlong, and Matthews; A.E. Moysey and Company; and, of course, Solloway Mills. A few days later the partners of the prominent Ottawa firm of Mowatt and MacGillivray were arrested. All were charged with conspiracy to defraud the public by short selling and bucketing. The Stobie, Forlong, and Matthews firm immediately went into receivership, a fate that ultimately overtook all the others.

The effect of the arrests on the oil and mining stock markets was devastating. By the time Solloway and Mills were convicted by Justice Ives in Calgary on June 23, 1930, the price of Home Oil stock was down to four dollars a share, United was thirty-five cents and Royalite was down to twenty-six dollars.

Public confidence in the financial world, which had been shaken so badly by the Wall Street crash, was destroyed by the trials of the brokers. It took ten days for the Solloway and Mills trial to run its course in Calgary. It was easily demonstrated by the evidence of the company's books that it had sold short as its customers bought stock. Mr. Justice Ives also found that the company had made it a practice of frequently taking a substantial net short position in shares it was urging its customers to buy. The defense contended it was forced to take a short position against customer purchases because there was no way of financing margin investments otherwise. In addition, it frequently took a short position in order to provide market liquidity which enabled orders to be filled quickly. The defense also argued strongly that the short selling against customer purchases was legitimized by general usage over many years by the mining brokers of Canada.

The most cogent argument for the defense was that margin trading provided capital for resource development that could not otherwise be obtained. Solloway noted a number of Alberta oil companies that became successful operators in Turner Valley with funds he had obtained from investors for them. And the Commercial Aviation Company, about which Premier Brownlee had so enthused, was the product of Solloway's spreading around of his own earnings from margin trading of oil and mining stocks.

The brokers were convicted out of hand by Judge Ives on four counts of conspiracy to defraud their customers. Solloway was fined $225,000 and sentenced to four months at hard labour in the Lethbridge jail; Mills, who was very much the junior in the company, was fined $50,000 and one month in jail.

With the conviction of Solloway and Mills and the arrest of the other Ontario mining brokers, finis was written to the mining and oil stock markets as Canadians had known them for twenty years. The Criminal Code was amended to outlaw short selling of stock. But the travail of Solloway and Mills was just beginning. At the close of the Calgary trial, they were arrested on warrants issued in Ontario charging similar offenses to those on which they had been convicted in Alberta. They went on trial in Toronto in October 1930, pleaded guilty, and were fined $250,000, which they paid. In November, new warrants were issued by Ontario and the men were put on trial again. The following month, they were arrested in Toronto on British Columbia warrants and taken to Vancouver. The following June, they were back in Toronto for another trial, this time before the judge and jury; they were acquitted. Then it was back to Vancouver to pay a fine of $100,000.

Solloway, in his book *Speculators and Politicians*, estimated that the trials cost him one million dollars in fines and legal fees, and he served three months of his four-month jail term. In that regard, he got off much lighter than his Toronto confrères. Eight other Toronto mining brokers were found guilty and the following sentences were imposed: William J. Smart and Maurice E. Young, (Home L. Gibson and Company), 3 years and 2½ years respectively; D.S. Patterson, (D.S. Patterson and Company), 3 years; Austin Campbell, of the same firm, 2½ years; Malcom Stobie (Stobie, Forlong and Company), 3 years, C.J. Forlong, of the same firm, 2½ years; James Hepplestone (A.E. Moysey and Company), 3 years; and W.T.H. Shutt, of the same firm, 2½ years.

Rene Dupont, former president of Corporation d'Obligations Municipales, of Quebec City, was sentenced to five years' imprisonment for "conspiracy to defraud the public." R.H. Mowat and D.A. MacGillivray, heads of a group of mining brokerage houses with headquarters in Ottawa, pleaded guilty to charges of conspiracy to defraud the public and bucketing, and each received a sentence of imprisonment of three years in Kingston Penitentiary.

In the quiet aftermath of the spectacular broker trials, and the easy reelection of the UFA government of John Brownlee of Alberta, the several provincial governments took another run at legislating morality into the brokerage business. Ontario even established a full-fledged Ontario Securities Commission to ride herd on the Toronto brokers. It appointed Colonel George Drew, later premier of the province, to head the commission. But when President Franklin Roosevelt raised the price of gold to thirty-five dollars an ounce from fourteen dollars, he set off another double-faced boom.

It unloosed battalions of prospectors into the north country and generated an even gaudier boom in mining stock than Solloway and friends had triggered. This time it was featured by slick coveys of super salesmen who were past masters of the bait-and-switch trade. By long distance telephone and door-to-door bell ringing, they descended on holders of solid bankable securities and government bonds and switched them into worthless shares of moose pasture gold mines.

Fifty years after Solloway, this footnote might be added: The hard-nosed United States Securities and Exchange Commission still permits brokers to sell short in order to make stock available to willing purchasers. "Making a market," Solloway called it. These brokers are called specialists or, in the vernacular, "odd-lotters." The minimum-size block of stock tradeable on the New York Stock Exchange is 100 shares. However, a system has been in place for many years to accommodate the thousands of investors who may wish to acquire a lesser number of shares, particularly of the higher priced stock. When Joe Blow places an order with his broker to buy 25 shares of IBM at $150 a share, the broker's floor trader at the stock exchange goes to the post where IBM is traded. There he locates the IBM specialist, a trader who has been registered as such by the stock exchange. That person is required to sell 25 shares of IBM at a quarter above the last trade reported. He will thereby go short 25 shares of IBM and will remain so until he has sold short an additional 75 shares, or enough to make up a "board lot." He can then buy 100 shares and balance his books.

All this still comes under the heading of "making a market" for the stock. In the process of doing so, the specialist will gain a profit if the market goes down while he is short. Or he will incur a loss if the market goes up. Intrinsically, it is what I.W.C. Solloway was doing fifty years before. Solloway's trouble was that he was doing on a gigantic scale what modern New York specialists are doing in miniature. Nor is that all. In the 1980s, the most respectable of Canadian financial institutions, who join together to underwrite the sale of large blocks of capital stock, buy and sell in the "after-market" to create a market for latecomers to the issue or to absorb surplus stock from some customers who over-bought the primary issue. They are, in short, making a market in a fashion no different in any important way from the one that landed I.W.C. Solloway and Harvey Mills in the Lethbridge jail in 1930.

In the context of the times, however, the conviction of the brokers was inevitable, if only on account of the excesses that occurred in their market-making. Although the debit balances in the accounts of all their margin-account customers did not exist in reality, they charged 7 per cent interest on the fictitious debt and posted the charge monthly. And when they closed out an account by simply crossing it on their books, they charged the clients commission on the transaction at the full stock exchange rates. Both practices are fraud.

There remains the matter of the lawyers involved in the Solloway Mills affair in Calgary. The fee that McGillivray and Helman earned from Solloway in their losing effort would not, in the nature of things, have compared with their fee for keeping Harry Bronfman out of jail in two places. Nevertheless it must have run well into five figures for Helman and that plus for McGillivray. For the prosecuting team, though McLeod, Sinclair, and A.L. Smith carried the main load, McKinley Cameron drew the same $10,000 fee that the other two were paid by the Government of Alberta for winning the case. Toward that winning, a substantial contribution was made by a young $3,500-a-year staff solicitor in the attorney general's office, J.J. Frawley, who went on from the Solloway case to a distinguished career in the public service of Alberta.

# Chapter Seven

# McPherson and Brownlee, an Underbrush Full of Liberals, and Nobody But Liberals

There is only one adequate word to describe the Brownlee case. That word is "unique." There is no other case in Alberta legal history, in Canadian legal history, even, that can match its multiplicity of fascinating aspects. For example, by decision of the Supreme Court of Canada reinforced by confirmation by the Judicial Committee of the Privy Council, it established a new high-water mark in the liberation of Canadian women. After Brownlee, it was no longer necessary for a seduced female to be made pregnant in order to sue her seducer for damages. Seduction, of and by itself, as defined in the Revised Statutes of Alberta, 1922, was adequate grounds.

It was the all-Canadian sex scandal of the 1930s and destroyed the political career of Premier John E. Brownlee, one of Canada's most respected politicians. Not only did Vivian MacMillan's story of her two-year dalliance with the premier impel the Calgary, Edmonton, and Lethbridge newspapers into breaking out their 72-point black type for eight-column front-page headlines, it made the front-pages in Toronto, Ottawa, Montreal, London, and Windsor. More, it was a story that ran to more than a thousand words a day in eastern papers at a time when a combined earthquake and flood in the West would have attracted scant attention east of Winnipeg.

It was the Brownlee case, in part at least, that copper-rivetted the lid on the coffin of the United Farmers of Alberta as a political force in the province. Then, too, it was the back-lashing word-of-mouth from the Brownlee case that shattered the hopes of the Alberta Liberal Party that it would come to power once John Brownlee was destroyed. Instead, the Liberals in Alberta became an endangered species when the farmers, disenchanted with the UFA turned not to the Liberals as an alternative but to the economic gospellers of Social Credit.

But would either have happened, would the UFA's once impregnable farmer constituency have been shattered, or would the Liberal Party have been discredited, if the McPherson-Mattern wife-swapping scandal had not erupted almost as a curtain raiser for the Brownlee affair? Connoisseurs of the prurient might argue that compared with the wife-swapping scandal of O.L. "Tony" McPherson, MLA, Brownlee's minister of public works, the Brownlee case was pretty tame, almost Sunday School stuff. The Brownlee trial ran for only six days while the McPherson trial extended over two weeks. Verbatim reporting of the Brownlee trial seldom ran to more than eight columns a day in the Edmonton *Bulletin*. The McPherson testimony ran to up to twenty columns.

It was the McPherson case that set the cat among the pigeons in the UFA caucus and had his fellow members disgustedly calling for his resignation. When that failed to happen, two members resigned from the caucus. Then when the MacMillans sued Brownlee for damages it sent a message rocketing across the Alberta skies that UFA politicians, despite the sanctimonious pose they had been striking all these years, were hardly much different from other politicians. To emphasize the importance of that point it is necessary to place both events in the context of the times, roughly the first twenty-five years of Alberta's existence as a province.

By the time Alberta became a province in 1905 the flow of immigrants from the United States, eastern Canada, and the United Kingdom was nearing flood stage. Thanks in part at least to a constituency map gerrymandered in Ottawa by Honourable Frank Oliver, the Liberals scored a whopping victory in the first provincial election and retained power without serious challenge for the next fifteen years.

One factor which may have helped keep the Liberals in power was the reluctance of conservative American immigrant farm leaders to risk their American citizenship by becoming involved in Canadian politics. A contributing factor to that decision was undoubtedly a pathological distrust, which many had developed before migrating to Canada, for all political parties and party politicians. It went much deeper than a normal once-bitten twice-shy reaction, to a point where they identified all political parties with fundamental evil. That can be seen from the catalogue of opprobrious epithets then commonly current among the Plains States farmers, some of which spilled across the border. Some examples: boodler, mugwump, scalawag, slush fund, pork barrel, bell ringers, shake-downers, rippers. The last three in particular are worth defining. They are synonyms for state legislators who introduced legislation merely to frighten business interests into making generous contributions to party coffers, after which the proposed legislation was abandoned.

For the Americans immigrating to western Canada, the disrepute of the politicians was well justified. Time and again the American farmers had turned to political parties to remedy grievances. Time and again they had been betrayed by the elected "tools" of the eastern banks, the railways, the grain speculators, or meat packers. Was the collective body politic of Canada as venial as States-side politics? Definitely not! But we did have our northern railways scandals, parliament buildings scandals, and rampant patronage in all levels of government.

What it added up to in Alberta and Manitoba was an inward turning of the farmers to their own self-help movements and away from politics. Nudged, pushed, and shoved by the American newcomers, they became deeply involved in farmer organizations patterned after American models. Out of all this evolved the United Farmers of Alberta, composed of farmers of deeply religious, mainly Protestant, persuasion. It was an organization that developed into a well-muscled arm of the social gospel and the moral reform movements. Thus the UFA led the struggle for the emancipation of women, female suffrage, child welfare, and above all for Prohibition.

When the end of the First World War brought a collapse of farm prices and excruciating debt problems, the focus of farmers' attention veered from the social to the economic-political problem area. At first the movement to convert the UFA into a political party was squelched by its leaders who were dedicated to the maintenance of the UFA as a class-action pressure group. When at last the decision was taken to nominate UFA candidates for the legislature, it was done in a way unparalleled in Canadian history. The UFA was not to become a political party in any recognized meaning of the term. Each UFA local selected a member to run for the legislature as a delegate of the local organization. If elected he had to follow the dictates of his organization or resign his seat. In the legislature he was to concern himself exclusively with the interests of the farmers. And what about the interests of city businessmen, trades unions, the professions? They could all elect their own groups to the legislature from city constituencies, bring in their own legislation and get it passed if it did not unacceptably impinge on the interests of other groups.

This was Henry Wise Wood's famous contribution to prairie political thought, the "group government" concept of legislatures without political parties or party politicians! A visionary, moonstruck, not to say crackpot idea? Certainly. But that did not stop the farmers of Alberta in 1921 and in Manitoba in 1922 from sweeping to power, to the shattering surprise of Liberal party administrations in both provinces.

The election results were even more astounding to the farmers themselves. In neither province did the United Farmers have any particular animus toward the Liberal governments. Their anger was directed instead toward the tariff policies of the federal government, against the railways, the grain companies, and above all the chartered banks. Their goal was not to replace the Liberals with another political party. It was to abolish the party system. For the first battle of what was expected to be a long campaign, the UFA would have been satisfied with the election of enough members to form a decent bloc of farmer representatives in the legislature. Hence it only nominated forty candidates in a house of sixty-one seats, and would have been pleased to have elected half of them. Instead it elected thirty-nine of the forty.

Alberta Liberals went into the 1921 election with thirty-four seats compared with nineteen Conservatives and a handful of Independents. They regarded the result as a foregone conclusion and the voting a mere formality after which they would go on governing the province as before. When the ballots were counted, the Liberals were down to fourteen seats, mainly in the greater Edmonton area and the Tories were reduced to a single representative by the UFA landslide.

In the aftermath of the elections it was generally assumed that the group government theory would be quickly wrecked on the shoals of impracticality. That happened in Manitoba where, after a couple of years of thrashing about, the farmers and Liberals came together in the Liberal-Progressive party. In Alberta, Premier Herbert Greenfield survived for four years before deciding politics was not for him. His successor was John Brownlee of Calgary, former solicitor for the United Grain Growers and the only non-farmer in the government. A skilled politician and an able administrator, he was under no compulsion to listen to overtures from the Liberals to form a Manitoba-type fusion. In the 1926 election he increased his support to forty-three seats, while the leaderless, drifting Liberals dropped to seven members.

Then came the 1930 election and the onset of the depression. Coupled with incessant attacks on the UFA government by the urban newspapers of Alberta over many years, it gave the Liberals cause for hope. Hope was shattered by the election returns which limited the Liberals' gains and UFA losses to only four seats. Still enjoying a margin of thirty-nine to twenty-two seats overall, the farmers' government clearly had no cause for concern. Curiously enough, it was during the run-up to that election the previous fall that the first faint whisp of a storm cloud began to form on the UFA horizon.

It happened in 1929 at the formal Armistice Day ball at the Edmonton Armory when the paths of Tony McPherson and his wife, Cora, crossed those of retired Major Leroy Mattern and his wife, Helen. McPherson, the minister of public works, was representing the provincial government and Mattern was the lieutenant-governor's aide-de-camp. Whether or not it was actually a double-barrelled case of love at first sight, it was certainly a reasonable facsimile thereof. Soon the couples were socializing back and forth and Helen Mattern was junketing around the province with McPherson on his electioneering jaunts.

McPherson was a wheat farmer from Vulcan. It was he who had led the movement to turn the UFA into a political party in opposition to the wishes of Henry Wise Wood. When the party came to power he was elected speaker of the Legislature. Then nudging fifty, McPherson's family life had been even more absence-prone than that of most politicians. The couple migrated to the Vulcan area soon after their marriage in 1908 and within a decade McPherson had nineteen hundred acres under cultivation and still found time to be a leader of the UFA during the war years. Then as his family grew he bought a house in Calgary to be closer to school for his boys and commuted to the farm, seventy-four miles away, when school was in session. In the winter, when the farm was shut down, McPherson was busy with UFA meetings. When he was appointed to the Brownlee cabinet, the family moved to Edmonton.

Nothing much is known of the Matterns except what came out at the trial. Their's was a wartime marriage in 1916 when she was in her early 20s and he was just over 30. After their whirlwind courtship he went off to the war and Helen went to New York to live. Mattern remained in England for some months after the war and eventually they were reunited in Edmonton. But not for long. After a long separation Helen decided in 1922 on a Reno divorce. Then she changed her mind and returned to Edmonton. They lived together in Edmonton thereafter where Mattern taught high school science and later became local manager for Western Canadian Airways.

Between Armistice Day 1929 and Dominion Day 1930, passions that had become aroused after the ball burst into flames. By the end of 1930, Helen was frequently found in the McPherson home, occasionally in bed with the minister. Meanwhile, Leroy Mattern would confess to his wife, who would tell McPherson, that he, Mattern, had been having his way with Cora McPherson. A wife-swapping gambit was about to be played.

For any politician, never mind a front-row cabinet minister, even to contemplate becoming involved in a divorce action, was unheard of anywhere in Canada, not to mention in the straight-laced environment of Alberta. In the context of the times, divorce was a nasty business that brought discredit on everybody—the aggrieved party, the guilty party, and even the lawyers involved. As a result, handling an action for divorce was viewed with extreme distaste by the established legal firms. It was not uncommon for a person seeking a divorce to be shunted from firm to firm before a lawyer willing to take the case could be found.

One reason for this situation was undoubtedly the fact that the sole cause for the dissolution of a marriage by legal action then was adultery—a violation of (a) Holy Writ, (b) minimal community standards of common decency, and (c) good taste. When there was a legitimate cause for action it was never enough for the culpable spouse to confess the transgression, it had to be proven to the satisfaction of the judge by the sworn testimony of a disinterested witness in open court. That involved the hiring of private detectives to act as peeping toms and catch the offending party in the adulterous act. And that was a time consuming and costly business, whether the action was taken before a Parliamentary committee, which was necessary in Quebec, and, until 1928, in Ontario, or before a supreme court justice on the Prairies after 1918. In the main, however, the 150-odd divorce suits a year then occurring in Alberta were uncontested. The offending spouse simply agreed to provide the suing spouse with the necessary evidence by arranging a convenient tryst for the benefit of the private detectives.

So considering the exalted position he held in Alberta politics, and in face of the nasty publicity a divorce action might well attract, it was almost unthinkable that McPherson would have contemplated a divorce. That he went to his friend and cabinet colleague, Honourable J.L. Lymburn, the attorney general, for advice on how best to obtain a divorce is indicative of the extreme heat the aroused passion was generating. The best advice Lymburn could give McPherson, when he had recovered from the shock of his colleague's disclosures, was to recommend that he retain Mayne Reid, one of Edmonton's most proper, stiff-necked and straight-laced lawyers, who, incidentally, happened to be Lymburn's partner. Reid would take the case as a favour to his partner, but he would most assuredly do whatever he could to avoid having his own involvement with a divorce action bruited abroad.

Whether Lymburn, looking fearfully over his shoulder at the political implications of a publicized divorce action, tried to dissuade McPherson from his contemplated action, or not, is lost to history. If he did, his argument fell on barren ground for, in a few weeks, Cora McPherson was persuaded to take a well-witnessed trip to Saskatoon with Roy Mattern. And not only one trip. On the first occasion the retained witness watched only until the pair checked into the hotel. The McPherson lawyers decided that was insufficient proof of adultery so a second safari had to be organized. This time the detective kept the pair in sight until they had entered the hotel room and he was able to swear they were there for the night. That set the stage for McPherson's shedding of his wife so he could marry Helen Mattern, after she, using the same evidence, obtained her divorce from Roy Mattern.

There would be no harm done politically, of course, if the divorce proceeding could be brought off without publicity. Then the only people who would become privy to the wife-swap would be immediate family members, intimate friends, a few neighbours, and cabinet colleagues. Ergo, the course of wisdom would be to arrange for the hearings to be held at a time and in a place off the beaten path of nosy newspaper reporters. All that was required to achieve that was a sympathetic judge who would be amenable to a suggestion to change court procedure. The amenable judge turned out to be Mr. Justice Thomas Tweedie.

Thomas Tweedie was everybody's favourite judge and boon companion. Not only was he an able judge learned in the law (he was a graduate of Dalhousie who had done post-graduate work at Harvard), he was a man totally without "side" and unfailingly courteous in court and out. A friendly giant of a man, he carried his robes and books in an ancient faded green bag, slung over his shoulder on a cane, like a tramp with a poke on a stick. He was the despair of Alberta haberdashers, for his taste in clothing was fixed as the stars—a blue suit, white shirt, and a flaming red tie.

Prior to his appointment to the Supreme Court of Alberta, Tweedie had been active in politics in southern Alberta, having served in both the Alberta Legislature and the House of Commons. So he was well aware of the almost fatal impact that involvement in an unsavoury and well-publicized divorce would have on a politician's career. And reporters would certainly become privy to McPherson's divorce suit if it was tried in a regular court room during regular hours. So Reid and Tweedie had a table dusted off in the judges' library, which was located in a remote corner of the Edmonton courthouse. It was in this seldom-used alcove that Mr. Justice Tweedie, ungowned in his blue suit and red tie, adjudicated the McPherson divorce during the noon hour on April 22, 1931. It was, he was later to insist, an open court because both doors to the room were open during the hearing. However, any stranger wandering the corridors of the building might well have been dissuaded from entering by the large, polished brass, "Private" sign permanently attached to the door. The chance of that happening was, however, remote indeed that day because the hearing was held at a time when the building was usually deserted.

Mr. Justice Tweedie granted McPherson a decree *nisi* on the spot and awarded him custody of the four children. Some weeks later, it was Helen Mattern's turn to cut herself loose from Roy Mattern, with the same body of facts used by McPherson in his suit. Meanwhile Mattern had been transferred to Winnipeg by Canadian Airways and Cora McPherson accompanied him. There she quickly discovered that Mattern not only had no intention of marrying her, but he was relishing his new single status to play the field.

In a panic, Cora wrote her ex-husband to report Mattern's behaviour. At first he simply answered her with suggestions that she be more aggressive and imaginative in her pursuit of her intended. Then, as her relationship with Mattern became impossible, she wrote McPherson that she was going to call off the divorce at the decree *nisi* stage and return to her home, and to McPherson, in Edmonton.

It was McPherson's turn to panic. He grabbed a train for Winnipeg where he bombarded his former wife with advice. She should not be discouraged by Mattern's coldness but pursue him with greater vigor. She should also seek religious consolation by resort to the Bible. To this end, he plied her with piles of inspirational religious pamphlets. Instead of her feeling devastated by the travail through which she was passing, he urged her to cherish the pain because she would emerge a much better person for having gone through it. He quoted the Bible to prove it. As for himself, there could be no turning back from his plans to marry Helen Mattern.

McPherson nearly had his cake, but things fell apart when he tried not to pay for it. Part of the pre-divorce deal had been that McPherson would pay his former wife $75 a month. The following year, when his ministerial stipend was cut from $8,000 a year to $7,000, McPherson cut his payments to Cora to $40 a month. Then when he married Helen in 1932 he dropped the payments entirely, and his former wife was reduced to penury and had to resort to private charity or public relief. When Cora wrote demanding a reinstitution of the payments, McPherson consulted Attorney General Lymburn again because he believed Cora's letter threatened blackmail. He decided to ignore the letter. Cora consulted a lawyer.

Until August of 1932 not a whisper of this affair had reached beyond the McPherson-Mattern family circles and McPherson's tight-lipped cabinet colleagues. In his remarriage, McPherson had scaled new heights of secrecy. He had the ceremony in Edmonton performed by his friend the Alberta movie censor who had only renewed his license to perform marriages the day previous. But when Cora McPherson talked to Harry White, a lawyer from Mundare, Alberta, the protective cloak of secrecy started to disintegrate. White was a committed Liberal Party worker and took the case to George Van Allen, a rising star in the Liberal Party, who in turn brought in Neil Maclean, another prominent Edmonton Liberal and one of the ablest barristers of his day. On October 15, 1932, a statement of claim was filed on behalf of Cora McPherson asking to have her divorce set aside because of fraud and collusion. The statement was ultimately amended to add the grounds that the trial in private constituted a violation of the law.

Accompanying the statement of claim was a lengthy affidavit signed by Cora McPherson in which she spelled out all the fleshy details of the events that led up to the divorce. S.B. Woods, whom McPherson retained, filed an objection to the affidavit with Mr. Justice Frank Ford. Ford, who was unquestionably one of Alberta's most learned judges of the time, was nonetheless also a rather inflexible man whose fuse was noticeably short when it came to equity rather than law. He ruled that the affidavit was entirely irrelevant and, within the meaning of rule 253, an abuse of the process of the court. He ordered it removed at once.

That was the beginning, not the end of McPherson's problems, and the problems of the UFA. As Woods would later complain, the affidavit soon made its appearance in a by-election in the Camrose constituency and the UFA was caught up in the Caesar's-wife-syndrome: she must not only be above reproach but must be *seen* as being above reproach. And here was an ornament of the UFA, which wore its righteousness on its sleeve, which gave thanks it was not a political party like other political parties, caught *in flagrante delicto*.

From the Camrose hustings the affidavit reached the Toronto weekly scandal sheet *Hush* which published it in three weekly instalments. *Hush* was a widely circulated publication, a forerunner of such as the *National Inquirer*, etc., and was sold on newsstands all across the country. When *Hush* broke the McPherson wife-swapping scandal to Albertans, McPherson lashed out with libel suits in all directions. He sued the CPR news agency for transporting the publication, he sued its Alberta distributors, and he sued each of the newsstands that offered the publication for sale.

So if the Cora McPherson law suit had been a theatrical performance, it could have been said of it that it had certainly been favoured with an immense amount of preliminary publicity when it opened before Mr. Justice Frank Ford on May 8, 1933. And throughout its fourteen-day run it never played to less than a capacity audience, predominantly female. The women left no doubt where their sympathies lay—with Mrs. Cora McPherson. Early in the trial, *sotto voce* comments by the women about some of the sleazier episodes being described by witnesses triggered protest from S.B. Woods, and drew stern rebukes from the bench.

In ancient Rome the authorities provided the population with "bread and circus" to divert attention from pressing governmental problems. The McPherson case was the Alberta population's Roman holiday at the depths of the Great Depression. The sordid details revealed daily satiated the most salacious appetites, even in the expurgated and summary form in which they were reported in the columns of the Alberta newspapers outside Edmonton.

In one instance, so the testimony went, in 1930 Helen Mattern took to accompanying Tony McPherson on his electioneering junkets around the province and Cora McPherson went along to "protect McPherson's reputation." Then when the minister took an extended vacation to Victoria with the two women, they slept three in a bed, with Helen in the middle. When they returned to Edmonton, Helen moved into the McPherson home and into bed with the minister. The arrangement allegedly—and understandably—drove Cora McPherson to the verge of a nervous breakdown. She had a sister, who was married to McPherson's brother in Great Falls, Montana. Eventually she asked her sister to visit her in an effort to solve the marital mess. The sister testified that McPherson tried to enlist her support in getting rid of Cora so he could marry Helen. When she refused, Tony and Helen openly concentrated on abusing Cora in an effort to drive her out of the family home.

As sorry a chronicle of infidelity as an Alberta court was ever likely to hear, surely. It was compounded in the public mind by McPherson's action in barring Cora's access to her children, and then by his cutting off even the picayune financial allowance he had granted to her. The final blow to his image came when he was reduced to blubbering incoherence under cross-examination by George Van Allen, and Mr. Justice Ford had to call a recess to let him get his nerves under control. The trial destroyed O.L. McPherson.

Nor was the moral issue raised by the divorce action the only public relations disaster for the government. Early in the examination for discovery, the lawyers for Cora McPherson discovered the "secret" nature of the divorce proceeding that Mr. Justice Tweedie had held in the judges' library. A separate action was launched to have the divorce set aside on the grounds that the proceedings had not been held in open court. That action failed when Judge Tweedie appeared at the hearing before Mr. Justice Ewing and told the judge he had declared the library to be an open court room for the purpose of the hearing prior to presiding at the action.

Judge Ewing dismissed the action and the Alberta Court of Appeal sustained him. However the fact that a member of the United Farmers of Alberta cabinet would stoop to a secret hearing of his divorce action was a head-shaking matter for the UFA rank and file, at a time when the "one law for the rich, another law for the poor" complaint was being actively agitated. Nor did it add any lustre to the legal system's posture of impartiality come what may.

The courtroom issue, incidentally, ultimately reached Privy Council in London where Cora McPherson was able to use the ancient *in forma pauperis* procedure to obtain a hearing. The Privy Council appointed the greatest British barrister of the time, Wilfred Greene, to represent her. Eventually it ruled that the principle of a right to trial in open court had indeed been violated. But it refused to set the divorce aside because a remarriage had occurred.

In the meantime, back in Alberta, Judge Tweedie had to put up with a good deal of often biting badinage over the episode. Once he mentioned to his friend the irrepressible McKinley Cameron that he was off to Edmonton for court hearings. To which Cameron remarked, "You better be careful Tom and don't get to holding court in the shit house!"

As for Cora McPherson's suit to have the divorce annulled on grounds of collusion, Mr. Justice Ford had little problem in dismissing the suit on the grounds that a party to a conspiracy could not win an action to benefit from it.

The case itself gives rise to this question: Was it the McPherson case that inspired the young medical-student-boy-friend of Vivian MacMillan, John Caldwell, to go for John Brownlee's jugular?

The McPherson case opened as noted, on May 8, 1933, with Liberal stalwarts Maclean and Van Allen again in the starring roles. As he would later be reported as saying, Caldwell had purposely selected a Liberal lawyer to hear the story he had to tell about Vivian and John Brownlee. Maclean had taken on the Cora McPherson case against one of Alberta's most prominent and powerful politicians, the minister of public works, obviously at substantial cost to himself, for this was long before the idea of such a thing as legal aid was even thought of. It was while Maclean was knee deep in the McPherson case that Caldwell broached the Brownlee case with him. It was likewise while Maclean was involved with the McPherson case that he agreed to hear Vivian McMillan's story.

In the Brownlee case, Vivian MacMillan sued for $10,000 and her father sued for $5,000 damages under the Alberta Seductions Act, section 5, RSA 1922. The jury in June 1934 found that she had been seduced by the premier and awarded full damages and costs to her and her father. Thereupon Mr. Justice William Ives stepped in, reversed the jury's verdict, and awarded judgment to Brownlee with costs.

As litigation moved from the trial court to the Alberta Court of Appeals, to the Supreme Court of Canada, to the Judicial Committee of the Privy Council, it set the Alberta legal profession on its collective ear. The robing room of the law courts buzzed with the pros and cons of Justice William Ives' charge to the jury, over his reversal of the jury's verdict, over the strategy and tactics of the Brownlee defense, over the legal rabbit tracks it made across the legal landscape.

While the lawyers argued among themselves, the general public got into the act. Subscription lists were opened in Edmonton to fund the cost of an appeal from the judge's decision. In short order more than two thousand dollars trickled in one, two, and five dollar contributions, egged on by critical editorials in the newspapers as far away as Toronto and Montreal.

The Brownlee case, as a case, began on August 3, 1933, with this letter:

The Honourable J.E. Brownlee, K.C.
Parliament Buildings,
Edmonton, Alberta.

Dear Sir:

We have been instructed to commence action against you for damages for seduction of Miss Vivian MacMillan.

We see by the newspapers that you are about to leave the province for three months and would be glad, therefore, if you would let us have the name of your solicitor, who will accept service on your behalf, of the statement of claim which we will be issuing within the new few days.

Yours truly,
(signed)
MACLEAN, SHORT, KANE

The shattering impact which such a letter would have upon Premier John Brownlee may well be imagined, and for two reasons. It came without the slightest inkling, the slightest warning of any kind. And it reached him almost at the moment when his career in public life was reaching its apex. He was, in fact, actually packing his bags for a journey to Ottawa to take his place on the Royal Commission on Banking and Currency, along with Lord Macmillan, the pre-eminent British jurist-economist; Sir Charles Addis, former director of the Bank of England; Sir Thomas White, Canada's wartime minister of finance; Beaudry LeMan, general manager of the Banque Canadien Nationale. That

Brownlee belonged in such august company is indicated by this fact: when the report of the Macmillan Commission came down a year later and recommended the establishment of the Bank of Canada, it was Brownlee's minority report alone that suggested the corporate structure which the bank ultimately took.

Born in 1884, the son of a small town Ontario merchant, Brownlee came to Calgary in 1909 after graduation from the University of Toronto. He became an articled student in the firm of Lougheed and Bennett, and after being called to the bar joined the firm of Muir, Jephson, and Adams. Very early in his career he made the acquaintance of Henry Wise Wood, the leader of the United Farmers of Alberta, and began handling legal work for that organization and for the United Grain Growers. Subsequent to his marriage in 1912, he left the Muir Jephson firm to become the full-time solicitor for the United Grain Growers, a position he held until his entry into politics.

So well was he regarded by the organized farmers that, when the UFA swept to power in the provincial election in 1921, he was Henry Wise Wood's choice for premier, though he had not run in the election. Passed over in favour of Herbert H. Greenfield, he was appointed attorney general and a seat was found for him in the Ponoka constituency. He was deeply involved in the organization of the Alberta Wheat Pool in 1923 and in the prolonged negotiations with Ottawa over the return of Alberta's natural resources. In 1925 he was the party's unanimous choice to succeed Greenfield as premier.

As premier of Alberta, Brownlee became recognized as an important voice for the West. From 1930 onward he was in almost continuous negotiation with Ottawa and the other western provinces over agricultural and fiscal problems. As the depression deepened, the full force of everything that was wrong with the Canadian financial and political system came to bear on Alberta. Wheat and livestock prices fell to levels where the cash return to the farmers would barely pay the costs of shipment to market. It was in part to allay the mounting public criticism of the financial system that Prime Minister R. B. Bennett set up the Royal Commission on Banking and Currency in May 1933.

The seducee in the impending suit, Vivian MacMillan, was a junior stenographer in the attorney general's office, the daughter of Allan MacMillan, mayor of Edson and the assistant foreman in the CNR Edson shops. Vivian MacMillan was then twenty-one years old and had lived in Edmonton since the fall of 1930 when she had enrolled at an Edmonton business college. When she graduated in 1931 she immediately obtained employment with the Alberta government. In the interval she had become so close a friend to the Brownlee family that she was regarded by Mrs. Brownlee and the two Brownlee sons "almost as a member of the family," coming and going as she pleased and taking part in family activities. She, in turn, described Mrs. Brownlee as "more than a mother to me." It was a relationship that began soon after her arrival in Edmonton and grew over the next three years.

Brownlee's reaction to the Maclean letter of August 3 was to contact M.M. Porter of Calgary, an old friend and close associate over many years in activities involving both the Alberta government and the Alberta Wheat Pool. One of the ablest of Alberta solicitors, Porter succeeded Brownlee as legal advisor to the Alberta Wheat Pool when Brownlee became premier, and the two were associated in the long struggle of the prairie provinces for the return of their natural resources. Porter immediately brought A.L. Smith into the case so that Brownlee had as high-powered a defense team as could be found within the Alberta profession. The letter also triggered a call from the premier to Attorney General J.L. Lymburn to alert him to the possibility that an extortion conspiracy was afoot. The attorney general got hold of Harry Brace, the superintendent of insurance, whose office had an investigative wing, and Brace hired three private detectives to start nosing around.

Brownlee also phoned Vivian MacMillan, who refused to see him; he also tried to contact her family without success. When he returned to the city later in August he and Mrs. Brownlee went out to Edson to try to see Mr. MacMillan to, in his words, "try to find out what I was being charged with; whether Vivian was pregnant and I was being accused." He found out at 11:00 A.M. on Friday, September 22, 1933, when Neil Maclean, Vivian's solicitor delivered the statement of claim to the clerk of the court, and made a copy available to the publisher of the Edmonton *Bulletin*.

The gist of that statement of claim was that Brownlee had become enchanted with Vivian MacMillan's "youth and innocence" on first meeting her at her parents' home in Edson, Alberta, in July 1930. He persuaded her—she was then just eighteen—to come to Edmonton to take a business course after which he promised her a government job. Once she enrolled at business college, Brownlee proceeded to seduce her whenever he desired—in the back seat of a government car parked on a lonely road, on a chesterfield in his office, and in a bed in his home, two or three times a week for the next two years. In one seven-week stretch he "insisted on having connections with her every night he was home."

That the statement was well designed to leave Brownlee's reputation in shreds can be illustrated by three paragraphs taken from it:

7. During the months of September and October, 1930, while driving in the country on different occasions at night, he told

her his wife was an invalid, that he and his wife had not lived together for years and that he was starved for affection, and unless the said Vivian MacMillan would give him her love he would be forced to resume marital relations with his wife, which would probably kill her. He told her that he had loved her devotedly from the first time he saw her and that it was her duty to give him the love he required. He told her that it was not wrong for her to have sexual relations with him but on the other hand was for the good of all concerned. He laughed at her old fashioned scruples. He told her that he was lonely and unhappy and needed a confidant and that he could not continue as premier unless he had her for a lover and confidant and that if she gave him the affection he had to have if he was to go on, that any thing he accomplished in the future would be owing to her. All the said statements made by the defendant were false and made only with the intent of accomplishing the seduction of the said Vivian MacMillan. At the same time the defendant by caresses, kisses and fondling exerted all his arts of seduction.

8. The said Vivian MacMillan was an inexperienced and innocent girl of eighteen and by his false statements, wiles, flattery and expert lovemaking the defendant managed to make the said Vivian MacMillan feel that it would not be wrong to be the defendant's confidant and sweetheart, but on the contrary it was her duty to save the unhappy, lonely premier for his important work to his Province and his Country and to save his wife from the danger of marital relations, and she yielded to his entreaties and was seduced by him on a lonely country road in October, A.D. 1930.

9. Therefore, from October, 1930, to June, 1933, the defendant required the said Vivian MacMillan to be at his disposal whenever he required her. He procured for her a position in the Provincial Government in an office close to his own. When the said Vivian MacMillan objected to doing his wishes the defendant threatened her with the loss of her position with the provincial Government.

Getting hold of the copy of the above statement so quickly enabled the *Bulletin* to score a clear scoop on its archrival, the *Journal*. Within an hour the *Bulletin* was on the street with an extra edition, trumpeting "Brownlee Sued for Seduction" with an eight-column headline. The statement of claim was summarized in the leading paragraphs of the story and then the statement itself was reproduced verbatim. Other urban Alberta dailies reported the gist of the story in their Friday afternoon regular editions and waited until the next day to run the text of the charges.

Brownlee was then in Ottawa with the Macmillan Commission and issued the following denial:

I have received the statement of claim by long distance telephone. While one regrets to have to face a case of this kind, still it will enable me to come to grips with rumors that have been spread throughout the province for some weeks. There is not a word of truth in any of the allegations against me and I will defend the action to the limit and hope to show before I am through the real cause behind it.

The enigmatic references in the statement—"rumors that have been spread abroad" and the "real cause behind it"—naturally increased public interest in the suit rather than otherwise. But when the premier entered his rebuttal to the statement of claim and filed a countersuit on November 10, 1933, it was far from the media event that the MacMillan charges had been.

This lack of equal treatment could not have been attributed solely to the anti-Brownlee, anti-UFA bias of the Alberta newspapers, although that bias existed. The Edmonton *Bulletin*, Calgary *Albertan*, and Lethbridge *Herald* were unmitigated Liberal party supporters. The Edmonton *Journal* and Calgary *Herald* were Conservative to the core. All five were therefore committed to the destruction of the farmers' government of Alberta and the Progressive movement federally.

But that Armistice Day weekend of 1933 was jam-packed with other news that diminished the importance of the Brownlee case. On Sunday, November 13, the German people went to the polls in a plebiscite-cum-general election and voted ninety percent in favour of Adolf Hitler and his Nazi party. And on Monday the Bennett government released the text of the eagerly awaited Macmillan Royal Commission report which urged the cancellation of the currency issuing privileges of the chartered banks and the establishment of the Bank of Canada. It was the *Journal's* turn that Monday afternoon to bring out an extra edition, this one on the Macmillan Report. It included the Brownlee rebuttal on the front page. The *Bulletin* only got around to the Brownlee denial the next day.

Brownlee denied each and every allegation in all the fifteen specific charges in the statement of claim. In addition he charged that "the statement of claim is false, frivolous, vexatious, scandalous and an abuse of the process of the court and the defendant will contend on or before the trial of this action that it ought to be struck out and expunged from the records of the court." Brownlee, moreover, had a counterclaim of his own.

Brownlee alleged that the suit was a result of a failure by Vivian MacMillan and her fiance John Caldwell to extract money from him by threatening him with the seduction story, which they wholly invented. In addition,

The defendants by counterclaim conspired with each other and with diverse persons to the plaintiff by counterclaim at present unknown to secure for the defendant by counterclaim Caldwell a reward or profit to be paid by one or more of his fellow conspirators in consideration of the defendants by counterclaim taking such steps as would be designed to bring into disrepute the character of the plaintiff by counterclaim.

The defendants by counterclaim having failed in their attempt to induce the plaintiff by counterclaim to pay money by threatening to bring an action making allegations to their knowledge untrue caused the statement of claim in this action be issued maliciously well knowing that its contents were untrue and caused it to be published in the press with the intent that the publication of its contents the public would be induced to believe the allegations contained therein and that the reputation of the plaintiff by counterclaim would be damaged thereby.

The trial itself did not begin until June 25, 1934, with Maclean and R.H.C. Harrison for the plaintiffs and Porter and A.L. Smith for the defendant, before Mr. Justice William Ives and a six-man jury. Vivian MacMillan took the stand once preliminaries were out of the way and spent a day and a half under examination by Maclean and the next day and a half under cross-examination by A.L. Smith. Midway through her testimony a halt was called while Judge Ives dealt with the lurid coverage of proceedings by the Edmonton *Bulletin*. Mr. Smith called the court's attention to comments on proceedings that were in contempt of court and, open as the newspaper was to the jury's eyes, highly prejudicial to the case for the defense. Among the statements he objected to were an eight-column headline in red ink: "Vivian testifies to harrowing ordeals," and the following:

> Facing with courageous mien the terrible ordeal of disclosing her frailities and indignities before a judge and jury, counsel, reporters and the public, Vivian MacMillan, who a few days ago had her 22nd birthday, told such a story in the witness box in the Brownlee seduction suit on Monday afternoon as was never told before in the annals of court records or in the pages of fiction.
>
> Facing this morning still greater ordeal of having her story given in the witness box Monday, remorselessly dissected by one of the greatest cross-examiners in Western Canada....

Judge Ives issued a peremptory order for Charles Campbell, owner and publisher of the *Bulletin*, and his star reporter and master of purple prose, J.S. Cowper, to appear to answer contempt charges. Brushing aside arguments by counsel for the pair for time in which to prepare an answer, Judge Ives fined Campbell $300 and Cowper $100 on the spot with alternatives of ten days and three days at hard labour, respectively.

The gist of Vivian MacMillan's testimony was that she had been lured to Edmonton by Brownlee with a promise of a government job after she completed a business course. Almost immediately after her arrival he had taken her for a ride in the country and seduced her in the back seat of his car. Thereafter over the next thirty months the seduction was repeated two or three times a week in the back seat of a car parked on a country road; in his office; in a twin bed he occupied in a room shared with his son, while his wife slept in an adjoining bedroom. In many cases MacMillan attached dates to places.

Under cross-examination her story began to unravel. A.L. Smith was able to show that Brownlee was frequently absent from the city when she had sworn he was seducing her. These absences in Winnipeg, Ottawa, Calgary, or rural Alberta resulted in one stretch of three months of almost daily "connections" being whittled down under cross-examination to less than ten days.

Though she pleaded physical discomfort, no evidence was ever produced that the experience had any deleterious effect on her health. No legislative building janitor could be found who had ever seen her entering Brownlee's office on Saturday afternoon, when the offices shut down and the cleaning staff moved in. No wayfaring stranger ever came upon them parked on a country road in a car with the engine running in the dead of winter. No evidence was introduced to corroborate her story in any detail. It was her story against his.

But as Chief Justice Harvey pointed out in his writing of the decision of the Court of Appeal, Smith's cross-examination had brought out inconsistency after inconsistency in her story: She had insisted that intercourse was painful and distasteful to her and had endured it only because of Brownlee's influence over her. That influence, she testified came to bear only when she was with him. Yet two years after the affair was alleged to have started, she had been home with her parents in Edson; they had urged her to stay home and give up her job in Edmonton. She refused, and returned to Edmonton, knowing the relationship would be resumed. In January 1933, she told her fiancé of the relationship. Yet she continued the relationship for several months. Even after Caldwell took her to the solicitor to prepare the damage action, she continued the relationship.

This was a period in which all people in public office were under siege by economic upheaval, from the prime minister of Canada to the chairman of the lowliest school board of the hinterlands. Wherever they looked and whenever they looked there was nothing but trouble compounding trouble. And additionally, for Premier John Brownlee of Alberta, during 1931 and 1932, his own UFA party was being torn apart by internal ideological dissension. Prominent members of both the provincial and federal groups had played significant parts in the Calgary and Regina founding meetings of the Co-operative Commonwealth Federation, a depression-model, Canadian-style, Fabian socialist organization. At the other end of the spectrum were growing numbers of zealots of the Douglas theories of Social Credit. The 1933 convention of the party turned into an ideological Donnybrook, with Brownlee at the centre of the storm.

Keeping his party from flying apart at the seams was problem enough. It was complicated by the continuing financial crises of his government and its relations with its municipalities, school boards, and medical institutions. Would such a multiplicity of concerns not have tended to vitiate the libidinosity of any fifty-year-old provincial political leader? An occasional dalliance as an escape from the awful reality of the Dirty Thirties? Perhaps. But two or three times a week, week in and week out, over two-and-a-half years in the social and political climate that prevailed?

The trial began on Monday and ground to a halt on Saturday morning. Then, without an explanation of any kind, Smith announced that the defense was abandoning its counterclaim and agreed to the dismissal of the claim with costs. He did not move that the case be taken from the jury on the grounds that no group of reasonable men could possibly find for the plaintiff on the evidence represented. Nor did Justice Ives withdraw the case for the same reason. Instead, after the opposing counsel had made their representations, Ives charged the jury to provide answers to four questions: Did the defendant seduce the plaintiff? If so, when? If so, did she suffer damage? Did Allan MacMillan suffer damage?

The jury retired at 3:55 P.M. and returned at 8:45 P.M. with its verdict. It found that there was seduction the first time Vivian went out with Brownlee, that she suffered $10,000 in damage, and that her father suffered $5,000 in damage.

Justice Ives then said, "Gentlemen of the jury, you are excused and you may go. I think I should say openly and publicly while you are present I strongly disagree with your answers. The evidence does not warrant them. You may go." After hearing from counsel for both parties he refused to enter judgment and adjourned court. Instead of waiting for Ives to enter the judgment, Brownlee resigned forthwith as leader of the United Farmers of Alberta and as premier.

After pondering the case over the weekend, on Tuesday Judge Ives entered his judgment as follows:

Upon the verdict being announced by the jury, counsel for the defendant moved for dismissal of the action on the grounds that there was no evidence of any interference with the daughter's services to the parent to which he was entitled and no evidence that the seduction in any way interfered with the daughter's ability to serve.

It is quite clear that the daughter left her home in Edson with the consent and approval of the parents and was accompanied to Edmonton by her mother. It is equally undoubted that no illness resulted from the seduction and no evidence that the ability of the daughter to render services was in any way interfered with.

In my opinion the law is well settled that damage is the gist of the action and I am also of the opinion that the damage necessary to found a right of action in the woman must be of the same character as gave the master the right of action, that is loss of service or at least an interference with the woman's ability to serve. I see nothing in our statute to convey a contrary intendment of the legislature.

In my view of the law the action must be dismissed with costs, including the cost of discovery and only one bill should be taxed.

No evidence being offered by the defendant on his counter-claim, it will be dismissed with costs including discovery.

Mr. Justice Ives' decision set off an unprecedented spate of editorializing in the newspapers across the country on the general theme of "If a judge can override the considered judgment of a jury, what's the good of a jury system?" The Calgary *Herald* expressed the general sentiment of most of the editors in the following editorial:

At the moment the Brownlee-MacMillan case is from some angles, at least, a proper subject for discussion by laymen. The jury of six men weighing such facts as were developed in the evidence, decided unanimously that the defendant was guilty of the charge laid against him.

Acting in line with instructions given them by the judge in his charge the jurymen considered damages and made an assessment thereof of $10,000.00 to the female plaintiff and $5,000.00 to the male plaintiff.

Those instructions, were most explicit, as it was proper they should be, the whole basis of and justification for the action being the matter of damages, as was indicated in the statement of the judge to the jurymen that "if no damage follows a seduction the action is not maintained".

Respecting damages the learned judge stated to the jurymen that they were entitled to assume the father had felt humiliation and had lost some service of his daughter, for which he would be entitled to damages. He told them that they might, if they felt the misconduct of the defendant deserved punishment, inflict exemplary damages, thus putting on the record their opinion in that respect. In the case of the female plaintiff the learned judge told the jurymen they were entitled to assume she would suffer at the hands of society, and that for this as well as for her illness, if they decided it was brought about by acts of the defendant, they were entitled to assess fitting damages.

Acting on these instructions the jurymen brought in a verdict for the plaintiffs and assessed damages. At once counsel for the defendant gave notice of appeal on stated grounds, which the judge asked time to consider, delaying entering of judgment in the meantime.

Tuesday morning the learned judge filed a judgment which set aside the verdict of the jury, dismissed the action against the defendant and assessed all costs thereof against the plaintiffs. The stated ground upon which this judgment was based in that under the law "the damage necessary to found a right of action in the woman must be of the same character as gave the master his right of action; that is loss of service, or at least an interference with the woman's ability to serve."

Assuming that the learned judge interprets the law correctly in this judgment, it is most unfortunate that before the case was handed over to the jury he had not exercised his right to withdraw and dismiss it, he evidently being of the opinion that the plaintiffs' claim had not been substantiated. It is equally unfortunate that he should have directed and instructed the jury on the question of damages in terms so out of accord with his own interpretation of the law, as indicated in his Tuesday judgment.

The province of Alberta has suffered considerable unfavorable publicity already over this case; it looks as if more of the same thing will have to be suffered before "finis" is written to it.

The *Herald* was certainly right about one thing—there would be more of the same.

Curiously enough, in all the public outcry over the Ives decision, no one seemed to have wondered why the counterclaim was dropped. During the trial a number of questions were left hanging in the air. In the main they centred on the details of $1,400 that Brownlee had paid to the attorney general's department in reimbursement for government expenditures investigating the alleged conspiracy against Brownlee involving the MacMillans and John Caldwell. It was these investigations which provided the evidence that convinced Porter and Smith that they had grounds for a counterclaim. And why was the counterclaim dropped so precipitously? The record sayeth not. But the story that surfaced soon after the trial, and was still being repeated twenty-five years later with minor modifications, went like this:

The $1,400 had been used to hire private detectives to zero in on Caldwell, probe into his background and, if possible, have one of them winnow his way into Caldwell's confidence. That was done. An RCMP shorthand reporter was secreted in a closet and took down a conversation between Caldwell and the detective in which the former outlined his plan to use Vivian MacMillan to blackmail Brownlee or, as an alternative, get the Liberal party to fund the law suit. The master plan of the defense was to produce the Mounted Police constable in court in uniform to testify to Caldwell's confession. On Friday afternoon, one story goes, a telegram was received from Ottawa interdicting the use of an RCMP constable in civil legal proceedings. That order blew the Brownlee defense clear out of the water and Porter and Smith had no alternative to dropping the countersuit.

Another version has a slightly different denouement. To wit: Prime Minister R.B. Bennett had the highest regard for Brownlee, vide his naming Brownlee to the MacMillan Royal Commission on Banking and Currency. He maintained a close watch on the case as the trial proceeded through H.R. Milner of the Milner Steer firm in Edmonton. (Milner was a power in the Conservative party and was Bennett's confidential consultant on all judicial appointments in Alberta.) Bennett knew of the defense countersuit strategy and, at the last minute, vetoed the use of the RCMP constable on the assumption that the jury would throw out the suit.

The story of the countersuit begins with the meeting of Vivian MacMillan and John Caldwell, a third-year medical student in the early autumn of 1932. Their association blossomed into romance and by Christmas they were talking marriage after Caldwell completed his medical studies. Thoughts of marriage nudged Vivian into confessing her alleged relationship with Brownlee. That blew the marriage plans as far as Caldwell was concerned. His interest in Vivian MacMillan as a potential bride evaporated. But his interest in John Brownlee as a target for an avenging angel named Caldwell mounted steadily until in early May of 1933 he went looking for legal advice. He got as far as the counsel for Cora McPherson, Neil Maclean, and the search ended.

If the acting out of the McPherson-Mattern morality play was bringing great gobs of aid and comfort to the Alberta Liberals, the sudden appearance of John Caldwell on the scene must have transported the party to cloud nine. The electoral fall-out from the McPherson affair might translate into the loss of seats by the UFA. But if Premier Brownlee himself could be similarly impaled it could mean a return of the Liberals to power.

This scenario was developed by McLean and Charles Campbell, publisher of the Edmonton *Bulletin*, at a Sunday morning meeting in the early summer of 1933 in the office of George Bell, publisher of the Calgary *Albertan*, with Bell and several prominent southern Alberta Liberals. By the time of the meeting the Edmontonians not only had Caldwell's story of the Brownlee-MacMillan relationship—they had Vivian's signed affidavit. What they wanted was for the Calgarians to become the nucleus of a group to raise a financial war chest to take care of their commitments to Caldwell.

It was, of course, the wildest of harebrained schemes because raising money for any cause no matter how worthy was nearly impossible in southern Alberta in the absolute depths of the Great Depression in 1933. But even had the plan had any hope of success, neither George Bell, nor any of the Liberals at the meeting, would have anything to do with it. That it offended Bell's sense of the fitness of things was clearly demonstrated by the subsequent action of the *Albertan* when the case eventually went to trial; the *Albertan* limited itself to sanitized and condensed versions of the proceedings.

On June 26, 1934, the *Albertan* published the following front page editorial:

### KEEP THE PRESS CLEAN

Certain of the Alberta newspaper press look upon the present unfortunate trial now going on at Edmonton as a heaven-sent opportunity to indulge their readers in an orgy of salaciousness. Ordinarily such a trial would be dismissed in a few words. The one under discussion, however, seems to have robbed newspaper managements of all sense of decency, and to distort all their perspectives. Hence this frantic endeavor to secure verbatim reports and to publish the grossest facts in the nude language in which they must be put to the court.

There is no justification for such a course. Because of the high public position of the defendant the facts must, of course, be published. The public, having rested its faith in the defendant, is entitled to know of what he is accused and of the answer thereto. But there is all the difference in the world between presenting the facts plainly and presenting a slow motion picture of all the alleged details. There is very little difference, in principle, between that and the vending of indecent photographs. Neither of them is fit for the home. The leering decadent who purchases his obscene literature in the back alley may gloat over this unexpected wealth. But why present it to our children?

The Albertan will not follow such a course. If this newspaper cannot be taken into the home without shame or humiliation it will not be published. In the interests of accuracy and fairness some details of the case in point must be presented. But The Albertan intends to derive no temporary and ephemeral circulation advantage by catering to obscenities and indecency. It is our belief that a very large proportion of the public is inherently decent in its reactions, does not want to read the elaboration of the facts such as a necessary to the court and jury, and not interested in strewing about the home page after page of the evidence in this case.

Getting the cold shoulder in Calgary did not discourage the

Edmontonians. As previously noted, Vivian maintained her relationship with Brownlee and his family for at least six weeks after her trip to Maclean's office with Caldwell and played a key role in the setting up of Brownlee for a "John Gilpin"-type car chase through the Edmonton streets on July 5, 1933.

The details of that car chase are spelled out in documents in the Lymburn and Brownlee files in the archives of Alberta. On July 3, Vivian had talked to Mrs. Brownlee about being a weekend house guest at their cottage at Sylvan Lake. Brownlee was to meet her to arrange details when he returned to the city on July 5. Unbeknownst to Brownlee, when he phoned Vivian and arranged to pick her up in front of the Administration Building to discuss the Sylvan Lake weekend arrangement, Caldwell and a person named Grieve were waiting with Vivian for the call. They took off for the meeting place, a few minutes distance from Vivian's rooming house. While Vivian waited for Brownlee, Caldwell joined Neil Maclean in a car which began to tail Brownlee's car after he picked up the girl.

Brownlee soon began to suspect that a car was following him. He asked Vivian what she thought and her reply was noncommittal. So while they talked about her visit to Sylvan Lake, Brownlee dipsied and doodled around the city, but the car stuck to his tail. Eventually he stopped, got the license number of the car and later traced it to Maclean. Vivian later begged off the weekend invitation to Sylvan Lake and that was the last Brownlee saw of her until the opening of the trial.

When he got her lawyer's letter of August 3, Brownlee recalled the car episode, put two and two together and called Attorney General Lymburn. It did not take long for the private detectives hired by Harry Brace to set young Mr. Caldwell up in their sights. They struck pay dirt rather quickly. One of the first things they discovered was that Caldwell had signed on with *Maclean's* magazine to head a crew of subscription canvassers for the summer once he had written his exams. But before he got started, he contacted Harold Davies, the *Maclean's* manager, and resigned with the explanation that he had a big deal on that would net him at least $25,000 and he had to work on it full-time.

In connection with the July 5 fox-and-hounds car chase, the following is a transcription of a hand-written memo in the Brownlee files in the public archives of Alberta:

Operator 3

Grieve, Caldwell and Maclean were in the first car which followed Mr. Brownlee's car and Mr. Howson and two others were in Mr. Howson's car which did not follow. Neilson mentioned several times that he recognized Mr. Howson. Grieve had called on Neilson to see if he would go on July 5th. Neilson refused, according to Neilson. Caldwell, Grieve and Miss MacMillan were at her boarding house when she made an appointment with Mr. Brownlee and arranged to meet him on 107th Street, changed to Administration Building. Taxi at 109th Street and 97th Avenue with driver, Maclean, Caldwell and Grieve. Howson across the street from Administration Building alone. Neilson did not wait until Brownlee picked the girl up.

The Howson referred to is W.R. Howson, the Liberal leader in the Alberta Legislature, later chief justice of Alberta. The following is a hand-written document in connection with Howson's relation to the case:

On July 30, 1933, Arthur Lessard told Katherine Medley (according to her declaration) that he was asked by someone whom she believed to be Mr. Howson if he wanted to see something exciting and of interest. He said he kept an appointment and was met by Mr. Howson and they proceeded in a car to the Administration Building where they parked. Another car was parked in the same area and in it he recognized Mr. Maclean and Mr. Caldwell. He said that Vivian MacMillan approached on foot and shortly after Mr. Brownlee in a car. Mr. Brownlee stopped and picked up MacMillan. Lessard said Mr. Brownlee proceeded over the High Level Bridge and that Maclean followed closely and Howson followed in another car. He said Maclean's car had the lights on but Howson's did not. Miss Medley further says that a week or so later Lessard told her Howson had said to him that in the future he was going to know nothing of the case.

On September 16, 1933, according to the statement, she again discussed the case with Lessard and he then definitely denied that Howson was in the car on the occasion mentioned but that he, (Lessard), had been picked up by Grieve and that Howson was not there at all and he denied ever having mentioned Howson's name to her, but if he did it was a mistake.

Miss Medley was a clerk employed by the Government of Alberta. Who was Grieve? Who knows? Who was Lessard? He was a resident of the Edmonton YMCA in 1933 and thereafter was not an Edmonton resident. Who was Operator 3? Probably one of the several people hired by Harry Brace to infiltrate the Caldwell-MacMillan conspiracy. That there was such an effort can be taken for granted from the following interchange between Maclean and Brownlee at the examination for discovery:

Q. Mr. Maclean: Do you know whether a detective named Burford had been acting for you Mr. Brownlee?

A. He wasn't acting for me.

Q. You have no knowledge of any investigation he has made?

A. Mr. Burford was, I believe, engaged by the Attorney-General's department, at a certain time to make certain inquiries.

Q. Have you any information that Mr. Burford paid a gentleman named Mr. Coffin $50.00 for an introduction to Mr. Caldwell, Jr.?

A. I have not.

Later on in the examination for discovery, Maclean asked Brownlee questions about a detective named Schwantje and got the same answers, and similarly, to a question concerning investigations by a detective named Dudley.

About all that is known about the $1,400, specifically, is that the attorney general advanced $500 for Harry Brace for incidental expenses on September 3, 1933. A month later Dudley had so gained Caldwell's confidence that Caldwell revealed the details of his plan to get $25,000 from Brownlee or someone else. The confession came in the course of his effort to obtain a loan from Dudley, pending his pay-off from the Brownlee caper. Dudley agreed to try to arrange a loan, made a date to meet later at his room at the Corona Hotel, and high-tailed it for Brace and the attorney general. The latter agreed to have Staff Constable Harold Allen of the RCMP hide in Dudley's room and, when the detective led Caldwell into repeating his story in detail, Allen, a shorthand reporter, could take down the conversation verbatim.

Here is a transcription of a longhand report from S.A. 999 (presumably "Special Operative") from the Lymburn dossier:

On October 5, 1933 John Caldwell came to "Dudley" and told him he was in a tough spot and needed some money. He said: "You have heard of the Brownlee case. I don't want you to think I am callous, but I'm going to make a lot of money out of that case—I am the man behind the case—I engineered the whole thing.... We have him sewed up tight and it is a safe gamble we will win and I will get the money.... But even if I don't win the case, I will be getting the money anyway."

He left and arranged to come back again at eleven. I arranged to have S/Cst. Allen concealed there. He came and talked again about the loan saying he would be in a position to pay in December after he gets his money from the Brownlee case. He told me what MacMillan had told him about Brownlee and herself, he said: "I hate Brownlee and I am out to get him and the innocent must suffer with him.... Mind you there are no politics in this as far as I am concerned. They are incidental to the case and crept in afterwards....Of course I was smart enough not to go to a Conservative lawyer like Milner....I went to a Liberal lawyer, Neil Maclean, and told him my story. I didn't tell Vivian I was going to see a lawyer about it. It was entirely my own idea....

Why, do you know that that article you read in the papers signed by Vivian and her father saying there are no politics behind the case? That was my idea, I wrote most of it myself.... No one knows that I am going to get most of the money from the case.... Politics have come into this thing. You can't keep them out but I won't be the loser by it. Of course this is all under the hat but I have been promised that if the Liberal party gets in, as they sure will do now, there is nothing I want I won't be able to get. When I get this money I am going to quit Varsity next year—Maclean and my Dad think it will look better if I go back this year and go to McGill.... I expect to get $20,000.00 or $25,000.00 out of this."

He also told Dudley they had given Brownlee ten or twenty days to settle but he had refused.

Where precisely would the money come from that would enable him to repay the loan he was negotiating with Dudley? And where, for that matter, would the money come from to pay for the substantial legal fees that would be incurred in prosecuting the damage action? Would it come, perhaps, from the same unknown benefactors who had retained the services of Van Allen and Maclean, both prominent Liberals, to take on the destitute Cora McPherson's suit against her ex-husband cabinet minister? Someone, perhaps, with a monumental vested interest in the destruction of the Brownlee government? The Liberal Party of Alberta, for example? According to Caldwell, it would take care of him handsomely whether they won the Brownlee case or lost. There can be little doubt, in the later, scribed-in-the-closet, conversation with Dudley, that Caldwell would have been pressed for names and details of where the money would come from to repay the loan.

But whatever became of Staff Constable Allen's shorthand notes?

Staff Constable Allen, long since retired, was interviewed at the Bow Valley Nursing Home where he resided on July 15, 1983. He refused to discuss any aspects of his work with the RCMP or to even admit he was involved in the Brownlee case. He had spent his career in the administration end of the RCMP and only participated in actual police work when getting something down in shorthand was involved. Was there any difficulty in getting things down in shorthand while hiding in closets or under beds? No, he said, you just had to make sure there was enough light to see the paper. And what became of the reports generally after he had transcribed his notes? Allen explained that a copy went onto his superior's desk and a copy went into the files. What did the inspector do with the report? The practice was to send it or take it to someone in the attorney general's department. Would a copy of the report have gone from the Edmonton RCMP to Ottawa as well? It would depend, Constable Allen said, on the nature and seriousness of events covered by the report. This was later confirmed by RCMP officials. If the Allen transcription did find its way to Ottawa, to the RCMP and to the Department of Justice, it would explain last minute instructions from Ottawa to the Brownlee defense not to use the testimony of an RCMP officer in a civil suit.*

The appeal of the MacMillans against the Ives judgment was launched on September 19, 1934, heard in mid-January 1935, and the majority dismissing the appeal was handed down at the end of the month. Chief Justice Harvey, who wrote the majority report, was scathing in his criticism of Vivian MacMillan's testimony. "It is," he said, "of such a nauseating character that I shall deal with it in the most general way possible and it seems almost as incredible that a girl could concoct such a story as that can be true."

Vivian's story was indeed ridden with contradictions but—. During the period in question she lived in several different rooming houses, always within easy walking distance of the Legislative Building where she worked. Brownlee lived on 88th Avenue, a five-minute drive across the High Level Bridge. On the late evenings when Brownlee drove Vivian home from his home, according to his wife's testimony, he would usually return within an hour and a quarter or an hour and a half. That was time enough, as often happened, for Brownlee to call on a man at the Corona Hotel, or pick up some papers at his office, before returning. It was also time enough for a trip out the Stony Plain Road and to park for a while.

Between the Brownlee trial and the Appeal Court verdict, Alberta politics roiled and boiled like a witches' brew. To some, the Brownlee case, coming so hard upon the McPherson case, proved that a moral decline had set in within the UFA and, in December 1934, two UFA backbenchers crossed the floor in protest to join the Liberals. And out in the constituencies there was little doubt that the McPherson-Brownlee sex scandals were affecting the party faithful. It was a malaise that ran deeper than anybody could have envisioned at the time.

Given the religiosity of the UFA constituency there is little doubt that the sex scandals were deeply offensive to the farmers. That being so, the Alberta Liberal Party had every reason to be confident that the votes of the disenchanted would fall to their candidates at the next election. It might all have come to pass except that the evangelists of a new religion, Social Credit, had already harvested thousands of new converts from within the ranks of the UFA faithful. And there was one other thing—the Brownlee case had put the Liberal party itself under a cloud of

*The story of how Porter and Smith were all set to put Staff Constable Allen on the stand to testify to what he had heard in the closet in Dudley's room was widely circulated in Alberta. That testimony would have nailed down the connection between young Caldwell and the Liberal Party. Years later, when I heard the story from Marsh Porter, I persuaded Honourable S.S. Garson, the federal attorney general, to ferret out any corroboratory material in the Department of Justice files. The search located nothing.

suspicion. The counterclaim was based upon the alleged existence of a conspiracy between Caldwell and "others" to damage Brownlee's reputation. Were the others the leaders of the Liberal Party of Alberta? Brownlee and his defense certainly thought so because the legal underbrush was full of Liberals, and nobody but Liberals.

In the hiatus between provincial leaders, W.R. Howson MLA was the Liberal house leader. He succeeded to the party leadership in October 1932. It was a clerk in Howson's office, according to S.B. Woods, who filed the original writ in the McPherson case. Charles Campbell, who bought the Edmonton *Bulletin* from Frank Oliver, was as equally dedicated to the cause of the Liberal party. It was Campbell's paper that turned the McPherson case firstly and the Brownlee case secondly into the media circuses they became. The Conservative Edmonton *Journal*, in contrast, took two days to decide whether it would report the McPherson suit at all. During the McPherson trial Campbell saw to it that McPherson's hometown of Vulcan and Little Bow constituency were flooded with *Bulletins*. Both Maclean and Van Allen were top level Liberals and the latter successfully contested one of the Edmonton seats for the party in 1935.

The McPherson case broke long before legal aid had been developed in Alberta. Van Allen and Maclean took on the foredoomed case for the destitute Cora McPherson with no hope of collecting a fee for their services. Indeed, it was a case where someone had to be putting up substantial expense money. One of Cora's sisters was prepared to testify on her behalf but not to come to Edmonton to do so. So a hearing was arranged in Great Falls, Montana, to which counsel for both sides and a court reporter travelled and spent a couple of days. Other witnesses for Cora McPherson were brought to Edmonton from the United States. Somebody was certainly providing a lot of the financial grease that put the McPherson show on the road.

Throughout this chapter the names of Brownlee and McPherson have frequently been coupled, which should not be taken to indicate that they were men of equal stature or prestige within the farmers movement of Alberta. Brownlee had grown immensely in stature during his premiership. One indication of that was his appointment to the Macmillan Royal Commission. When the McPherson case broke, it was not long before demands for McPherson's expulsion surfaced in the UFA caucus. When the Brownlee case broke, the executive of the UFA went into emergency session immediately and unanimously expressed its confidence in and support for him.

Clearly there were enough loyal Brownlee supporters within the UFA and within the Alberta Wheat Pool to make sure that the counterclaim story of a Liberal conspiracy was spread far and wide among the farmers of Alberta, and to keep the details circulating. There was no similar upwelling of sympathy or support for McPherson. Indeed just the reverse was true. Following Brownlee's resignation as premier, his successor, Honourable R.G. Reid, reappointed all Brownlee's cabinet except McPherson. Following his crushing defeat in the Little Bow constituency in the 1935 election, McPherson disappeared from public life.

The Liberals did very badly indeed in 1935 and it is hard to believe that part of the explanation did not lie in the "roorback" syndrome. This Americanism describes a political development in which there is reaction against a party that attempts to discredit another party's candidate by resorting to "dirty pool."

Not only did the Liberals fail to attract the voters who deserted the UFA by the thousands, they lost ground themselves, winding up with only five seats compared to the thirteen they held at dissolution. A case in point was the Ponoka riding where Brownlee had been elected by acclamation in 1930. He was defeated in 1935 by a political neophyte, Mrs. Edith Rogers, the Social Credit candidate and the only woman to be elected in 1935, by 2,295 to 879. The Liberal candidate managed to poll only 696.

Following the loss in the Alberta Court of Appeal the solicitors for Vivian MacMillan carried their case to the Supreme Court of Canada. There on March 1, 1937, the decision followed the reasoning of the dissenting justices of Alberta and restored the verdict of the trial jury. It rejected the position of the Alberta Court of Appeal majority that a tort had to be proved to sustain a claim for damages. Vivian MacMillan was awarded $10,000 and costs. It was Brownlee's turn to appeal and he did so to the Judicial Committee of the Privy Council. In June of 1940, it confirmed the judgment of the Supreme Court of Canada.

By this time the reputation of John Brownlee had been completely rehabilitated. He had retired from politics after his defeat in 1935 and returned to the practice of law. He was almost immediately re-appointed solicitor for the United Grain Growers (UGG), an action in itself indicative of the faith of the farm leaders in his integrity, to say nothing of the proof of the effectiveness of the widespread circulation of the "inside story of the counter-claim." Brownlee was elected to the Board of Directors of the United Grain Growers in 1942 and served on the boards of a number of food industry companies. In 1948, when R.S. Law retired from the UGG, Brownlee was elected to succeed him as president and served until his death in 1961 at the age of seventy-seven.

Among his honourary pall bearers were Former Chief Justice Clinton Ford; Justice M.M. Porter; Premier E.C. Manning; Honourable Douglas Harkness, minister of defense; George

McIvor; R.W. Milner; Senator T.A. Crerar; and other prominent farm leaders of the West.

That John Brownlee managed to rise unscathed from the ashes of his political career to a position of eminence in western Canada cannot be gainsaid. The extent to which public revulsion against the Liberal Party's role in the McPherson-Brownlee imbroglio contributed to the Social Credit triumph in 1935 must remain one of history's conundrums. The party's failure to prosper even when the auguries were favourable, on the other hand, is convincing evidence that its involvement, no matter how peripheral it may have been, was a public relations disaster.

There remains to be added only one footnote in the form of the longest unamended and least-used of all Alberta statutes. It is the Seduction Act which was first passed by the North-West Territories Council in 1903 and re-enacted by the Alberta Legislature in the revision of the Alberta Statutes in 1922, by, incidentally, the United Farmers of Alberta government of which John Brownlee was attorney general. It was re-enacted, word for word, except for minor paragraphing and syntax tidying-up, at each subsequent revision of the statutes until and including the revision of 1980. Here it is:

REVISED STATUTES OF ALBERTA, 1922
THE SEDUCTION ACT
CHAPTER 334

1. This Act may be cited as *The Seduction Act.*

2. The father or, in case of his death the mother, whether she remains a widow or remarries, of a unmarried female who has been seduced or for whose seduction the father or mother could maintain an action if the unmarried female was at the time dwelling under his or her protection, may maintain an action for such seduction, notwithstanding that the unmarried female was at the time of her seduction serving or residing with another person upon hire or otherwise.

3. (1) Upon the trial of an action for seduction brought by a father or mother it is not necessary to prove an act of service performed by the party seduced, but her act of service shall in all cases be presumed and no evidence shall be received to the contrary.

   (2) Notwithstanding subsection (1), where a father or mother of an unmarried and seduced female had before the seduction abandoned her and refused to provide for and retain her as an inmate, then any other person who at common law might have maintained an action for the seduction may maintain such action.

4. A person, other than the father or mother, who by reason of the relation of master or otherwise would have been entitled at

common law to maintain an action for the seduction of an unmarried female may maintain such action if the father or mother

(a) is not resident in the Province at the time of the birth of the child born inconsequent of the seduction, or

(b) is resident in the Province but does not bring an action for the seduction within six months from the birth of the child.

5. Notwithstanding anything in this Act, an unmarried female who has been seduced may, in her own name and in the same manner as an action for any other tort, maintain an action for seduction and in any such action she is entitled to such damages as may be awarded.

# Chapter Eight
# The Oil Boom

In a matter of forty years, the petroleum industry went from being the least regulated of all Canadian enterprises to becoming, as some might say, the most over-regulated enterprise in Christendom. From beginning to end, the Calgary bar was an inextricable part of the process of going from one to the other, (probably first defining the term "oil well" as being "a hole in the ground surrounded on all sides by law suits"), and because it did, Calgary, and not Edmonton, became the oil capital of Canada.

Such pioneer ornaments to the bar as Sir James Lougheed, R.B. Bennett, and Eric Harvie were all shareholders in 1914 in the Dingman well that made the discovery of crude oil in Turner Valley. It was Mr. Justice A.A. McGillivray, the most famous of Alberta barristers, who, as a royal commissioner, provided the foundation and the framework for Alberta's regulatory system. And between 1925 and 1940, there was no one who was anybody in the Calgary bar who was not a director of at least one oil company and counsel for several more.

But it all began for these purposes in 1913 when Richard Bedford Bennett was already on his way to becoming the biggest somebody of all. So it was when W.S. Herron noticed escaping gas near Sheep Creek and followed his hunch at least far enough to have a sample analyzed, that he knew that Bennett was just the man to invite to a picnic at the site southwest of Calgary. Accompanying them was A.W. Dingman—as cagey an Ontario entrepreneur as Bennett was a New Brunswick lawyer—and when Herron lit a match over the gas pocket and a flame erupted strong enough to boil their coffee, both men knew that this was a place where money could be made. Bennett hurried back to town to assemble the syndicate of businessmen that would become Calgary Petroleum Products Company; Herron traded a parcel of his land in exchange for a modest amount of money and a 25 percent interest in the new company; and Dingman started drilling at the Turner Valley picnic site.

Within weeks the location was the target of curious sightseers, and within months their ranks were swollen by frenzied would-be speculators reacting to *Herald* stories about a predicted bonanza. And, when at last word of the Dingman Number 1 discovery reached Calgary from Turner Valley on May 14, 1914, that discovery set off a speculative orgy in Calgary unequalled for either the instantaneous intensity of the public's participation, or its fundamental fraudulence. Near-bankrupt real estate promoters converted their Eighth Avenue and Ninth Avenue premises, overnight, into oil stock supermarkets while the legal fraternity worked overtime documenting the incorporation of scores of new oil companies.

The city directory for 1914 listed 226 oil mining companies, thirty-two oil brokers and four separate stock exchanges. The speculative mania ran through the summer and well into 1915 before it gradually petered out. The First World War, the essential fraudulence of most of the promotions, and the lack of success of the companies that did drill wells combined to squelch the boom. By the end of the war only twenty-one oil companies and two brokers survived, and the latter were exclusively occupied selling government bonds.

One reason for the extravagance of the boom was the ease with which anybody could get into the "oil mining" business. The title to the natural resources of Alberta was still vested in the federal government. All that one needed to obtain a twenty-one-year lease on the petroleum and natural gas rights underlying a quarter section of land was eighty-five dollars—five dollars for a filing fee to be paid to a clerk in the government land office along with eighty dollars for the first year's rental at fifty cents per acre per year. With that lease in hand the promoters could, and did, organize a 500,000 share company, set aside 150,000 shares of the stock for themselves as vendors of the eighty-five dollar lease, and proceeded to sell the rest of the shares to the public for fifty cents or one dollar a share. (Blue sky laws to protect unwary investors had not yet been invented.)

Meanwhile Calgarians who rattled their way over the rutted mud trails to the site of the Dingman well discovered that its oil was unlike anything resembling the heavy, sticky black stuff usually associated with oil wells. It was so impregnated with natural gas liquids that it could be poured directly from the well into a Model T gas tank and the car would run. The first order of business for the Dingman people was to build a processing plant to separate the gas from the oil before the latter could be trucked to market. The second order was to get on with the drilling of a couple of more wells within a quarter mile of each other and the discovery well.

The nature of the Dingman discovery made it particularly propitious for the Canadian Western Natural Gas, Light, Heat, and Power Company. It was then embarked on a campaign to persuade Calgarians to switch from coal-fired furnaces to natural gas heat. Unhappily, the gas supplies it had discovered between Lethbridge and Medicine Hat kept petering out as the demand increased. In the beginning, the Calgary Petroleum Products Company, which drilled the Dingman well, simply piped the waste gas away and burned it. When the third well was completed successfully, the size of the flares burning around the clock called stark attention to the wastage of gas that could well have been used in Calgary. The two companies negotiated a contract to build a gas line to the town of Okotoks to connect with the trunk main the gas company had built from Bow Island to Calgary.

Unfortunately, the absorption plant was scarcely into full operation when it caught fire and burned to the ground late in the fall of 1920. That was the end of the Calgary Petroleum Products Company. The receipts from its production had been barely sufficient to pay for the drilling of the follow-up wells. The insurance it carried on the plant was insufficient to rebuild it, even if the steadily declining production from its wells had justified the expenditure. Then, Imperial Oil, which had a small refinery under construction in Calgary, entered the picture.

Five years' experience with the Dingman wells had given rise to a theory that if a well was drilled into deeper formations better reservoirs would be found. Imperial was prepared to finance such a well. So Calgary Petroleum Products became Royalite Oil Company, in which Imperial became the major shareholder by supplying the funds to reconstruct the absorption plant and drill a deep well a mile north of the discovery well.

It took Royalite two years to complete the well into the Mississippian limestone to a depth of sixty-five hundred feet. It blew in on October 14, 1924, as a high pressure wet gas well, however, and not as a conventional oil well. But it was a world class "gusher" nonetheless. When a great gust of gas hit the surface that afternoon, the drilling crew rushed to pull the drill string from the hole and close the shut-off valve on the wellhead. Then they watched in mounting concern as the wellhead gauge showed the pressure in the well casing rising at the rate of one hundred pounds a minute. When it got to a thousand pounds to the square inch they fled the rig and watched from a safe distance as the mounting pressure blew the casing out of the hole and through the top of the derrick. After blowing out of control for a week, the well caught fire and burned for a month before it was finally brought under control.

It was then possible to determine that it was a well to answer every wildcatter's prayer. The 17 million to 20 million cubic feet of gas a day it produced also yielded five hundred barrels of natural gasoline or naphtha. Enough gas, in short, to supply the needs of a city the size of Calgary. The gas company and Royalite immediately got together and negotiated a deal that would become a festering sore in the ear of every independent producer in Turner Valley for years to come. Royalite became the *exclusive* Turner Valley supplier of natural gas to the Canadian Western Natural Gas, Light, Heat, and Power Company in *perpetuity*.

The oil stock boom triggered by the Royalite well was more restrained and less larcenous than the Dingman boom had been. The corporate structures had changed but little. The promoters were still creaming off a third of the treasury stock for their leases and the commission to the salesmen was still a generous third. The public in 1925–1926, unfortunately, was still suffering from the once-bitten twice-shy syndrome and, in the economic doldrums of the 1920s, money was less plentiful than it had been in 1914. What the promoters needed was sales of shares in 1,000-share blocks to finance the drilling of hundred thousand dollar wells. What they got were sales in the 25, 50, and 100 share blocks. As a result few promotions were adequately financed and it was common for drilling to be halted several times while financial coffers were recharged. (Indeed, it was not until I.W.C. Solloway and the Toronto brokers discovered Turner Valley in 1928 that the real boom in oil stocks occurred. See Chapter 6.)

Mainly what happened after Royalite Number 4, was that a rush of 1914 investors began searching through trunks and bureau drawers for their long forgotten stock certificates in the hope they were among the companies being resuscitated. There were, indeed, some survivors—McDougal-Sequr, Illinois Alberta, McLeod, Mid-West, Dalhousie, Okalta, Herron-Elder, some of whom had actually found oil and had money in the bank with which to resume operations.

The development that took place after the Royalite Number 4 went on production was more the product of internal combustion, than the result of the promotional excesses of stockbrokers. There was first of all the arithmetic. Every few weeks the newspapers would carry reports that, over the past month, Royalite had produced naphtha at the rate of six hundred barrels a day. At four dollars a barrel, that was generating income at the rate of seventy-two thousand dollars a month. And that did not count the twenty thousand dollars a month it was obtaining from the natural gas. That all this was certain to continue into the foreseeable future was indicated by the new fourteen-inch gas line being constructed from Turner Valley to Calgary.

Figures of such magnitude were bound to appeal to the businessmen of Calgary and soften them up for the approach by colleagues trying to put an oil company together based on some favourably located crown leases. The names of prominent Calgarians became the names of Turner Valley oil companies—Spooner, Devenish, MacLeod, Davies. The names of the business leaders— Pat Burns, R.J. Hutchings, F.R. Webster, and others, turned up on the director roster of Turner Valley oil companies. And the names of all the most prominent Calgary lawyers became regularly associated with oil company business. R.B. Bennett was a director of Imperial Oil and his partner, Alex Hannah, was general counsel for half a dozen companies, including Royalite and Dalhousie. Among the other names to occur frequently in connection with Turner Valley activities were H.P.O. Savary, W.C. Fisher, A.M. Sinclair, D.A. MacDonald, McKinley Cameron, H.D. Patterson, Alec Hannah, Gordon Egbert, D. Austin Lane, O.H.E. Might, M.M. Porter, L.H. Fenerty, Fred Shouldice, and A.L. Smith.

But with the possible exception of Bennett and L.H. Fenerty, who were both introduced to Turner Valley by W.S. Herron, the list of oil-wise legal veterans could be reduced substantially in those early days of 1920, and those who were still stubbornly scratching for a foothold in the valley numbered few indeed. By 1928 when D.P. McDonald (later to become chief counsel for Westcoast Transmission) arrived in Calgary looking for an articling position, the veterans were hard at work, each representing clients greedy for a piece of the action, which unfortunately was tied up tight as a tic by the big landholders. McDonald remembers four of them—Porter, Fisher, Harvie, and Sam Helman—with undiminished awe. They wheeled and dealed their way through the oil and gas business of the 1920s with a zeal akin to religious fervor, yet despite their common interests they had little use for one another personally.

McDonald found his first legal position with Porter's firm, but cut his wisdom teeth in the oil business with W.C. Fisher, who was to be his long-term law partner. Until the early twenties Fisher's practice had been distinguished only by the fact that he was one of the few lawyers who actually welcomed divorce cases, but he earned his page in the legal legends of Alberta when he penned his famous drilling contract that agreed "to drill in a husbandlike manner." When he discovered how easy it was to sell oil mining shares in the farming communities of southern Alberta, Fisher's entrepreneurial side took over. He managed to get a twenty-acre lease in north Turner Valley, organized a company that he called Model Oils and when Model Number 1 produced condensate at the rate of one barrel to 5,000 cubic feet of gas it made it the lowest gas-oil ratio well in the valley. But, despite his good fortune Fisher was only too aware that until the big companies were made to free up their virtual monopoly of the market outlets little could be accomplished in the way of expansion for the independents.

McDonald, as Fisher's junior, spent long hours cooling his heels in competing lawyers' outer offices, trying doggedly to set up meetings that neither party wished to attend, and desperately seeking to mend the ruffled feathers of peacock-like egos. If Porter refused to speak to Fisher, Fisher wouldn't talk to Helman, and nobody wanted to deal with Harvie. It got so bad that Fisher took to sneaking out of the office, leaving McDonald to barricade Harvie and his client in with the documents until the client agreed to sign. "I found that no matter what kind of a deal you had with Harvie at five o'clock, if he had a chance to think about it overnight, you had to make the deal all over again."

The four of them may have fought and scrapped their way through those early decades, but their respect for one another's abilities was great and those coming along behind learned a good deal. Not only did they counsel the oil companies, they took active interest as shareholders in the companies' operations. Thus, for example, when a group of dissident MacLeod Oil Company shareholders staged a protest against a group of directors, Bennett, Hannah and Cameron all turned up at the meeting and took sides in the controversy.

As the old companies became reactivated and new companies were organized, the Calgary legal fraternity found its services in demand, modestly, again. With the real estate market quiescent, farm prices depressed, and the general level of business activity slowed to stagnation, the law had become a hand-to-mouth sort of profession for many practitioners. Suddenly legal services were needed to transfer leases, negotiate contracts, and put syndicates together.

For the large companies like Royalite, Imperial, and others, the ordinary lawyer-client relationship prevailed when it came to setting and collecting fees. But, with many of the companies, the lawyers were frequently persuaded to take blocks of stock in lieu of fees. In some cases, in later years, such arrangements would prove to be extremely lucrative for the more fortunate lawyers. Much more often, the stock certificates provided only memories of things that might have been. Art Smith, the son of A.L. Smith, recalled that after his father's death a bulky file filled with such certificates turned up among his father's papers.

On the other hand, many lawyers had the chance to cash in handsomely after the Toronto brokers moved in late 1928. Some actually did take their profits. D.P. McDonald recalled his own experience in 1929 as an articled student with the Brownlee, Porter, Goodall, and Rankin firm. A worried secretary asked his advice about what she should do with the thousand shares of Dalhousie Oil stock she had bought at thirty-five cents. It was then selling for eight or nine dollars. Should she sell or not?

"It so happened I had been instructed that very day to retrieve a stock certificate for several thousand shares from the vault for one of the partners and take it to his broker's. He had sold his stock so I felt confident in advising the secretary to sell hers," McDonald recalled.

The partner was M.M. "Marsh" Porter who, four years earlier, had devised a plan for amalgamating several small companies into Dalhousie Oil Company, an Imperial Oil subsidiary. For his services he was allotted seventy-five hundred shares of Dalhousie stock at a nominal value of forty cents a share. Four years later he sold them for nine dollars a share. It was M.M. Porter in the mid 1920s, who came up with a proposal that more profoundly affected the history of the oil industry in Alberta than any other suggestion ever to emanate from the Calgary bar. It was a formula for revising the federal government's petroleum leasing system.

Marsh Porter was counsel for the Hudson's Bay Company which owned 1.6 million acres of mineral rights on the Prairies. These leases, left over from Confederation, were widely scattered, mainly in sections eight and twenty-six of the surveyed townships between the Red River and the Rockies south of the North Saskatchewan River. The Bay made an arrangement with the Marland Oil Company of Oklahoma to come up and investigate the potential oil structures under its holdings.

In those days, before geophysical science was applied to oil findings, companies had to rely on clues supplied by surface geology to locate favourable drilling sites. When Marland geologists fanned out over southern Alberta after Royalite Number 4, their comings and goings quickly caught the attention of local speculators who filed on forty-acre leases surrounding the Hudson's Bay holdings. The result was that when Marland moved in to drill a wildcat, it often found itself surrounded by local speculators eager to cash in on its discovery. As Porter complained to Charles Ross, the superintendent of petroleum for the federal government, "This is all wrong. It doesn't give the legitimate oil companies a fair chance to complete a broad geological study before the speculators have pock-marked the whole countryside with their leases."

Porter's proposal: Give the legitimate oil companies who were seriously trying to find oil a fair chance to complete a geological examination of a spread of land. A prospecting license on 100,000 acres, similar to those granted to mining sourdoughs, would do the trick. Once they completed their geological work they could take their data back to the government and say: "This area and this area look quite favourable and we want to drill wells on them." The government could then take back the 100,000-acre prospecting license and issue a 160-acre, 640-acre or 6,400-acre drilling lease.

Ross took Porter's plan to Ottawa and eventually sold it to the government and it was taken over by the Alberta government in 1930 with the transfer of resources. When interest in Alberta's oil potential increased following the Turner Valley Royalite discovery in 1936, it was the prospecting reservation system that drew the oil companies of the world to the province.

In the interval between Turner Valley Number 4 and Turner Valley Royalite Number 1, a revolutionary new oil finding tool had become available to the wildcatters—the use of geophysical technique to locate favourable structures at depth. The reservation system was ideally suited for the new technique. And it was this system, though it was substantially modified as a result of further Porter agitations, that filled and refilled to overflowing the Alberta government coffers with cash from reservation and lease sales.

The rules that governed the actual drilling of oil wells in the 1920s were as casual as those governing the sale of shares. Indeed, as long as the annual rental was paid, the government did not care whether a leaseholder ever got around to actually drilling a well. If a well was drilled the ordinary rules governing the operation of steam engines applied. If oil was discovered, stipulated measures had to be taken to avoid waste and damage to the environment. That was about it. If a discovery was made, it followed automatically that a second well would be drilled. There was no limit on the number of wells that could be drilled on a forty-acre lease. In the early oil days of Texas, Oklahoma, and California, two or three wells on a single acre were not uncommon.

In Turner Valley such concentration was not even approached, but, by standards established later, the early wells were hopelessly congested. A half mile west of Royalite Number 4, fourteen wells were punched down on an eighty-acre tract. One operator managed three wells on a ten-acre lease. The importance of this for the legal profession is this: interests in the various wells were frequently farmed out from one company to another and then another. It took a great deal of tricky legal footwork to keep all interests sorted out, both as regard to income and liabilities, and, more importantly, when interests were sold or hypothecated to banks for loans.

From 1926 onward, there were seldom less than forty wells drilling in Turner Valley. Those that were successful were mainly completed as wet gas wells. In 1929, however, Home Oil completed three substantial crude oil wells four miles south of the Dingman discovery in a new productive horizon. By the end of the decade there were thirty-five wells in production in the valley with an output of almost four thousand barrels of naphtha and 500 million cubic feet of natural gas per day. The liquid production was piped to two refineries in Calgary but 85 percent of the natural gas was piped away from the wellheads and burned.

The light from the burning flares, concentrated as it was in a narrow corridor seven or eight miles long, bathed the area in a golden sunset that lasted all night, a spectacular glare that could be seen from Calgary, thirty-five miles away. Indeed it was the

Turner Valley pyrotechnics that captured the promotional attention of I.W.C. Solloway on his visit to Calgary in 1928.

For the people of the Calgary area, however, it was the sense of
smell and not sight that kept attention focussed on Turner Valley.
The process being used to separate the natural gas from the
naphtha or natural gas liquids made no pretense of doing anything
else, so the heavy impregnation of hydrogen sulphide that emerged
from the wells with the gas was still in it, and in the naphtha,
when it went off to market. Or, in the case of the surplus gas, in
the gas when it was flared into the atmosphere.

There was, therefore, no mistaking the cars that were running
on gasoline made from Turner Valley oil. The clouds of exhaust
permeated with the smell of rotten eggs attested to that. And the
villagers of Turner Valley and Black Diamond lived with tarnished
silverware, to say nothing of the tarnish that quickly coated the
silver coins in the pockets of the visiting drummers. In Calgary, it
was not uncommon for householders to get strong whiffs of
sulphur from their stoves or fireplaces as a batch of extra-sour gas
was fed into the system. This was a problem that went unsolved
until Royalite completed construction of a sulphur extraction
plant in 1929.

As the drilling pace accelerated in 1929, so did the amount of
natural gas being wasted. It was the spectacular pyrotechnics as
well as the malodorous atmosphere that got the attention of the
Alberta government when it obtained ownership of its natural
resources and became the Turner Valley landlord in 1930. With
title to the natural resources it also took over several key employees from the Dominion government, including several geologists
and engineers who had been long concerned with the gas wastage
in Turner Valley. So one of the first acts of the provincial government was to establish a petroleum and natural gas division under
the department of lands and mines. Then it passed the Oil and Gas
Wells Act which, for the first time, gave government engineers
authority to regulate drilling and production of wells on freehold
land.

Almost simultaneously, the Calgary city council decided that
Calgarians were paying too much for the poor quality gas they
were getting, in face of the huge gas surplus that existed. On
March 17, 1931, it instructed the city solicitor, L.W. Brockington,
to appear before the public utilities board to request a reduction in
gas rates. At the board hearings an immense amount of engineering data was produced to demonstrate that between 1924 and 1931
approximately 250 trillion cubic feet of natural gas—more than a
third of the total reserve of the field—had been wasted. Perhaps
the most telling figures were those for the current production in
1931. In April that year 512,190,000 cubic feet per day were being

wasted while the total amount used was only 35,626,000 cubic feet per day.

The first step after the hearing was the appointment of the Turner Valley Gas Conservation Board. It sought to put Turner Valley on a scientific production system, based on a scheme worked out by a team of technical experts. Each well would be given a production allowable based on its gas-oil ratio and the size of its lease. The overall objective was to cut the gas wastage in half by setting a ceiling of 200 million cubic feet per day on the natural gas production of Turner Valley.

When one of the producing companies, Spooner Oils Limited, received the first order from the board, its immediate reaction was to call in its lawyers and challenge the constitutionality of the order of the courts. In that suit, H.S. Patterson and McKinley Cameron represented the company, A.L. Smith, the conservation board, and W.S. Gray and J.J. Frawley, the attorney general.

As the company said in its statement of claim, the order would put it out of business. Spooner had a thirty-acre lease a mile north west of Royalite Number 4 on which it had drilled a total of five wells. Good wells when they were drilled in 1926 and 1927, the gas-oil ratio had risen over the years while the naphtha content declined until, in 1931, production was down to less than a hundred barrels a day for the lease. And it was taking 16 million cubic feet of gas to produce one hundred barrels of naphtha. Because of that gas-oil ratio, the board ordered the Spooner production cut back to 4.7 barrels a day.

Spooner carried the case through the Alberta courts to the Supreme Court of Canada, which ruled that Alberta was indeed within its constitutional power in taking steps to prevent waste of natural gas. Even with a limitation of 200 million cubic feet per day production from the Turner Valley field, 80 percent of the gas was still being flared, and this offended many of the oilmen's sense of the fitness of things as much as it did the government's. (One of these men was Frank McMahon, whose Pacific Petroleum Company had found some crude oil production wells to the south of the Turner Valley wet gas wells. In 1934, he went off to England to try to enlist the financial support of the Anglo-Iranian and Royal Dutch Shell Companies in constructing a natural gas pipeline to Vancouver.)

By 1932, the Great Depression had a grip on all Canada, including Turner Valley. Drilling dropped off by 85 percent, production of gas and naphtha remained steady but prices to the producers were reduced by almost 50 percent. Nevertheless, a modest stream of cash still flowed into the oil company coffers and lawyers with oil industry connections at least had solvent clients. For the balance of the profession, the depression years were an unmixed disaster as they were for all professions.

During 1931 and 1932, many mortgages were forecloseable and some bills were collectable with sternly worded "lawyer's letters." There were occasional divorces to be litigated. Then came debt adjustment acts and worsening unemployment. Creditors gave up trying to get blood out of stones and credit itself dried up. Then, when everything in Calgary was reaching zero-bottom, fortune smiled. The Turner Valley Royalties well blew in Turner Valley in 1936 and another oil boom was on. And this was a boom for lawyers as well as for wildcatters.

Turner Valley Royalties was the amalgamation of two ideas that had been kicking around the oil patch for years. One was a geological theory that if drilling was carried downdip to the west it would miss the wet gas cap on the limestone formation and penetrate into the zone below where crude oil was located. The other idea was that the gun-shy investors could be lured back into wildcatting with the offer of direct payments of oil out of any production discovered. (The Bonanza Oil Company had publicized the royalty idea far and wide in 1927 but its promotion came to nothing when it failed to find any oil to divert to its royalty owners.) Turner Valley Royalties was the promotion of R.A. Brown, the manager of the City of Calgary electrical utility; George Bell, owner of the Calgary *Albertan*; and John Moyer, a Calgary lawyer, all of whom had been active in the 1920s Turner Valley developments.

The royalties plan required a lot of legal paperwork—drafting trust deeds, special drilling contracts, and sales contracts, agreements with trust companies, and so on. With success came the usual flurry of new companies to be incorporated, new joint ventures to be negotiated, new titles to be registered—all grist for the legal mills. The Royalties boom, in fact, came just in the nick of time for the Calgary legal fraternity, for the Great Depression had side-swiped everybody's practice, as it had decimated the ranks of students entering the profession. E.M. Bredin, a former Calgary city solicitor, recalled that there were less than twenty students in his graduating class of 1939 and that there were only six in the class that followed. M.E. Jones was in that class and articled to E.J. Chambers at a salary of twenty-five dollars a month. Articling, in those days consisted of opening mail, running messages, and answering the telephone. Minuscule as Jones' salary was, it was more than most firms could afford.

By the second anniversary of the Turner Valley Royalties discovery, fifty-nine new oil producers had been brought into production. Turner Valley's annual combined oil and naphtha production zoomed from sixty-six thousand barrels to six million barrels. This meant that Turner Valley by 1935 was able to supply all of Alberta fuel needs along with those of British Columbia and Saskatchewan. So as an even larger surplus of crude oil loomed on the horizon, Alberta enacted a new Oil and Gas Resources Conservation Act and established a new conservation board with greatly increased powers, including that of pro-rating production to market demand. Then in 1938 it established the royal commission headed by Justice A.A. McGillivray to investigate the entire operation.

The McGillivray Commission quickly became the forum for the ventilation of all the long-standing grievances of the Turner Valley oil and gas producers. The gas purchasing monopoly of Royalite oils, through its marketing arrangements with the Canadian Western Natural Gas Company was roundly attacked. So were the monopolistic practices of Imperial-Royalite and British American Oil. The hearings of the commission went on, intermittently for over a year, with the leaders of the Calgary bar in steady attendance. Harry Nolan represented Imperial Oil, Eric Harvie was counsel for British American, and J.E.A. Macleod, James Mahaffey, L.H. Fenerty, A.L. Smith, and J.E. Brownlee regularly attended.

Outshining them all, however, was a Rumanian-Canadian non-lawyer from Saskatchewan, Leon Plotkins. He had operated a bulk wholesale and retail oil business in Saskatchewan before coming to Calgary in the early 1930s where he built a small tea-kettle refinery in East Calgary called Lion Oils. He also did some speculation in Turner Valley leases. Early in his career he had consulted D.P. McDonald, who as a partner of W.C. Fisher, was also managing the affairs of Fisher's Model Oil Company. Plotkins retained McDonald to draft some leasing agreements for him.

After studying the agreements overnight, Plotkins returned to McDonald's office full of complaints. He was so articulate in his summary, and specific in what he required, that McDonald's reaction was, "Mr. Plotkins, you don't need a lawyer. You know more about how those agreements should be drafted than I do. Draft your own agreements. And, if the time ever comes when you get into court, act for yourself as well."

The time came for Plotkins at the McGillivray Commission. His bill of complaints included Imperial-Royalite refusal to allow him access to the pipeline to Turner Valley for his oil supply, forcing him to move the oil he bought in Turner Valley by tank car. Nor would either Calgary refiner sell him gasoline in bulk for resale at retail in his several small service stations.

The McGillivray Commission hearings were split into two segments. The first dealt with the pipelines that carried the natural gas and crude oil to Calgary. These hearings began in January 1939 and were concluded in early April.

When the hearings turned to the investigation of oil pricing by Imperial-Royalite, Leon Plotkins really came into his own. Earlier, in recognition of Plotkins' special knowledge of the oil industry in all its phases, he had been invited to become a special counsel to the commission, along with J.J. Frawley. This gave him the right to participate in the cross-examination of the technical witnesses called by Imperial Oil and Royalite. Plotkins used his counsel status to bait the Imperial Oil witnesses unmercifully. He was obviously Calgary's greatest living expert on the international machinations of Standard Oil of New Jersey, the parent company of Imperial Oil, Royalite, and literally scores of other companies operating around the world.

It was Plotkins' contention that the posted field price for crude oil in Turner Valley was set by Imperial Oil to best serve the continental interests of the Standard Oil Company of New Jersey, just as other Jersey subsidiaries set the price in other fields in the United States. As the hearings proceeded, he demonstrated he knew more about the way in which Jersey, and Imperial Oil, operated than many of the expert witnesses Imperial Oil trotted out.

He also demonstrated a remarkable knowledge of the inner workings of the Calgary operations of Imperial Oil and Royalite. Thus when Royalite tendered audited financial statements from Price Waterhouse of its operating costs, Plotkins told the commission to ignore them. Royalite, he said, kept two sets of books, one set of forms for its parent company and another for the auditors.

In making the charge Plotkins obviously believed he was getting back at Imperial for "dirty tricks" somebody had been playing on him since the McGillivray hearings began. First there was the mysterious appearance of a Canadian customs officer with a bill for forty thousand dollars for duty on crude oil he had been importing from Montana. Who could have known about this importation except Imperial-Royalite? Then there was the sudden shutting down of eight of his retail service stations for selling gasoline for less than Imperial stations were charging, in violation of recently passed provincial regulations of retail trade in the province. (The closing order was soon rescinded and the customs claim was later reduced to two thousand dollars.)

For Harry Nolan, the counsel for Imperial Oil, Plotkins' allegation of the two sets of books was the last straw. He stormed from the room and marched backed to his office where he dictated a blistering letter to his clients about the way proceedings were going and the way McGillivray was allowing questions that were giving Imperial Oil the worst of it in the press reports. Apparently there was some reference in the letter to having pressure exerted on the newspapers to tone down the reportage. The following day, or shortly thereafter, Plotkins arose to complain to McGillivray that Mr. Nolan was bringing pressure on the newspapers to tone down their reports of the hearings. Nolan exploded out of his chair to demand proof of Plotkins' charges and to have witnesses produced to collaborate them. McGillivray also demanded the identity of Plotkins' source of information. Plotkins hedged. He would first have to counsel himself and ask the person who provided him with the information for consent to identifying the informant.

Then Plotkins took the offensive. He demanded that the commission order Imperial Oil and Royalite to file certain documents with the commission. He would need these documents to sustain his charge about influencing the newspapers. For the second time in two days, Harry Nolan stormed out of his chair and out of the court room. The document that Plotkins was fishing for was the letter that Nolan had written to Imperial Oil in which he had made several uncomplimentary references to McGillivray and his handling of the commission hearing. Obviously, the same snake-in-the-grass employee of Imperial Oil or Royalite who had snitched to Plotkins about the duplicate sets of records had told him about the Nolan letter. Nolan, paling at the thought of what that letter would do to prejudice his own standing before the commission, to say nothing of Imperial Oil's standing, and his own standing with Imperial Oil, had to circumvent Plotkins' effort to reveal it to the commission.

Now Harry Nolan was not usually a man to act precipitously. As son of the notorious Paddy Nolan, young Harry had been groomed in the traditions of Calgary's legal community and it was always expected that he would assume his father's place at the bar. However, the times conspired to slow his course, and when Paddy succumbed from too-much-of-a-good-thing, studious young Harry was but a schoolboy. He made his way to the new university at Edmonton, however, and excelled at every endeavour. He was president of the literary society, an editor of the *Gateway*, a member of the debating team and president of the student's union. *And* he played football well enough to be awarded the "Large A" by the athletic association. When he graduated in 1915, crowning all other prizes was the announcement that Henry Grattan Nolan had been awarded the Rhodes Scholarship—the first Alberta native son ever to receive that honour.

The year 1915, though, found the world at war and Harry was not long in England before he enlisted at the Inns of Court officer training corps, and the following two years he spent with the Forty-ninth Canadian Battalion in France. Finally, after being awarded the Military Cross and suffering a wound serious enough to have him sent back to England, Harry returned to Oxford to resume his scholarship, and in 1922 he was called to the bar of England from Gray's Inn.

Such potential could hardly escape the notice of R.B. Bennett, and if young Nolan was not actually piped off his returning train, he was most certainly warmly welcomed into the Bennett firm—

no doubt with the understanding that he would in time succeed to Bennett's throne. As heir-apparent, Nolan had been long acquainted with the Imperial Oil and Royalite files. Now with his name at the top of the letterhead, his hasty flash of temper was both out of character and much to be regretted. So, chastened and somewhat frantic, Nolan went back to his office after supper to see what could be done to salvage the impending disaster. Could some precedent be found to exclude the letter as evidence?

Now as most everyone knows, the only warm bodies left to fuel the late night fires in legal offices are those of the articling students (who aren't paid enough to enjoy the evening hours anyway). Young Mister Maclean (Mac) Jones, fresh out of law school, was the only one around to greet Mr. Nolan as he set to work briefing the law. Nolan commandeered his services, called in another lawyer, and all three worked at the problem until eleven o'clock. "We hadn't found anything helpful, and it didn't look like we were going to, so the others left, but I thought I'd stay around for a while because it was such an interesting subject," Jones recalled. "I began to get a glimmer of hope and I went to all the digests of cases—Canadian and English—and finally, after working all night, I found a case in the early nineteenth century *English Re-prints* which was strongly supportive of our position. By eight o'clock I had all the case reports up and when Mr. Nolan walked in and asked, 'Well, where do we stand?' I was able to tell him that the letter wasn't admissible. 'Good,' he said, 'show me the case law.' "

What Jones had unearthed was a high court decision in England in 1835 which first established the principle of confidentiality of lawyer-client relationships. Nolan had barely enough time to read the head notes before he had to be at the commission, so he told Jones to pack up the books and bring them along. "I trailed dutifully behind," Jones recalled. "I had lined up the books on the counsel table and retreated to the shadows, when Mr. Nolan did a very nice thing. 'My Lord,' he said, 'I would like to introduce my associate, Mr. M.E. Jones, who is going to be with me in this matter from now on.' "

While Mac Jones sat in shock at his side, Nolan argued brilliantly for two hours and at last McGillivray ruled that the letter was not admissible and that it would not come before the commission.

Jones, now senior partner of Bennett Jones, in recalling the skirmish, acknowledges the very great favour afforded him by Nolan's generous introduction to the powerhouse of the bar. "There I was—a rank student—sitting beside the outstanding trial lawyer of the time. And I'm sure it was largely due to his influence that I was given a raise to forty dollars a month and asked to stay on with the firm as an associate."

Later in the day Plotkins produced the source of his information about Royalite's inner activities. It was Miss Ellis MacAskill, of 517–13th Avenue, who had been a Royalite secretary for thirteen years, until she had abruptly resigned the previous week. Her grounds? She had become completely disenchanted with what she said was the gulf that separated what Royalite was telling the commissioner and the actual facts of its relationship with the Turner Valley producers and gasoline consumers. After Miss MacAskill's testimony, the McGillivray hearings ground slowly to a halt until the final report was published early in 1940.

Among the recommendations of the commission were that the crude oil pipeline from Turner Valley to Calgary be declared a public utility and its throughput charge be reduced from fifteen cents a barrel to under ten cents. It also recommended that all customers, like Plotkins' refinery, be entitled to move their crude through the pipeline and that it be required to build a connection to his refinery. For the Turner Valley gas producers, the commission urged the government to legislate an end to the Royalite monopoly and that the gas production of the entire field be unitized and pro-rated among all the wells in the field. The commission recommended that a three-man conservation board be placed in full charge of oil and gas production in Alberta; that each oil well be given a daily allowable based on engineering data relative to gas/oil pressure, spacing, bottom hole pressure, producibility; that the field production be based upon market demand.

With the adoption of McGillivray's bill of particulars, the era of unfettered free enterprise ended for the Canadian oil business. As time passed there would be more and more rules and regulations emanating from more and more boards and commissions. All grist for the legal fraternities' mill. For the moment, however, there was a war on and the federal government moved in almost immediately to countermand some of the major decisions of the new conservation board. The board, for example, had established a twenty-thousand-barrel per day ceiling on oil production in Turner Valley. The federal oil controller countermanded the order and ordered production to be increased to twenty-five thousand barrels a day. Then Ottawa decided to establish an explosives factory in Calgary for the munitions industry and ordered an increase in the amount of natural gas the field could produce. Ottawa also went into the wildcatting business with a company called Wartime Oils which drilled a number of marginally successful oil wells.

By the end of the war there were one hundred wells in oil or gas production in Turner Valley. In addition to producing oil and gas, Turner Valley was the magnet that attracted several international companies to Alberta. Shell Oil made a major discovery of natural gas in the Jumping Pound area west of Calgary. Standard Oil of

California drilled several small oil wells in the Taber area. Gulf Oil was wildcatting in the Pincher Creek district and several discoveries were made in the Tilley area. It was not, however, until the Leduc discovery of 1947, and most notably the Atlantic Number 3 blowout and fire at Leduc in 1948, that Alberta edged its way onto the world oil map and, more particularly, caught the eye of the American oil industry.

The advance parties from Los Angeles, Dallas, Tulsa, Houston, Pittsburgh, to say nothing of Baton Rouge, Midland, Casper, and Denver, reached Calgary and stopped. Hughes Tool, Continental Supply, Oilwell Supply were already established in Calgary. So were Shell, Gulf, and Calstandard, all of whose staffs vouched for the fact that the natives were friendly, and that Calgary was where the action was. For the newcomers, there were immediate priorities—finding a place to live, renting an office, hiring somebody to answer the phone, arranging for a briefing on land leasing rules. And, for all of these, the services of a lawyer could be required, or at least be useful to have.

In Calgary there was a substantial reservoir of legal talent ready, able, and willing to be of service. Its members had been exposed to the oil business from kindergarten to post-graduate courses in geology, chemistry, and engineering by attendance at the McGillivray Commission hearings. They had absorbed about all there was to absorb about natural gas, reservoirs, and economics at the hearings of the Dinning Commission in 1948. But most of all, the senior members of every legal firm in town, from personal involvement with the Turner Valley companies, knew all it was necessary to know about the government oil and natural gas leasing system.

It was not only petroleum industry expertise that the immigrant oilmen required, however. They needed offices in which to hang their hats and homes in which to live and they discovered a desperate shortage of both in Calgary. As a result of the Social Credit Government's repudiation of its bond interest obligations, mortgage money had fled the province prior to the war; house building had ceased and there wasn't a house in Calgary to be rented in 1949. When the government changed its mind about interest, mortgage money slowly returned, but there was a shortage of materials as well as skilled workers, so house building was also in the doldrums. Immigrating companies were forced to buy homes for their staffs instead of renting; they needed the lawyers' services not only to draw deeds and register titles, but to recommend realtors and advise on the selection of districts in which to locate.

Nor was that all. What vacancies there were in office space in Calgary were scattered in several dozen buildings, in small offices. When Shell Oil came back after 1949 and started rehiring

John McKinley Cameron,
Calgary, 1918. Glenbow
Archives, NA-4691-6

*Automobile near the location of
the gunning down of Cst. Steve
Lawson, Coleman, Alberta, 1922.*
Glenbow Archives, NA-4691-5

*The Alberta Provincial Police office and residence of Cst. Steve Lawson,
Coleman, Alberta, 1922.* Glenbow Archives, NA-4691-2

*Mrs. Florence Lassandro, 1922.* Glenbow Archives, NA-3282-2

*Testing sand at Home Oil No. 1 Well, Turner Valley, Alberta. Major James R. Lowery is on the left.* Glenbow Archives, NA-2335-7

*John E. Brownlee, Premier of Alberta, 1925–1934.* Glenbow Archives, NA-1451-11

*Vivian MacMillan and parents, Edmonton, 1934.* Glenbow Archives, ND3-6747

*Mrs. John E. Brownlee, 1908.*
Glenbow Archives, NA-2547-8

*Courtroom interior, Edmonton,*
*1933.* Glenbow Archives,
ND3-6464-5

*Group at the Dingman Discovery Well, Turner Valley, Alberta, 1914.*
Glenbow Archives, NA-2335-4

*Discovery Well, Turner Valley, Alberta.* Glenbow Archives, NA-4139-1

*A group at a meeting of the Indian Association of Alberta. From left to right: seated—Senator James Gladstone, Ruth Gorman, John Laurie. Standing—John Samson, Albert Lightning.* Glenbow Archives, NA-4212-154

*Henry Grattan Nolan, c. the early 1940s.* Glenbow Archives, NA-1371-8

*Dr. John Lee Laurie, Calgary, 1957.* Glenbow Archives, NA-2554-1

*Ruth Gorman and Chief John Samson, Calgary, 1960.* Glenbow Archives, NA-2557-17

*A. A. McGillivray, Calgary, c. 1928.* Glenbow Archives, NA-2982-2

*Sam J. Helman, Calgary, c. 1928.* Glenbow Archives, NA-2982-1

staff, it had to rent office space in half a dozen buildings to accommodate them. Again the services of lawyers were needed to negotiate leases and assist in the purchase of office buildings.

To the incoming American oilmen, Alberta and the Canadian oil industry were very easy to get used to. The Alberta terrain is similar to that in parts of Texas, Montana, and Colorado. The geology is similar and all the tools and equipment were identical. And, given a Louisiana-East Texas accent or two, there were no problems with the language. Where there was a world of difference was with land titles. Two landmark legal cases, which incidentally concerned Canadian companies on all sides, acted as storm signals to alert the newcomers to the imperative need to pay meticulous attention to details and legal niceties in all their land management.

The Borys case involved the definition of petroleum, no less. Michael Borys was a Leduc area farmer who bought his land from the CPR in 1906. In the sale, the company reserved all coal, petroleum, and valuable stone. In 1918 he transferred the farm to his son. At the time of the Leduc discovery, CPR leased the petroleum rights it had withheld from Borys to Imperial Oil. When Imperial discovered oil, Borys applied for an injunction against removing the natural gas with the crude oil because natural gas was not reserved to the CPR in the title. Sam Helman and Harry Nolan represented the CPR and Imperial Oil, respectively. The case wound itself through all the Canadian courts and eventually got to the Privy Council. The ultimate decision was that natural gas in solution was part of the definition of petroleum but that natural gas by itself in a gas cap was not. If petroleum was saturated with natural gas and the gas acted as the agency that forced the oil to the surface it was incidental to the right of the owner of the petroleum to "capture and take" the substance to which he had acquired title.

Another case involving the oil business then was the Turta case. It was based on a mistake made by the Alberta Land Titles Office in failing to include the reservation of petroleum when the sale of a piece of farm land was recorded on the Land Titles Office books. In 1908, one Podgorny, acquired a 160-acre farm from the CPR with the faulty deed to his land. Ultimately he sold the land to Anton Turta with the coal being reserved to the CPR but not petroleum. Neither of the immigrant farmers could read English so neither was aware of the mistake. However in 1942 the Land Titles Office made an audit of the titles and discovered the mistake in the Podgorny-Turta title. So a correction was made in the office records but nobody notified the farmer of the change. At this time the Imperial Oil Company was putting a large land-spread together prior to the Leduc discovery. It came upon the corrected title in its land titles searches and included it in the leases it took up from the CPR.

When Turta took a look at his title after oil was discovered, he consulted George H. Steer of Edmonton and suit was filed to have him declared owner of the petroleum. Once again Helman appeared for the CPR and Nolan for Imperial Oil. The Supreme Court of Canada ruled by a vote of six to three that Turta was a bona fide purchaser from the first owner and was the owner of the petroleum rights. One consequence of the Turta decision was that an important change was made to the Land Titles Act to make provision for damages to innocent parties when mistakes were made in recording mineral titles. In addition, land titles activities became more and more intensified throughout the years as checking and double-checking the registering of options, caveats, and transfers increased in demand.

But all this is ahead of the story. For the Calgary legal profession, the Great Depression was all over by 1949. One sign that it was over for good was the emerging indication that new regulatory agencies for the oil and gas business were in the offing which would require increased legal presence all down the line to help manoeuver the concomitant flow of paper work. The first such sign was the entry of the federal Parliament into the picture. When the first surplus of natural gas developed, it sparked interest in building a pipeline to export the surplus. Then, when the surplus of crude oil developed, an interest arose in a crude oil pipeline to serve Saskatchewan, Manitoba, and British Columbia. Ottawa decided it was time to prepare to control interprovincial pipelines, if, as, and when they became a reality. In 1949 it passed the Pipelines Act of Canada to license the construction of interprovincial and international pipelines by companies which had to be incorporated by special acts of Parliament.

The second sign was the enactment by a special session of the Alberta legislature in 1949 of the Natural Gas Preservation Act which provided that any company seeking to export gas from Alberta must first apply for a permit to do so from the Oil and Gas Conservation Board, which had to hold public hearings before permits could be granted. Alberta, meanwhile, had adopted the recommendation of the Dinning Commission that exports of gas should be permitted only after the needs of Alberta had been assured for fifty years.

The first company to become activated was Frank McMahon's Westcoast Transmission Company. In May of 1949 he hired D.P. McDonald as general counsel and had the company incorporated by act of Parliament. McDonald, as noted, began his law career in 1929 and cut his wisdom teeth in the oil business as manager of W.C. Fisher's Model Oil Company. He was counsel for several Frank McMahon companies, including the Canadian-American

Bear Exploration Company that spent five million dollars looking for oil and gas in northern British Columbia and Alberta. He had also been counsel for the Dinning Commission of 1948. Soon he would be one of a group of senior Calgary barristers who would live out of suitcases as they bounced from regulatory board meetings in Calgary, Ottawa, and Washington, and to a number of points between.

The sudden and steadily mounting oil company business caught the Calgary bar in a seriously under-manned condition and none more so than the Porter Allen firm. Like the other major firms, it went hunting for reinforcements. Marsh Porter, who was a vice president as well as counsel for Home Oil, was also counsel for the Alberta Wheat Pool. It was while attending a royal commission hearing on the grain trade in Ottawa that he broached the subject of hiring another barrister to lawyers at the commission. Several of them suggested the name of Ross MacKimmie who was then practicing in Sydney, Nova Scotia, after recently graduating from Dalhousie University, which was Porter's alma mater. MacKimmie had impressed the lawyers as a young man with a future. Porter was not so sure. What could a young man with a future be doing practicing in Sydney, Nova Scotia? But the endorsements were so strong that he invited MacKimmie to come to Calgary as his guest to be interviewed, scout the country and see if he was interested.

"With Calgary and me, it was love at first sight," MacKimmie later recalled. Then he returned to Sydney to ponder the offer Porter had made. The pondering took a lot longer than Porter had expected and, eventually, after several weeks he pressed MacKimmie for an answer. It was only later that Porter learned that MacKimmie was sold on moving to Calgary immediately. But no canny Nova Scotian was likely to rush off from an established position in Sydney to a preferred position in Alberta without carefully investigating the people dangling the lure. As a relative by marriage of the Royal Bank, he waited until he got the bank's report on the stability of the Porter Allen firm before committing himself.

The young Albertans who had interrupted their university law studies to join the armed services were then emerging from law school to discover that finding a firm to article with was no longer a problem. The Calgary law firms were out recruiting students. Two of the first to be picked up by Porter Allen were F.R. Matthews and S.H. Wood.

In 1949 the Fenerty firm had consisted of L.H. and R.L. Fenerty, W.A. McGillivray, J.M. Robertson and R.D. Freeze. By 1952 D.C. Prowse, W.R. Brennan, and D.C. Medhurst had joined the partnership. Over the same period the Macleod firm grew from J.E.A. Macleod, H.W. Riley, N.D. McDermid, and K.S. Dixon with the addition of A.D. Bessemer, W.H. Patterson, P.A. Ferner, Eric Harvey, Weston Brooks, William Chipman, R. McCullough, and John MacDonald. The Bennett firm of H.G. Nolan, E.J. Chambers, O.H.E. Might, and G.M. Peacock, which had been static for twenty years, added M.E. Jones, R.G. Black, J.J. Stratton, H.F. Gain, J.H. Laycraft, C.S. Molyneux, and J.S. Woods.

The impact the incoming tide of American oil companies had on the Calgary bar was many-sided. One immediate effect was on the fee schedule. D.P. McDonald recalled that during the operation of the Bear Exploration Company, he had on many occasions rendered legal service to some of the American partners. He had naturally billed them for such services at the going Alberta rate. One of his American clients had returned his invoice with the comment that his company was accustomed to paying twice that much when its American lawyers performed a similar service. He suggested that Mr. McDonald adjust his invoice to conform to American standards.

The truth was that the wage and price ceilings imposed by the Canadian government during the Second World War had caught Alberta with wage and salary levels still hovering near the mid-depression lows, although some modest recovery was achieved during the postwar era. A measure of that recovery may be illustrated by a couple of actual experiences. When William Egbert completed his articling with the Porter, Allen, MacKimmie firm in 1954, he was invited to stay on with the firm on a salary of $200 a month. Having only recently married, Egbert needed more than that, so he canvassed the field and accepted an offer from H.W. Riley at $300 a month. D.P. McDonald, by experience and reputation was one of the leaders on the Calgary bar in 1949. At that time his usual fee for consultation was $10 an hour for run of the mill cases. When he became associated with Westcoast Transmission, his charge was $100 a day for work done in Calgary, but if he were required to spend extended periods on the road, the fee would be $200, plus expenses, of course.

Equally important to the impact on fees was the expansion of the use of in house lawyers by the petroleum industry, a development that would lead to bitter rivalries in years to come. Not only did the new companies put lawyers on their payrolls, they provided them with the tools with which they plied their trade, the costly libraries no lawyer could do without.

As previously noted, the oil industry in Alberta was still very much in its infancy when Leduc was discovered and Atlantic Number 3 caught fire. It was an industry of individual companies doing their own thing and operating their own wells. As the costs of getting leases on which to drill skyrocketed with Redwater, several companies pooled resources to bid for leases against the big companies, the Home–Anglo–C & E team for example, or the

General Petroleums team. But the latter-day sophistication of oil field operations had not yet filtered across the border from the United States, where whole catalogues of standardized forms had been devised for putting deals together. It was deemed to be more efficient to have lawyers added to landmen-geologist-engineer teams of company employees than farming out a lot of documentation preparation to "over-town" lawyers in private practice.

Indeed the in-house lawyers in practice increased in numbers at least as quickly as the over-town law firms expanded. A.W. Hendricks was one of the earliest petroleum industry in-housers. He joined Shell Oil long before the Leduc boom hit. He was a medical dischargee from the armed services in 1944 as a result of an eye injury and, instead of going back to Bennett Hannah, he opted to take a job with Shell as head of its legal and land departments.

After the discovery of the Jumping Pound wet gas field west of Calgary, Hendricks was responsible for putting one of Alberta's first field unitization agreements together. Jumping Pound was a very deep field and drilling to production was expensive. Instead of punching down wells on every forty-acre lease over a sixty-four-hundred-acre spread, Shell worked out an arrangement to minimize the number of wells drilled. This was done by dividing production from the field among all the leaseholders within the unit area, regardless of whether wells were drilled on their leases or not. Because there was much involved—CPR land, Hudson's Bay Company land, freehold leases, and a large block of land in the hands of a Calgary company—a great deal of drafting and redrafting was involved in the ultimate completion of the unit agreements. Later the drafting of unit agreements became an important part of the work of all legal departments.

The bulk of the work, however, began as and remained related to what could be broadly called real estate transactions. In addition to registering titles and filing caveats, the legal departments drafted the documents required in settling claims of farmers for damage done to their land, for leasing of surface rights such as for access to well sites. The in-house lawyers could complete these phases of the business in much less time and for a lot less money than the over-town solicitors could do.

Ed Bredin, who resigned as Calgary city solicitor in 1958 to become head of the Mobil legal department, summarized it this way: "There isn't a business anywhere that generates the amount of legal work the oil business does. You have to trace all the farm-outs on a freehold lease to complete it. There are the farm-out agreements that have to be traced from one company down through another, through the amalgamation of companies. All this has to be individually researched and documented."

With the rapid spread of field activities in all directions, the demands on the time and talents of the legal departments naturally increased. The Shell company, which was typical, went from being a one-lawyer department in 1950, to two in 1951, then to four, to five, and to six. Expansion was slowed, however, by the fact that each new lawyer came to the companies unacquainted with any phase of the oil industry. So they all had to go through an articling regimen before they could fully begin to earn their pay.

The influx of American oil companies thus created an unprecedented demand for the services of Calgary law firms, but the same newcomers made it difficult for the established lawyers to meet their demands by competing with them for the services of unattached legal talent. Gradually the situation sorted itself out in this way: the in-house lawyers did the overwhelming bulk of the solicitors' work while the over-towners had a near monopoly on the barristers' work.

The demands on the barristers' time were quickly complicated by expansion of the functions of the conservation board which was then composed of I.N. McKinnon, D.P. Goodall, and George Govier. Because only Goodall had oil industry experience, the board felt its way very carefully indeed through a minefield of technicalities which had to be mastered before decisions could be made. And millions of dollars hung on all its decisions because the competition was fierce between the oil companies for pipeline franchises, gas treatment plants, gathering systems, and for production quotas of oil and gas.

So the barristers found themselves working twelve-hour days. They participated in the interminable meeting of the conservation board during the day, and then went back at night to be briefed by company experts on the fine points of pipeline through-put mathematics, line pipe dimensions, cost of service calculations, not to say millidarcy decimal points and porosity percentages. All with the intentions of unhorsing the expert witnesses of rival companies at the hearings on the morrow.

In no area of economic activity did the competition ever approach the intensity it did than in the struggle for the natural gas pipelines to take Alberta gas to the four corners of the continent. And, it began with the beginning of the post-Leduc boom and continued unabated for almost a decade.

In actual fact, the first serious attempt to export natural gas from Alberta predated Leduc, and it originated in New York and not in Alberta in all. The moving spirit was A. Faison Dixon, a partner in the geological firm of Brookaw, Dixon, and McKee which had been pioneer developers of the US natural gas markets. After a study of Alberta geology, Faison interested the investment firm of Morgan Stanley in a pipeline to move Alberta gas to Seattle, Portland, and Vancouver through Washington state.

After incorporating the Northwest Natural Gas Company,

Dixon approached the Alberta government to outline their plans. The meeting gave rise to the question of whether Alberta had enough gas to meet domestic needs and allow for exports as well. Eventually the Dinning Commission was appointed to provide answers to the question. Northwest came forward with a tremendous volume of technical information in support of the position that Alberta reserves were adequate. Late in the hearings Frank McMahon came forward to present the "Canada First" viewpoint. He said there was a tremendous need for natural gas across the prairies to Winnipeg and in British Columbia including the metropolitan Vancouver area. McMahon argued for giving first chance to Canadian pipelines serving Canadian markets. When the Dinning Commission put the whole question of gas export on the back burner, McMahon concentrated on exploration, particularly in the Peace River area where, in 1951, the Fort St. John field was discovered.

The Dinning Commission was the indirect progenitor of a brand-new growth industry in Calgary in which the legal profession became an active participant. It was called economic forecasting—in reality a far-out guessing game in which the participants tried to compute (a) the total deliverable quantity of natural gas in underground reservoirs of Alberta, and (b) how much natural gas Alberta would need over the next fifty years. The answers were sheer guesses, of course, but over the next decade hundreds of thousands of dollars would be spent paying engineers to run figures through calculating machines, and then more hundreds of thousands paying lawyers to convert the engineering guesses into briefs to be submitted to the Alberta Conservation Board, first, and then to the federal Department of Transport in Ottawa, the federal Power Commission in Washington, and the Borden Royal Commission, here, there, and everywhere.

What began as a very simple idea—building a large steel pipeline to move Alberta natural gas to consumer markets elsewhere—became, almost overnight, the most complicated and convoluted exercise imaginable. As Ross MacKimmie, D.P. McDonald, and others have noticed, it became a learning experience for everyone involved, the members of the conservation board, the lawyers who had to draft the briefs being presented, and even for the engineers, geologists, and accountants who supplied the crude data for the presentation.

From the McGillivray Commission onward, regulatory bodies adopted procedures all their own. Less and less importance was attached to legal precedence and more importance was attached to the presentation of bales of factual material. All the material for hearings was prepared by the professionals—the engineers, geologists, economists, market experts, bankers, and so on. What consumed hours and stretched into days were the conferences between the company barristers and the technical experts in preparing the submissions. The expert witnesses had to be briefed and coached in the way their testimony and cross-examination could be turned to the interest of the client.

Despite the endless pursuit of data, the hearings before the regulatory bodies were adversarial in the extreme. Petroleum production and transportation tends by the nature of things to be monopolistic, whether it is well operation, local gathering and local transportation, or major processing, trunk line distribution and international pipelining. Before each hearing, four or five rival companies vied for permission to operate the monopoly facility, for to the winner of the franchise went millions in operation profits.

The barristers' role, of course, was to not only prepare the witnesses for their presentation but to familiarize them with the overall strategy and ultimate goals of the company. Brilliant though many of the technical experts were in their special field, many were not able to assess the relevance of some of their material to the main presentation. What all this meant was that the solicitor-barrister relationship that existed in the practice of civil law had no place in the oil industry practice. The counsel on the firing line at the regulatory board meetings could not rely on a core of solicitors to prepare briefs for them to present to court. They had to do all their own homework, and in the process develop a degree of patience unknown in any other profession. Without exception, the regulatory bodies dragged their feet right up to their hips, for, in face of the huge sums involved in almost any decision any board would make, no board ever acted precipitously. Nor was any board ever satisfied with the original factual basis any applicant ever proffered for their consideration. All this was particularly true of Canadian provincial and federal boards.

For many of the members appointed to these boards, it was a learning experience at the kindergarten level. A member appointed for his engineering expertise, for example, might know next to nothing about the impact of interest rates on cost of service. As a result what seemed to everybody to be cut-and-dry hearings stretched over weeks and into months until the board members understood. In addition, because lawyers were presumed to be political animals, they were expected to keep their antennae at the ready to pick up changes, however subtle, in the political climate that might have an impact on a project. Lawyers with a political "in" in Edmonton, Victoria, Regina, Ottawa, and Washington were frequently valued consultants for Calgary counsel for the pipeline companies. But, most of all, it was a learning experience for the pipeline promoters who, if they had even suspected what the cost in time and money would be over a period of five years, would never have been caught dead with a gas pipeline promotion.

Despite the stand taken by the Government of Alberta that no gas would be exported until Alberta's long-term requirements were in place, there was no doubt in the minds of the sponsors of Westcoast Transmission or Northwest Natural Gas that enough gas would soon be proven up to permit export. So in January 1950, they moved to complete the first formality, to obtain approval of the Board of Transport Commissioners to build interprovincial lines. That body ruled they were in a cart-before-the-horse situation; that no application could be considered until Alberta approved export.

Meanwhile, the pipeline business was attracting a lot of attention. Clint Murchison of Dallas, Texas, sent emissaries to Calgary to retain the services of Porter and Allen and to launch the Canadian–Delhi Pipelines project, to construct a line to Toronto and Montreal. H.R. Milner of Edmonton joined with D.D. Baxter and the Calgary and Edmonton Corporation of Winnipeg to launch Western Pipelines to build a line to Winnipeg and thence south to the United States. Another American company, Fish Engineering of Dallas, incorporated Prairie Pipelines Limited which wanted to serve the southwest United States. Finally there was another H.R. Milner promotion, Interfield Pipeline Company, which would gather all the gas within Alberta and deliver it to the export company that won government approval.

All this created an interesting situation for the Milner Steer law firm when the conservation board in 1950 got around to hearing arguments for and against gas exports from Alberta. The Canadian Western Natural Gas Company, which served southern Alberta, and Northwest Utilities, which served consumers in Edmonton and north, were both represented by G.H. Steer and resolutely opposed all exports from the province. Western Pipelines, seeking gas export for the Winnipeg-Minnesota line, was represented by R.C. Martland who was a partner in the Milner Steer firm.

No matter what decision was ultimately made by the conservation board, H.R. Milner would have all the bases covered. However, as noted, decisions were not something that came easily to the conservation board. It spent most of 1951 hearing individual submissions from the rival pipeline companies. Then it heard submissions from special interest groups. Then it heard submissions of all the companies together. It was not until 1952 that a decision was made to permit Westcoast to draw on its gas discoveries in the Peace River area for its export line to Vancouver and the lower mainland.

For their presentations to the conservation board, the companies all had to come prepared with technical data of endless variety and complexity. This meant that they had to have specialists on hand to testify to chemical constituency of natural gas from various fields, engineering details of gas processing plants, construction of river crossings, engineering details of pipeline construction, and financial experts who were capable of explaining the complexities of pipeline financing.

As Ross MacKimmie once put it, in pondering the skyrocketing expenses being faced by the pipeline promoters because of the tedious pace of board hearings, "There would be dozens of engineers, geologists and financial people eating their heads off in the Palliser Hotel, waiting for weeks to give evidence, and this was all money down the drain unless you got an authorization. As I have said, for a guy from Nova Scotia (accustomed to dealing in very small sums of money), contemplating those kinds of expenditures on a dream was hard to become accustomed to."

Yet, though the Alberta Conservation Board hearings moved at a snail's pace, it was no slower than the other boards with which the pipeliners had to contend. Take for example when Westcoast Transmission needed an export market in the United States to make its project feasible financially even after it got its permits from Alberta. This meant it had to go through more hearings in Ottawa to obtain permission to export and still more hearings in Washington to get permission to import gas from Canada into the United States. The hearings before the US Federal Power Commission between February 16, 1953, and March 1, 1954, consumed 192 days, with twenty-eight thousand pages of testimony and six hundred exhibits. Westcoast's ten witnesses were on the stand for 93 of those 192 days. It took D.P. McDonald, for example, five days to make his evidence-in-chief. He then spent the next nineteen days being cross-examined by counsel for rival interests. As for the National Energy Board, it was no better or worse than the others. The first hearing of the board began the day after New Year's and was over the day before St. Patrick's Day.

As far as the legal profession was concerned, the public hearings were only the surface manifestation of the endless burning of midnight oil. Leaving the public hearings completely aside, there was an immense amount of work drafting watertight legal agreements between an almost infinite number of game players. Long before the pipeline application became a reality, gas purchase contracts, gas processing contracts, gas moving contracts had to be negotiated in three- to ten-sided deals. Then as the pipeline approached reality, many such agreements had to be renegotiated and then re-renegotiated all over again when interest rates rose or the value of Canadian currency declined.

So the personnel of Calgary law firms expanded from five partners to ten partners and five associates, to ten partners and ten associates and so on, to the forties and fifties. At the same time, oil companies without an in-house lawyer became less and less numerous while those with full-fledged legal departments multiplied.

Inevitably the gulf that separated the two widened and animosities developed, particularly when it became apparent to the in-house lawyers that they were coming to be regarded by their over-town confreres as second-class citizens. When, at election after election, no in-house lawyer was ever elected a bencher, despite the fact that several stood for the office, the suspicion arose that one group was ganging up on the other. A movement developed by the in-house group to vote as a block in support of one of their own number. Nothing came of it.

It was not just a thirst for the prestige of being a bencher that was causing the in-house lawyers to complain at being cut off from the benchers. Some of the company lawyers felt they had real grievances that should be ventilated by the ruling body of the bar. One complaint was over the excessive fees that were sometimes charged for oil industry work by the private practitioners. There were occasions when work that was worth but a few hundred dollars was charged in the thousands. And there were occasions when the work was less than satisfactorily performed.

It is ironic that as time passed the legal work generated directly by the oil industry was hardly more important than the work it generated indirectly. Calgary's population doubled between 1950 and 1960 and doubled again by 1975, thanks mainly to the oil industry impact on the economy of the city. In the quarter century-long boom, the demand for legal services on the part of the real estate interests also doubled, redoubled, and quadrupled. So did the services required to draft construction contracts, long term office leases, and the breaking of long-term office leases. Inevitably, with unparalleled prosperity, there came doubled demands for lawyer assistance in resolving family disputes in the divorce courts. Finally, as a result of the government enforced oil industry depression, bankruptcies went dominoing across the economic landscape, and the need for legal service for the foreclosing mortgage companies and screw-tightening chartered banks doubled and redoubled.

And it was the oil industry that did it all.

And it was the oil industry, incidentally, that was responsible for the last appeal from the Supreme Court of Canada to the Privy Council in London. It was made by the highest octane group of Canadian lawyers ever to make an appearance before that august body over an issue of little consequence, though it did have its complexities.

The stage for this one takes some setting:

The judiciary committee of the Imperial Privy Council, from long before Confederation until 1949, was the final court of appeal for Canada. It was in fact, if not in actual form, the citizen's last appeal to the foot of the throne of earlier times. Her Majesty, by the Grace of God of the United Kingdom of Great Britain and Ireland and the British Dominions beyond the Seas, Queen, Empress of India, Defender of the Faith, had neither the time nor the expertise to decide all the knotty legal problems her subjects wished to pose for her. So she deputized the cream of the British law lords to hear the problems and advise the monarch how to decide the matters.

Over the years the law lords sitting in far off London had rendered what were politely described by Canadian politicians as perverse judgments on matters of grave Canadian import. So in 1949 the government of the day prevailed upon the Parliament at Westminster to abolish appeals from the Canadian Supreme Court to the Privy Council. Naturally a date had to be chosen, after which no law suit that was started could be appealed to London.

Enter W.G. Morrow in 1945 with a client who had lost a mechanics' lien case in the trial division in Alberta, won it by a three to two majority in the Court of Appeal, and then lost it five to nothing in the Supreme Court of Canada. Rummaging around in his files and what not, Morrow discovered that, incredibly, in face of the time it took to get to trial, the writ had been filed back in 1949, two days before privy council appeals were abolished. He had represented the defendant in the mechanics' lien suit and he could carry the appeal to the Privy Council if his client would stand the expense.

The nuts and bolts of the case were these:

A marginal well had been drilled on the edge of the Leduc field and it could not be made to produce commercial qualities of oil or natural gas. So after having a service company work over the well several times without success, the owners abandoned the well without paying the service company for its work. So the mechanics' lien was filed against the well and simply sat on the title as the years ticked away. New production procedures were eventually developed, the well was brought into profitable production, and the well service company brought suit for its unpaid bill.

Morrow then persuaded William Stevenson to join him in appealing the case to the Privy Council and have their names perpetuated for all time in the legal history of Canada. To represent the respondent service company, J.H. Laycraft recruited Ross McKimmie and J.V.H. Milvain for his team. While the rest of the group went off to rent the wigs they wore for their Privy Council appearance, Morrow, with a better sense of the historical significance of the occasion, bought a new wig to have as a permanent keepsake of the occasion. In no Canadian court did the case take more than two days—one and a half in the Supreme Court. In

London the five law lords, Simonds, Reid, Radcliffe, Tucker, and Denning sat on the case for five days before confirming the judgment of the Supreme Court of Canada.

*Chapter Nine*

# Queen Mother Morning Star, the Non-Practicing Lawyer who Scalped Indian Affairs

The impact that Calgary lawyers, in the practice of their professions, have had on the course of Alberta history has been important and varied. Ironically, it was a lawyer who had long since abandoned the active practice of the profession who cut the widest swath through the lives of more people than any lawyer in active practice. It was doubly ironic that that lawyer was a woman, at a time when women were regarded as aberrant intruders in the courtrooms of the land.

Her name is Ruth Peacock Gorman, a.k.a. Mountain White Eagle Woman, a.k.a. Queen Mother Morning Star. Not only did she spearhead the campaign that saved thousands of Indians from possible expulsion from their reserves at the hands of the federal government and the Department of Indian Affairs; she later took on the even more powerful Canadian Pacific Railway and torpedoed its Calgary track relocation plan.

Ruth Peacock came to the practice of law at the irresistible insistence of her father, Colonel M.B. Peacock. He was the fourth generation of his family who had practiced law in Canada and he had his heart set on his daughter becoming the fifth. She had no burning career ambition in any other direction but the last thing she wanted to do was to become a lawyer. So she intentionally flunked her high school Latin exam and became ineligible to enroll at the law school. Peacock sternly ordered her into a summer of Latin tutoring and a repetition of the exam. She flunked it for the second time. However, she eventually graduated from the University of Alberta in 1936 with a Bachelor of Arts degree. It was only then that her father discovered that that degree made her eligible for the law school there even if she did not have Latin. In she went and, curiously enough, after a five-year struggle against the law, she took to it like a fish to water and obtained her degree in 1939. In the process she also became a dedicated feminist.

It was difficult enough for the young male lawyers graduating during the depression to find lawyers to hire them as articling students, even when they were prepared to work for nothing. The handful of women who graduated from the University of Alberta had it even harder. Some of them had their entry into the profession delayed for over a year because male lawyer prejudice against women lawyers barred them from articling openings. Ruth Peacock, who married classmate John Gorman soon after their graduation, was luckier than most. She articled with her father's firm, Peacock and Skene. Once in practice she quickly discovered just how pervasively the dice were loaded against women lawyers. For example, because she was a woman she was barred from the men's robing room; the only place where she could change was in the women's toilet, which was frequently occupied by a police matron with a couple of women prisoners in handcuffs.

She also discovered that there were no essential facilities anywhere in Alberta for women prisoners in police stations, jails, or prisons. Women in prison spent their lives in cells in total idleness, except for the occasion when they were required to darn and patch the laundry for the men prisoners. The plight of women in custody became an item at the top of Ruth Gorman's list of changes to be made when, with the birth of her daughter, she abandoned her legal career to become the resident troublemaker of the Local Council of Women. (It was the pressure from these Calgary women that ultimately persuaded Premier William Aberhart to bring in a dower act that bore a remarkable resemblance to a document drafted by Ruth Gorman and the Calgary women.)

Opting out of a career in law did not mean that Ruth Gorman was abandoning her interest in either the law or public affairs. When she discovered the Local Council of Women it meant only that she was abandoning the court of law for the court of public opinion. And when the Local Council of Women discovered that in Ruth Gorman it had, as her mother described her, a "lawyeress," in its midst, it moved immediately to appoint her "convenor of laws."

The Local Council of Women was organized in 1895 by the *crème-de-la-crème* of Calgary society in response to a request by the Countess of Aberdeen, wife of the governor general, who had sponsored the organization of the National Council of Women. Madam Rouleau, wife of the Supreme Court justice, was the first president, Mrs. James Lougheed and Mrs. J.D. Lafferty were vice-presidents, while Mrs. Horace Harvey, Mrs. Amos Rowe, Mrs. D.W. Marsh, Mrs. J.R. Costigan, and Mrs. George MacDonald composed the executive.

The organization, however, made few ripples on local affairs until 1912, when Mrs. R.R. Jamieson, Alberta's first woman magistrate, headed up an executive that put it on a permanently active basis. With her were Mrs. George Kirby, Mrs. William Pearce, Mrs. P.J. Nolan, Mrs. Pat Burns, Mrs. P.S. Woodhall, Mrs. F.S. Jacobs, Mrs. E.A. Cruickshanks, and Mrs. Glass. The rejuvenated council eventually claimed fifty-one affiliated organizations at a time when a new militancy was gripping women's movements everywhere. The affiliates included women's church groups of every denomination, the suffragettes, the temperance legions, educational groups, and trades unions.

Mrs. Jamieson's passionate concern with improving the living conditions of women and children was reflected in the achievements of the Local Council of Women under her leadership. Among them, the enfranchisement of women in 1916, establishment of legal aid for women in distress, particularly for immigrant women, domestic servants, and unwed mothers. It succeeded in having women named to government boards and got a local consumers' league going, and a humane society. It campaigned vigorously for public health laws and for protection of babies from effects of venereal disease. It anticipated Ruth Gorman's concern for women prisoners by agitating for and getting a police matron appointed.

During the First World War, it was involved in all manner of patriotic projects and in particular with the needs of soldiers' wives, and widows' pensions. By the Second World War it expanded its goals to include greater concern with working conditions and the creation of provincially funded family planning clinics.

It was, in short, just the kind of an organization that was suited to involvement in the kind of causes that were troubling Ruth Gorman—things like the need for improvement and expansion of Calgary's parks system, and improvements in the police line-up system to shield women witnesses from possible retaliation from identified criminals. Above all, there was her mounting concern for the social problems of Indian women, particularly those in Calgary and environs.

M.B. Peacock had acted for the Indians in the early 1930s when an attempt was made by white hunting groups to curtail the hunting rights of Indians. Charges were actually laid against Indians for killing game animals on their reserves. Peacock had taken their case to the court of appeal and won. He was repaid for his efforts by being made an honourary chief of the Sarcees and, when he had taken his daughter along for the ceremony, Ruth was also honoured with the title of Mountain White Eagle Woman. Said John Laurie, "Inasmuch as you have long been an honourary Indian, don't you think it is about time you became actively involved in helping the Indians with their problems?" It was after the death of her father in 1943 that she became actively involved herself with the Indians.

The concern of the Indians at the time derived from the fact that while they were subject to the Indian Act, few of them had ever seen it and none of them had ever read it. In practical terms, they were the subjects, even prisoners, of the Indian agents on the reserves, who sometimes seemed to interpret the act in a way that most suited their own interests. Moreover, there seemed to be a lack of consistency between reserves in the enforcement of the act. So John Laurie concluded that what the new Indian association needed was to have its leaders become informed on the Indian Act so that they could make effective submissions for changes to the government. Laurie was a Calgary school teacher who devoted his life to the interest of the Indians and was responsible for the formation of the Indian Association of Alberta in 1944.

Laurie invited a group of Calgary lawyers to attend a round-up of southern Alberta Indian chiefs to explain the Indian Act to them. Ruth Gorman, though she was no longer in active practice, was one of the lawyers Laurie invited to the convention he was holding in the Paget Hall of the downtown Anglican Church.

Until this point Gorman's interest in Indians, apart from her concern for the Indian women in the clutches of the law, had been casual at best. Indeed, she had occasionally taken a dim view of the way her father allowed the Indians to clutter up his office. She had not even read the Indian Act herself and was totally unaware of the problems on the reserves. But Laurie was so persuasive, and he promised that two other lawyers would attend and carry most of the load, that Gorman gave in and went off to study the Indian Act.

Unhappily, the other lawyers failed to show up for the meeting so Gorman had the podium to herself. It was a tedious and difficult meeting because everything had to be translated into the Cree, Blackfoot, and Sarcee languages. After an all-day session that went on long after dark, they were not halfway through the Act. An adjournment was called and arrangements were made to resume the following morning. About noon the second day, a tired and hungry Gorman suggested to Laurie that it was time for a lunch break. Only then did Gorman discover that the Indians had come to Calgary without money, that they had had no breakfast and had spent the night bedded down on the floor in the bus station. Gorman emptied out her purse for enough money to buy a supply of chocolate bars and drinks to get the Indians through to the end of the meeting. And when the meeting ended Ruth Gorman signed on as the unpaid, unofficial legal counsel for the Alberta Indian Association and full-time dust-disturber for the province's treaty Indians. In addition to her role as unpaid, unofficial counsel to the Alberta Indians, Gorman also signed on as their unofficial agitator in white society. She became a frequent speaker on the problems of the reserve Indians to women's groups and letters-to-the-editor writer. It was not only the abject poverty of the Indians that inflamed Gorman's social consciousness; it was her discovery of the way in which seventy years of reserve life had been so destructive to Indian self-respect and initiative.

In the beginning the intention of the Government had been to provide the Indians with reserves on which they could convert from successful buffalo hunters into successful farmers. To this end they were provided with more land per Indian, in many cases, than white settlers started out with and were provided with white instructors and up-to-date equipment. But, when the conversion process failed, government policy drifted into maintenance of the Indians at a subsistence level. Super-paternalistic regulations evolved over the years to a point where the Indians could not even raise their own cattle or sell their produce from the reserves. The Indians became the subservient subjects of the Indian agent whose word was law and whose ire was to be avoided at all costs.

It so happened, circa 1948–1950, that the federal government was also having some second thoughts about the Indian Act, thoughts which would soon imperil the very existence of status Indians as status Indians. Behind these second thoughts was an expanding consensus in Ottawa that the basis of the national Indian policy should be to speed the social and economic integration of the Indians into Canadian society. There was also concern with the "de-Indianizing" mixed marriages taking place among the Indians and whites on reserves in the proximity to large urban centres.

It was a process, of course, that had begun with the arrival of the first fur traders and had increased with the growth of contact between the whites and the Indians. Sometimes the relationships were casual in the extreme with the offspring of the contacts integrating into the Indian bands of their mothers. In other cases trading post employees married Indian women and raised families at the trading posts and in the settlements that grew up around them. Intermarriage between Indians and whites was far from unknown in the early years in Alberta. Several prominent chiefs on the Blood, Blackfoot, and Sarcee reserves married white women and took them back to their reserves to raise families, which matured and married and raised families, which matured— and so on, ad infinitum.

Why something that had been a fact of life for two hundred years should have suddenly surfaced as a critical problem in postwar Canada is unclear. Perhaps the return to the reserves by the hundreds of Indians who had served in the Second World War, and came home with war brides, had something to do with it. In any event, on some reserves in Ontario and Quebec, voices were being raised strongly against the racial mixing that was taking place on the reserves. This agitation reached Ottawa at about the same time that the bureaucracy was discovering that the Indian birth rate was shooting up faster than that of any other racial group in the country. If the Indian birth rate were to continue rising so sharply, the government foresaw gigantic financial problems looming in the future. So, putting some brakes on Indian population growth was in the minds of the government when it set about amending the Indian Act in 1950.

The reserves were established for full-blooded Indians. The government felt that it was time to re-establish that condition and the first step in that direction, after passage of the new act in 1951, was to enumerate by registration all the Indians on the reserves. Commissioners were to be dispatched to the reserves to do the registering, but with instructions not to register any persons in the following categories:

1. If there was illegitimacy in their ancestry.
2. If any suspicion existed that there was white blood in their ancestry.
3. If ancestors had joined the wrong band.
4. If an ancestor had accepted half-breed scrip or cash payment in lieu of land after 1870.

If this bill of particulars did not spread consternation through the Indian reserves of the West, the Indians simply were not paying attention. Marriage, for example, among Indians was a ritual different from the Christian service. And it differed from tribe to tribe. Among the plains Indians polygamy was practiced and the number of wives a chief might have depended on his ability to support them. Crowfoot, the distinguished chief of the Blackfoot, had eleven wives during his lifetime, though he seldom had more than four at once. And as there was no recorded marriage, how could any of the grandchildren prove that they conformed to Indian Act legitimacy? The disqualification because of ancestral white blood left Indians open to banishment from their reserves on the mere suspicion that there had been a dalliance generations back with persons of white blood.

The scrip disqualification was even more serious. After the Red River insurrection, as the government was proceeding with organizing reserves for the Indians, it also had its eye on getting the half-breed buffalo hunters permanently settled on their own land. The instrument for doing so was a system of land grants under which each member of a family became entitled to up to 240 acres of land which could be selected once surveys were complete. In the meantime the entitlements were recognized by the issuing of scrip, a certificate, to the heads of half-breed families.

But as Indians and half-breeds all looked alike to the undiscerning eyes of the incoming white settlers, many Indians were persuaded to apply for scrip and then trade it to the whites for a fraction of its worth, often for only a bottle of whisky or two. Furthermore, none of the Indians realized that by accepting the scrip they extinguished whatever aboriginal rights they had to their former buffalo hunting grounds. Thus many an Indian, awakening from a hangover brought on by the sale of his scrip, found himself barred from a reserve and incapable of integrating into either the white society or the half-breed community. The problem of the status-less Indians became so vexing that the government in 1882 repealed the scrip disqualification and allowed the affected Indians to return to the reserves. Now, seventy years later, in 1951, the government was changing its mind and visiting the sins of the grandfathers upon third and fourth generations.

As the special commissions prepared to move out to the reserves for their hearings, something else was discovered about the new Indian Act. There was a provision that any Indian's right to inclusion on his reserve roster of qualified Indians could be challenged by his fellow Indians. If any group of ten electors of his reserve challenged him on any one of the four points, the registrar had to examine the charges. But no evidence was required to back up the charges. They could be based on the wildest hearsay. An adult Indian might swear that he had heard as a child that the grandfather of another Indian had accepted scrip. If the registrar accepted the testimony he could strike the names of all the descendants, perhaps forty or fifty people in all, from the band list and they would be expelled from the reserve.

Honourable Walter Harris, the minister of Indian affairs, explained that it was the intention of the government to remove from Indian status all Indians who failed to qualify, even those with 15/16ths Indian blood. Nor was this all. Consistent with the overall objective of integrating the Indians into Canadian society, a plan was developed to encourage even the full-blooded reserve Indians to leave the reserves. If they would do so, each Indian was guaranteed that he would be given a pro-rata share of the assets of his band. That was hardly an incentive for most Indians whose bands had little trust fund assets. But in the cases of some of the oil-rich reserves in Alberta it could run to several thousand dollars. Taking that choice would, of course, remove the Indians from the reserve forever, along with all the members of their families.

There were other ways of losing band membership. If an Indian had special talents and moved off the reserve to develop them, he could lose his reserve status. If he should vote in a municipal election while off the reserve, he faced a similar fate. One rather famous case of an Indian caught up in such machinations was that of Gerald Tailfeathers, a well-known Alberta Indian artist. John Laurie had spotted Tailfeathers' raw talent on a visit to the Blood reserve. He persuaded the young artist to enrol in the drafting course at the Southern Alberta Institute of Technology in Calgary and took him into his home to live. When he completed his course, Tailfeathers got a steady job as a draftsman in Calgary while he continued to pursue his career as an artist.

After some years Tailfeathers reached a point in his career where he decided to devote himself to his painting and to establish himself in a home-cum-studio in Calgary. As an Indian he would have been eligible for a government housing loan on the Blood reserve. He approached the Department of Indian Affairs for a loan to finance the home in Calgary. It was then that he discovered the "compulsory enfranchisement" provisions of the Indian Act. Indians who left reserves and achieved any manner of success in the urban environment were encouraged to abandon their status as reserve Indians by seeking enfranchisement. But if they refused, as Gerald Tailfeathers refused, and remained off the reserve, the Indian affairs department could force their enfranchisement and thus prevent their ever returning to their reserve. As an artist whose milieu was his Indian heritage, Tailfeathers was aghast at the dilemma which faced him. In the end he returned to the reserve where he died prematurely, some say a broken man.

The Canadian Parliament rewrote the Indian Act with a minimum of debate, and its passage in 1951 caused nary a ripple on the public mind. There was nothing precipitous about the enforcement of the new provisions, and it was not until well into 1952 when commissions were appointed to carry out the registration of the individual Indians.

The nature of the proceedings guaranteed there would be an eruption of bad blood on the Indian reserves of western Canada. The procedures were an open invitation to families who harbored grudges against other families to get even by laying charges under sections 11 and 12 of the new Indian Act. And that was what happened on the Hobbema reserve in 1952 when two Indians became embroiled in an argument over who had stolen whose horse. The dispute escalated in bitterness until it became a shouting match reminiscent of the famous feud of the Hatfields and McCoys. But instead of reaching for guns, one of the feuders reached for blank forms to be used in charging that his opponent was a descendant of an Indian who had accepted scrip back in the 1880s. The signatures of ten other family members were placed on the form and the wheels were set in motion to exclude John Samson and his family from the reserve—and not only his immediate family; it applied to all his cousins, aunts, uncles, and their families as well.

When the authorities got everybody sorted out and listed, no less than 27 male adults and a total of 122 persons were involved. That turned the Hobbema proceedings into the making of a *cause célèbre*, whereas, elsewhere in the West, the hearings had attracted almost no public attention.

In the main few people were involved and many of them accepted their eviction and did not appeal against the registrars' orders. Very little attention was attracted to the Hobbema case in its early stages either.

When the attempt to evict the Samson band came to trial before the recorder at Hobbema, the enormity of the government's action guaranteed it public attention. The 122 Indians constituted ten percent of the reserves' population. On expulsion they would be entitled to about one million dollars from the tribe's trust fund which had been built up from royalties on oil and gas production on the reserve. But they would all lose their homes, livestock worth an estimated three million dollars, and all claim to future oil royalties. But worst of all they would be evicted from their reserve homeland environment and banished to an utterly alien white society. Nothing like this had happened in Canada since the Acadian expulsion from Nova Scotia two hundred years before.

At the first hearing before a commissioner appointed by Ottawa, the Samsons were represented by John Laurie and Ruth Gorman. The evidence against the band was a telegram from Ottawa which stated that John Samson had applied for scrip. From a legal point, that was all the evidence needed to expel the band. But Gorman, more to stall for time than for any other reason, demanded that the complainants produce the actual evidence of that application in court. It was sheer inspiration, for when the documents arrived some months later they showed the words "application refused" opposite the noted application. The commissioner had no choice but to reject said application.

Ottawa, however, refused to accept defeat graciously. Instead, it passed an order in council amending the act to provide that the defendants had to prove their ancestors had *not* taken scrip, an obvious impossibility. It ordered the case to be reopened in February 1956, two years after it had first come to trial. This time the Samsons were represented by Ruth Gorman's husband, J.C.

Gorman, Robert Barron of Calgary, and A.F. Moir and Joe Brumlick of Edmonton, all former classmates of Ruth Gorman and, like her, unpaid volunteers for the duration of the struggle. The registrar reversed the judgment of the previous commissioner, ordered all the Indians' names struck from the band roles, and eviction proceedings to be started.

There was one more avenue of appeal open. It was to a judge of the district court of Alberta. Gorman had decided that the enormity of the crime against the Indians justified an appeal to an even higher court—the court of public opinion. She began this appeal rather tentatively, making speeches to women's groups and activating the Local Council of Women on behalf of the Indians. But when the Hobbema registrar delivered his judgment Gorman set off a publicity drive that soon assumed cyclonic proportions. In the end, it was an aroused public opinion that blew the offending sections clear out of the Indian Act and helped to defeat the Liberal Government in the 1957 general election.

In launching that campaign, Gorman had a problem. The Indians had thirty days in which to file an appeal against the judgment of the registrar. But as soon as the appeal was filed the case became *sub-judice* and newspaper and other public agitation would be doused. So while Gorman announced that the decision would be appealed she decided to delay filing appeal papers until the last possible moment. Technically, the case then was not before the courts so public excursions and alarums were perfectly in order. On her return to Calgary, Gorman's first call was on Basil Dean and Dick Sanburn, publisher and editor, respectively, of the Calgary *Herald*. Not only did they promise editorial support for a campaign to have enforcement of the act against the Indians halted, they assigned a senior reporter to write a series of articles exposing what was taking place. Dean also telephoned a crony on the *Times* of London and got the British press interested in the issue.

Then Gorman moved in on her old classmates to lobby them to start resolutions condemning the Indian Act through the bar associations. Her Local Council of Women took a strong stand and went back to their twenty main affiliates to spread the word and stir up letter-writing campaigns. Seldom before did Alberta react with such unanimity as it did to the case of the 122 Hobbema Indians. The rush to go on record opposing what was going on turned into a stampede. The Social Credit Government, the Alberta Women's Liberal Association, the Conservative Association, the Calgary Labor Council, the First Baptist Church, the Catholic Women's League, the Anglican Diocese of Calgary, the Home and School Association, all rose in anger to make their feelings known.

In the meantime a real problem was developing with the

Indians themselves. If the Indians accepted the verdict of the registrar, the Indian affairs department would continue their living allowances until the formalities were completed for their expulsion from the reserve. But if they appealed the award their rations would be cut off. John Laurie was able to launch a successful campaign to raise funds from the other Indians to support the Samsons pending the appeal.

Very early in the Hobbema case, Gorman had renewed her contacts with Douglas Harkness, Conservative member of Parliament for Calgary North and the Conservative Indian affairs critic, and he thorned the flesh of Honourable Jack Pickersgill with barbed questions about the campaign against what Pickersgill insisted on calling the "non-Indians" on the reserves. For his part Pickersgill stonewalled the issue by emphasizing that the Indians still had an appeal to the courts open to them and he urged "that woman" to get on with the appeal and let the courts decide the issue rather than in provoking public unrest. But Gorman was not about to take any advice from a Liberal politician, let alone the minister responsible for Indian affairs. Instead, she persuaded the Indians to carry their appeal to the foot of the throne, to appeal to Queen Elizabeth herself.

From the beginning, the prairie Indians have maintained a very special attitude toward "their" Queen. Their original treaties were with Queen Victoria's representative, the governor general. The assurances they had received during the negotiations with Canadian authorities came, in Indian eyes, from the Queen herself and not from Ottawa politicians. So, while the Hobbema appeal to the district court was still in limbo, Gorman's team drafted the appeal to Queen Elizabeth and fired it off to the governor general for transmission to Buckingham Palace.

Would the governor general, The Right Honourable Vincent Massey, actually send the appeal to the Queen? Or would he follow protocol, open the letter and bring the matter to the attention of the government for advice? Would anybody in the government bring it upon themselves to open a letter addressed to Her Majesty the Queen? Such questions as these enlivened the debate over Indian affairs during the bleak January days of 1957. And they brought that redoubtable royalist, Conservative leader John Diefenbaker into the fray in the House of Commons.

The governor general opted for long accepted protocol. He referred the matter to the prime minister's office for advice. It sent his query to Honourable Jack Pickersgill. His advice was that the matter was still before the courts in Canada and the appeal to the Queen should go no farther. The noisy Conservative opposition now had another handy argument—interfering with the Queen's mail—for attacking the Liberal Government of Prime Minister Louis St. Laurent.

When the final date for launching an appeal loomed danger-ously near, Gorman completed the necessary formalities on February 4, 1957. Chief Judge Nells V. Buchanan of the Northern Alberta District Court was named to hear the appeal which began at Hobbema on February 26 and ended on February 27. In a judgment delivered on March 1 an end was put to the department's ancestor hunt and to the notion that the government could get rid of the Indian reserves by integrating the Indians into white society.

It was a curious judgment in many ways, based very little on principle and very much on technicalities. Somebody, in preparing the case against the Samson band, had come up with a new way to spell "scrip"—script. Somebody else, who was charged with responsibility for posting a notice containing the names of all the Samson band, had posted it in a place not stipulated in the regulations. The regulations required that the protesters be "elec-tors" and no evidence was presented that the protesters were in fact electors and not ordinary members of the band. Regulations referred to ancestors who had taken scrip. The pleadings referred to "forbearer"—a non-word. For all these far-out technicalities Judge Buchanan found that there was no valid application to disqualify the Indians and reversed the registrar's ruling.

The fallout from the Hobbema trial was immediate and varied. Pickersgill's comment was that he was delighted with the outcome of the trial because he had always felt that "these people who have always been regarded as Indians should continue to be regarded as Indians." The general public bafflement with that reaction was best described by a Calgary *Herald* editorial which read:

> It is difficult to understand how Mr. Pickersgill can be delighted with the outcome of this case, after his own department instituted the action of re-opening the file against the Hobbemas, after it had been closed once before.
>
> Moreover, if he felt they should always be regarded as Indians it was his clear duty to introduce an amendment to the Indian Act removing those sections liable to prejudice an Indian's status, and long before this time. The Hobbema case has been pending for five years, and Mr. Pickersgill could have ended it at any stage since he first assumed the portfolio he now holds. Mr. Pickersgill cannot defend himself on the strength of a lack of protests in the past. The records show the Leader of the Opposition, Mr. John Diefenbaker, objected vigorously when it was first introduced. The Indian Association of Alberta, through its representatives, protested the contentious sections long before the act was presented to Parliament.

The reaction of the Indians, as the Buchanan-induced euphoria wore off, was to lay plans for a monster celebration on the Hobbema reserve to which they invited tribal chiefs from all over

Alberta and Saskatchewan. Curiously enough, by the time the case eventually got to a decisive stage, the dispute over the horse was settled and friendly relations between the disputants were restored. After an evening of dining and dancing, Ruth Gorman was called front and centre, presented with the traditional feathered headdress and formally installed as Queen Mother Morning Star of the Cree tribe.

When the Conservatives of John Diefenbaker defeated the Liberal Government of Louis St. Laurent later that year, Gorman was invited to become an advisor on the revision of the Indian Act. Then the prime minister offered her a senatorship and when she backed off he chose Gladstone of the Blood Indians. Her reputation as a civil libertarian went far afield and she was soon involved in efforts to have Canada become a signatory of the United Nations Charter of Rights. She was an advisor in the drafting of John Diefenbaker's Canadian Bill of Rights. Along the way she served as chairman of the Canadian Bar Association Civil Liberties Committee.

Hard on the heels of the imbroglio over Indian status came the federal election of June 10, 1957, which saw the defeat of twenty-two years of old Liberal administration and the accession to power of John Diefenbaker's Conservative party. The extent to which the row over the Indians had an influence on the outcome of that election was never determined. A much greater factor was surely the two-months-long series of confrontations over the trans-Canada pipeline bill. As far as eastern Canada was concerned, the Indian Act was very much a side issue. But John Diefenbaker once confessed to Ruth Gorman that he was sure that the effort to banish the Indians from their reserves was good for five seats in western Canada. If that was an accurate assessment, it could well be argued that it was those seats that provided the margin that tipped the Liberals from power and slid the Conservatives in. In that election the final seat count was Conservatives 112, Liberals 105, ccf 25, Social Credit 19 and others 4. If those five seats had gone to the Liberals there is certainly some question of whether the Liberals would have resigned or sought an alliance with one of the other parties. So is it too much to say that the Hobbema affair led at least in part to the election of the first Conservative Government in twenty-two years?

The election ended the Indian affairs department's efforts to clear the Indians from the reserves. The new Conservative Government eventually got around to redrawing the Indian Act. In the process Ruth Gorman and Chief John Samson of the Hobbema tribe played a vital role as advisors to the Senate committee which was charged with redrafting the act. Needless to say, it eliminated sections 11 and 12.

The struggle which ended at Hobbema affected thousands of

Indians from coast to coast. If it had not been for John Laurie and Ruth Gorman, uncountable thousands of Indians would have been evicted from their reserve home and dumped on the white communities to subsist and die on provincial welfare rolls.

By contrast the Canadian Pacific Railway's Calgary Re-Development Plan affected only Calgarians and, in the main, well heeled Calgarians at best. It was a project that came in like the power and the glory with all trumpets blaring. And it went out like an adolescent practical joke that backfired. Never before in Calgary had the unveiling of a project been greeted with such universal outpouring of enthusiasm as the unveiling of the Canadian Pacific Railway redevelopment plan on April 5, 1963. A year later it was abandoned by the city council in the manner of a spinster who had reached for a chocolate and found a can of worms.

At the beginning, the announcement of the "$35 million face lift for Calgary" took up half the *Herald*'s front page. It featured artists' renderings of new developments, centred by a clutch of CPR vice-presidents and Mayor Harry Hays gleefully contemplating a model of the new convention centre that would be the centrepiece of the new development. The vice-presidents were quoted predictors of a glowing future for Calgary, a new city even. The project drew an instant endorsement by both local newspapers, the Calgary aldermen (one of whom called it "a dream come true") and the chamber of commerce. Straw polls of the man on the street were nearly unanimous.

Behind all the enthusiasm was the fact that the CPR main line and railway yards that cluttered the heart of the city had constituted an unmitigated nuisance for as long as the oldest citizens could remember. Its east-west main line and north-south branch line divided the city into isolated quadrants. Its rail traffic created endless vehicular delays at its surface crossings. The subways under its tracks frequently flooded in summer showers. Its spur tracks and downtown railway yard made expansions and development of the downtown core a planner's nightmare.

Relocating the CPR, therefore, was a will-o'-the-wisp that engaged city aldermen periodically, but the immensity of the task was awesomely intimidating. Nothing came of any of the talk until in the early 1960s when the CPR discovered the extent of the real estate holdings it had title to in the cities of western Canada, most of it in the centre of downtown commercial areas. In Calgary, it amounted to over 120 acres in a long narrow strip running from the eastern to the western boundary of the city, between Ninth Avenue and Tenth Avenue. In 1962 the CPR embarked on a study to see what could be done to turn this trackage into commercial building lots.

It was quickly determined that the freight yards could easily be moved to another large tract of CPR land east of the city. But the cost of redirecting the CPR main line around the city could have cost twice as much as it would gain from downtown real estate. As it happened, the city planners had also been doodling with plans to reroute the railway and sent these plans off to the railway in 1962. One of the alternatives was to move the tracks one thousand yards to the north to a route along the southern bank of the Bow River. The closer the CPR looked at the city proposal the better it liked it.

A deal was quickly made with the Calgary mayor and city commissioners. The city would provide the CPR with a new right of way on the Bow River bank from Fourteenth Street West to Sixth Street East. It would also build an eight-lane freeway along the south side of the new trackage. Cost for land acquisition for both projects would be shared equally. The city undertook to build a new convention centre adjacent to the Palliser Hotel. The CPR was to build a new station including a massive bus storage facility where the city would be committed to storing its buses. The CPR would clear off its 120 acres of track-strewn land and open it for commercial construction, if, as, and when a demand developed for more office space in Calgary. That would add 80-odd acres of land to the tax rolls, and the project, when fully developed, would add an estimated two million dollars a year to the city's property tax income.

The only dissenting voice in the chorus of cheers for the project came from a local engineer with a vested interest that was at odds with CPR. He was G.M. Kernahan and he was trying to locate a site for a Hilton hotel midway between the Palliser Hotel and the Bow River. If the convention centre was to be located adjacent to the Palliser Hotel it would erase Calgary's name from a list of potential Hilton hotels. The Palliser Hotel was located on CPR right of way and hence exempt from city taxes. No tax paying hotel could compete with it for convention business, Kernahan said.

Somewhat slower off the mark was the Local Council of Women. Several years earlier it had become interested in beautifying the banks of the Bow River, which, over several downtown stretches, had come to resemble auxiliary garbage dumps. At that time it had urged the city to establish a buffer zone along both banks of the river between the high water mark and commercial construction. While the city was rushing to sign the agreement with the CPR, Ruth Gorman got the Local Council of Women into emergency session to fire a shot across the city's bow. In essence it said, "Hey, don't forget our buffer strip! If you go ahead with this deal be sure to keep the railway tracks at least a city block away from the river bank!"

In the euphoria of the moment, nobody at city hall paid any attention. Nor was any attention paid to J.C. Sproule, whose office building sat smack in the centre of the new right of way. He blasted the city for rushing into a deal that regional planning experts had not even seen. And it was a deal that would get the city involved in a raft of costly lawsuits for damages done to Calgary businesses, including his.

Despite the heckling, the city unanimously approved the agreement with the CPR on May 23 and the civic officials went into a prolonged huddle to work out the details. And while a substantial body of opposition to the scheme began to build among the owners of nearby real estate, it was overwhelmed by the strident chorus of support from the Calgary *Herald*, the Chamber of Commerce, Trades Union Council, and the Downtown Business Association.

Away from the euphoria, however, a mere wisp of the beginning of a cloud was forming, a cloud that would ultimately develop into a thunderhead of trouble for the project. At the behest of its convenor of laws, the Local Council of Women fired off copies of its greenbelt resolution to a score of local organizations with the suggestion that they bring the matter to the attention of the membership of each group. The extent of the notice paid to the resolution by the membership was never ascertained. But over the next sixty days the city hall was the recipient of a number of letters opposing the project, along with a petition demanding that a plebiscite be held prior to council's committing the city to the project.

In becoming embroiled in a campaign for river bank beautification, the Local Council of Women was latching onto an issue with which everybody in Calgary could identify. The Bow River, as long as nobody looked too closely, was in truth one of Calgary's most eye-pleasing sights. And the notion that the banks should be cleaned up and landscaped was one that surfaced periodically at service clubs, junior chamber of commerce, and community meetings. Everybody in Calgary had a godfatherish interest in the Bow River, though nobody had ever felt under urgent compulsion to do anything about its refuse-strewn water edges.

With her local council stalwarts alerted and in action, Gorman touched bases with her cohorts from the Indian wars, particularly Robert Barron and William Morrow, and it was a case of "once more, dear friends, into the breech!" And with passions aroused! Barron's family was already heavily invested in downtown real estate. Morrow came to represent a number of property owners on both sides of the river whose interest was severely affected by the proposal. Plans were carefully laid to dry-gulch the project when the opportunity became propitious.

The summer and early fall of 1963, however, was not a time for mounting a public clamour against the project. Too much public attention was elsewhere. The CPR project was unveiled, indeed, on the eve of a federal election in which the government of John

Diefenbaker was toppled. In that election, Mayor Harry Hays had been a successful Liberal candidate in Calgary South and he was soon sworn into cabinet as minister of agriculture. That left the mayor's chair vacant and the city lapsed into a state of mild torpidity for a short time.

Eventually the Calgary city council elected one of its own, Alderman Grant MacEwan, to succeed Hays. It was almost like electing the night to succeed the day. Hays was a hard-driving, forceful character as befitting one who had been one of Canada's most successful auctioneers before he had been lured into civic politics only two years previously. MacEwan, a former professor of animal husbandry and dean of agriculture, was the thoughtful, reflective, deliberate type; the consensus man. No less committed to the CPR project than Hays, he was prepared to move with great deliberation and a lot less drive than Hays.

In an aftermath of the federal election, the Manning Government also went to the polls, in June, to renew its overwhelming mandate for another five years. Then, as summer moved into fall, attention was diverted to an alternative proposal put forward by G.M. Kernahan and a team of engineers. The proposal: leave the right of way where it was and sink the rails twenty-five feet below the surface through the centre of the city. That would free the right of way for development over the railway line, similar to what had taken place in Chicago and New York. The CPR rejected that suggestion out of hand, but it still had to take time off from the nuts-and-bolts negotiations taking place with the city to produce an argument against it.

More serious for the CPR were efforts being made by the city administration to obtain some important concessions. One of the most powerful arguments in favour of the project, from the city's point of view, was that the removal of the tracks would improve access to the city centre. The subways under the tracks at Second Street East, Second Street West, and Fourth Street West could be filled in and converted into ordinary streets. A half dozen other streets that dead-ended at the tracks could be continued as through streets. On this point the CPR dug in its heels. It wanted to develop a park adjacent to its Palliser Hotel at Second Street West where the old subway was located. No crossing there. Nor would it give any commitment when the tracks would be removed so that level crossings became possible. Nor would it estimate when the flour mill at Third Street would come down.

So by the time the civic elections rolled around in October several crises had arisen and the project threatened to collapse. The troubles were usually overcome by the city's backing off. Curiously enough, during the civic election, the project was not made an issue by any of the candidates. Nobody ran on an anti-project platform although Roy Deyell and Dave Russell, who were only lukewarm toward it, both were elected to council.

In the meantime three engineering consultants who had been hired to run over the agreement in very general terms all gave it their approval. It would ultimately gain the city two million dollars a year in taxes, would make it possible to develop a new master plan to govern the city's growth. After several minor crises, a draft agreement for submission to the Alberta legislature was approved after a stormy debate in council on January 22, 1964. In that hearing Alderman Jack Leslie was joined by aldermen Runo Berglund, Roy Deyell, and Dave Russell in seeking radical changes to the agreement, the most important of which was to force the CPR to include a timetable for getting rid of the main line tracks and freight yard. As the agreement stood, completion of the deal would leave the railway with two tax-exempt lines running through the city instead of one for as far as anyone could see into the future. But all changes were voted down and the agreement went off to the legislature with what Alderman Russell described "as much vitality as a wet noodle."

The chamber of commerce, taking cognizance of the increasing opposition that was being heard, announced the formation of a special propaganda arm, the Calgarians for Progress Committee, headed by Carl Nickel, one-time member of Parliament and prominent oilman. Its job was to accentuate the positive in every nook and cranny of public opinion that could be reached. That included interviewing the men and women in the street, whose positive opinions were publicized in the *Herald*, and making speeches to any local organizations that would listen.

Ruth Gorman was also out making speeches, as was Robert Barron and Mark Coulson, a University of Alberta, Calgary, geography professor, and Alderman Dave Russell. It was not the track-removal deal per se that Gorman inveighed against, but the way it favoured the CPR in practically every aspect. In any event, the agreement went to the legislature where changes had to be made in sections that were at variance with the city's charter. One section in particular concerned the amount of land the developer of the right of way gave up for community purposes. Another was exemption of the CPR from the city's expropriation rights.

After first reading, the bill authorizing the changes went to the committee of the whole for a public hearing which opened on March 3. The city was represented by Mayor Grant MacEwan, Commissioner John Steel and an assistant city solicitor, John DeWolfe. Spokesmen for both proponents and opponents of the project had their say, and William Morrow called for the appointment of a royal commission to assess the worth of the project to the city.

Morrow contended the project was much too complicated for

judgments to be made without an intense and detailed examination by experts. He suggested a commission headed by a judge, that would include a planner, an engineer, an architect, and an economist. Then Robert Barron launched an attack on the agreement as a legal document which had the appearance of having been drafted by the CPR lawyers and which gave the company all the best of it. The wording of the agreement seemed to make the city liable to substantial damage claims in amounts impossible to even estimate.

Premier E.C. Manning was quite blunt: he was not interested in the merits of the deal, whether it was good, bad or indifferent for the City of Calgary. That was up to the city council to decide. But he was deeply concerned about the Barron criticism of the ambiguity of the drafting of the contract. He wanted the opinion of Carson MacWilliams, the city solicitor, on that point.

Mayor MacEwan pointed out that Mr. DeWolfe, the assistant solicitor was present and could reply to Mr. Barron. Premier Manning insisted on hearing Mr. MacWilliams, so the city solicitor was asked to come to Edmonton immediately. He came and threw proceedings into an uproar when he expressed agreement with Mr. Barron and said it was "the most one-sided agreement I ever saw."

In the months in which negotiations had been going on, his department had never been asked to express an opinion about it, only to draft documents as instructed. The solicitors were only concerned with crossing t's and dotting i's, not with the substance of the matter. "You do not speak unless you are spoken to," MacWilliams explained, because they were not concerned with policy.

However when aldermen had asked him privately what he thought of the agreement he had told them what he thought the city was giving away. He had expressed his deep concern for "injurious affection" claims for damages. "We are out in the dark on that one, I don't know what it may cost and I don't think anyone can tell you."

Mr. MacWilliams devoted some time to a clause in the agreement which stipulated that land that was used for "railway purposes" was to remain exempt from city taxes. He described the words "railway purposes" as "most elastic" and said the city would be in court every time they came up. He recalled the unsuccessful efforts of the city to tax the commercial telegraph business owned by the railways.

The solicitor insisted repeatedly, however, that policy was not his responsibility. His department was not concerned with it, only with insuring that agreements achieved the ends desired by the city council, though he agreed with Mr. Barron that certain clauses were ambiguous. But the fact that MacWilliams found so much fault with the project was manna for Gorman's legions.

In the end the agreement made its way through the legislature with only one additional major imbroglio. At one point near the end of proceedings, Ian Sinclair, senior vice-president of the CPR, threatened to abandon the plan unless provisions of the Alberta Planning Act were modified as applied to the contract. The act called for a total of 20 acres out of the 120 involved to be turned over to the city for parks and other purposes. Mr. Manning himself took a hand and reduced the acreage contribution to a $350,000 cash payment and the deal cleared its final hurdle.

Legislative hurdle, that is.

While the agreement was still in Edmonton, Ruth Gorman decided the Local Council of Women should become more actively involved and persuaded the executive to sponsor a public debate on the project. The gas company auditorium, which seated about three hundred, was engaged, and proponents of the scheme were invited to attend and speak their piece as well as were the opponents. Neither the Calgarians for Progress or J.R.W. Sykes, the CPR spokesman, attended the meeting, which jammed the auditorium far beyond capacity and spilled over into the corridor. Mayor MacEwan and several aldermen strongly defended the deal, and Gorman, Barron and Professor Mark Coulson attacked it. The crowd was overwhelmingly on the side of the opposition. The mayor was booed when he started to speak and heckled throughout his talk as he outlined the concessions made by the CPR and the advantages that would accrue to the city. The highlight of the meeting was the announcement by Alderman Ernie Starr that he was changing sides. He blasted the Calgarians for Progress Committee for pressure it was putting on council on behalf of the CPR and for sending out tons of printed material that had never been shown to council.

Nothing much happened as a result of the Local Council of Women's rally. The *Herald* had demanded editorially that MacWilliams be fired for his testimony before the legislature but Mayor MacEwan said that would not be done and deplored any descent into personalities. (MacWilliams, who was sixty-eight, had been appointed city solicitor only four years before.)

After the legislature agreed to the changes demanded by the CPR, the agreement cleared the legislature on April 15. There remained then only for the city council to decide whether to proceed with a plebiscite of the electors or to submit a money by-law to the ratepayers to raise the nine million dollars the project was now estimated to cost. Even with Alderman Starr's defection, there was still a solid seven-to-five majority on council for the project. Commissioner John Steel even checked in with the opinion that the council could proceed with the project without either a plebiscite or money by-law.

Would the project have passed the electors if it had been submitted? The city council had good reason to doubt it, for over the years Calgarians had developed a contrariness streak when it came to supporting aldermanic initiatives, particularly where money was involved. The project, nevertheless, had powerful supporters like the chamber of commerce, the business community, and Carl Nickel's lobby group—and it had lots of available funding. But the question was never to reach a decision.

While the council was dithering with the plebiscite question Alderman Dave Russell exploded a small bomb. He announced that his opposition to the project, as mild as it had been, had cost him his job. The senior partners of Rule, Wynne, and Rule, the architectural firm that had employed him for nine years, "let him know" that his stance was an embarrassment to the partnership. Then they told him there was an opening in the firm's Kelowna office which was offered to him. Then it was suggested that perhaps he had not paid enough attention to the solid arguments in favour of the plan and he should have a talk with Max Bell, the publisher of the *Albertan* and reputedly the largest single shareholder of Canadian Pacific shares. An interview was arranged with Max Bell who was friendly and very civil, but not particularly convincing to Russell. Russell refused the Kelowna offer and was then, on May 20, fired out of hand.

The firing of Russell fluttered the dovecotes of the Local Council of Women like a fox in a chicken coop. Gorman was off in a trice to organize another public meeting. Not in the gas company auditorium, which was declared off limits to the group after the last unruly affair. Instead the Central High School auditorium was engaged for a protest meeting. But not to protest the firing of Russell or to argue about the CPR project. The meeting was called to "examine the state of morality of Calgary's public life." Were there forces operating in Calgary which were pressuring Calgary elected officials to serve special interests instead of the public good?

The meeting was held on June 9, and Ruth Gorman's agitating art quickly became apparent from the social complexion of the people who attended. Everybody who was anybody in the world of doing good was on hand, for example, Bill Wearmouth, past president of the Calgary Federation of Community Associations; John Long, Calgary chairman of the Community Planning Association of Canada; Adrian Berry of the Calgary Council of Community Services. All spoke vigorously for the following resolution:

> Be it resolved that we at this meeting demand that the City Council and the provincial government institute an impartial

judicial inquiry as to whether civic employees or elected officials have been influenced in their expression of opinions in regard to current civic matters over the past two years. The inquiry should dispel rumors and distortions and growing fear as to the loss of our domestic rights and government.

As an afterthought, almost, the meeting also took a sideswipe at the *Herald* and the *Albertan* for the unfairness of their coverage of the news of the project and for their misleading and biased editorials.

But even while the morality mass meeting was waxing indignant, there were signs in the wind that the relocation project was fatally flawed. From the very beginning, the discussion of track relocations had been confined to an area between Fourteenth Street West and Sixth Street East. At the eastern edge was a large block of land owned by the CNR on which an express warehouse was located. Preliminary indications were that the CNR was prepared to do a land switch to enable its property to be part of the new CPR main line. West of Fourteenth Street there was a Hudson's Bay Company warehouse hard by the river bank. It would have to be moved.

When the city in late May got around to looking westward from Fourteenth Street it came upon all kinds of problems. The warehouse was only the first one, and it discovered to its horror that the CPR expected the city to pay the full shot for whatever it cost to move that warehouse. Then out of the blue came word from the CNR that it placed a figure of six million dollars on the cost of moving its eastside warehouse.

In a panic City Council named a three-man committee to rush off to Montreal to consult the CNR and to get the CPR's agreement to share the cost of these land acquisitions, and other land west of Fourteenth Street as well. The word the Calgarians got was that Calgary was on its own, totally, when it got to problems west of Fourteenth Street and in connection with the CNR claim as well. After a microscopic examination of the agreement, the city council's experts came to the same conclusion. A special meeting of council was held on June 22, 1964 and by a vote of ten to three, the city abandoned the project.

The Local Council of Women had again demonstrated that you can indeed fight city hall, provided always that you have a nonpracticing lawyer like Ruth Gorman as convenor of legal affairs.

# Chapter Ten

# Of Representational Allowances and Judicial Accoutrements

There is a concept abroad that ideas, once the excogitative processes are complete, take on lives of their own, flit about, and come in for landings in the most unexpected places. The idea of conferring fringe benefits on salaried employees is a case in point. The concept surfaced early during the Second World War, when wage and salary ceilings were rigidly enforced. The original fringe benefits were probably limited to providing protective clothing for industrial workers—gloves for steel workers and welders, coveralls for automobile paint shop workers and packing house employees. As time passed, the fringe benefit concept exploded in all directions, from entitlement, to medical and dental plans, to free coffee for work breaks. Forty years later the idea floated into and through the Canadian Parliament, and a thousand-dollar-a-year clothing allowance for judges was born.

Sometimes ideas collide in mid-air and rub off on each other, which may explain the actual form the idea of a judicial allowance took. It could be it came from the conviction of the Government of Alberta that appearance counted, that clothes made the man, that public men should look the part when they are performing their duties. And if all this costs money, it is money well spent. The decision of the Government of Alberta to give a judicial clothing allowance predated that of the Government of Canada by at least a couple of years, and one may very well, lacking proof to the contrary, have been the precedent for, or at least have influenced, the other.

In the spring of 1979, the Alberta government rewrote the Legislative Assembly Act and not only gave all the MLAs whopping salary increases but added a number of fringe benefits for travel, attending committee meetings, and so forth. Later that fall it came back to the legislature for some additions. Among the November amendments was a provision for the payment to the president of the Executive Council on and after November 1, 1979, a representational allowance at the rate of five thousand dollars per year. When reporters wondered aloud what this was all about, it was explained that it was a clothing allowance for the premier. When eyebrows were raised at the size of the allowance— five thousand dollars a year? —for clothes? —it was further explained that the money would be used to defray other expenses, especially for formal occasions, such as visits from foreign heads of state.

The drafters on this amendment were obviously expert philologists who had gone back to a middle-English adaptation of a French word—*representation*—which meant presence, bearing, air, appearance, and used this word to describe a clothing allowance. Curiously enough, when the Honourable Jean Chrétien, minister of justice, on June 12, 1980, arose to introduce the new Judges Act, he said that among its new features would be a provision "for reimbursement for major representational expenses, such as the price of purchases of judicial robes and the likes, that are necessary incidental to the proper performance of the office of a judge."

Had Mr. Chrétien been reading Premier Lougheed's mail? Probably not because the new Judges Act had been kicking around Parliament Hill for the better part of two years. The Canadian Bar Association had long been lobbying for a new Act, and in December 1978, the Honourable Jacques Quinn, then minister of justice, had promised to proceed quickly with the passage of the new Act whose contents seem to have been generally agreed upon at that time. So, because the draft changes had been widely circulated even before Quinn's announcement, it may have been the drafters of an Alberta act who lifted the phrase from the proposed federal legislation. But which was representational allowance chicken and which was egg is less important than the fact that the amendments to the Judges Act passed through Parliament on March 6, 1981, and received royal assent on March 18. Curiously enough, by this time the phrase had been dropped from the section in favour of more straight-forward language. Section 20(1) reads:

> Every judge in receipt of a salary under this Act is entitled to be paid up to a maximum of $1,000 each year for reasonable inciden-

tal expenditures that fit and proper execution of his office as a judge may require, to the extent that

(a) such expenses have actually been incurred by him, and

(b) he is not entitled to be reimbursed therefore under any other provision of this act.

As the new act covered expenditures made during the fiscal year ending March 31, Calgary judges dug out the receipts for their expenditures for the past year and fired them off to Ottawa. Here, it is necessary to note that superior court judges do a complete clothing change prior to entry into court. In each judge's office there is a clothes closet in which the courtroom costumes are hung. These include, judicial robes, judicial vests, shirts, collars, white tabs (ties), striped trousers, director's jackets, and black shoes.

Because of the price escalation that took place over the years, the thousand dollar allowance would barely cover incidental expenses if law book purchases and legal periodical subscriptions were also covered. For example, a silk judge's gown was price-listed back in 1979 by Harcourts at $395, waistcoats were $125, and black striped trousers at $75. Shirts were somewhat less—in the $45 to $55 range. A woman's court skirt with tabs attached was available at $18. Black belts cost $8 and robe bags were listed at $35.

When the judicial expense accounts reached the office of the commissioner for Federal Judicial Affairs in Ottawa they inevitably attracted gimlet-eyed scrutiny by the appropriate federal department minion in charge of judicial expense accounts. Out came the official blue pencil to mark a large question mark opposite two particular items—shoes and belts. Ultimately, the upper reaches of the judicial bureaucracy solemnly ruled that white striped trousers were necessary expenditures, the black belt to hold them in place was not. Neither were shoes.

Two things happened. First the judges were notified of the disallowance of their claims for shoes and belts. Then Chief Justice Bora Laskin and the executive of the Canadian Judicial Council took it on themselves to get into the act. They addressed a letter of interpretation of the new allowance to the acting commissioner for Federal Judicial Affairs, and sent copies of the letter to all Canadian superior court judges.

Herewith the letter:

Ottawa, Ontario
K1A 0J1
March 25, 1981

Mr. Andre Laframboise
Acting Commissioner for Federal Judicial Affairs
Lord Elgin Plaza
66 Slater Street
20th Floor
Ottawa, Ontario
K1A 1E3

Dear Mr. Laframboise,

The Executive Committee of the Canadian Judicial Council thought that it would be helpful to you and to your office if we gave our views as to the types of expenditures which should be allowed under s. 20(1) of the amended Judges Act. That provision provides "for reasonable incidental expenditures that the fit and proper execution of his office as judge may require" and allows a maximum of $1,000 for each year on an accountable basis.

We have considered what might appropriately be brought within the terms of this provision and our list which is not intended to be exhaustive, is as follows:

(1) judicial robes
(2) judicial vests
(3) shirts, collars and tabs
(4) striped trousers
(5) director's jacket
(6) cleaning of these items
(7) garment bag and book bag
(8) law books and law-related books and subscriptions to legal periodicals and law-related periodicals.

The Judges of the Supreme Court of Canada should be entitled, in addition, to provision for a morning coat having regard to their duties as deputies of the Governor General.

We do not think that personal items such as shoes and other furnishings or luggage should be included in the items to be covered by the $1,000 allowance. There appear to have been some extravagant suggestions made as to the use of this allowance and it is for this reason that the Executive Committee felt that it would be appropriate for us to give you our views on the kind of expenditures which should be permitted under s. 20(1). I would be glad to discuss this matter with you should you think it advisable to do so. A copy of this letter is going to each member of the Canadian Judicial Council.

Sincerely

Chairman.

The decision on the shoes and belt evoked scarcely more than a Trudeauian shrug among the Calgary judiciary. Chief Justice William McGillivray, whose claim for reimbursement for a new pair of shoes was disallowed, accepted the ruling with equanimity. So also did Justice Frank Quigley, the resident free spirit of the Calgary Court House, almost. Until, that is, the Bora Laskin letter came in. Then he blew his stack!

This was not something Frank Quigley could ever keep to himself. So it was not long before the judicial corridors were echoing with reverberations from side-taking in the shoes versus no shoes controversy. Naturally, the argument drifted into the barristers' robing room and into the nether reaches of the legal profession.

Ultimately and inevitably, given Frank Quigley's streak of puckishness, a tongue-in-cheek letter to the Canadian Judicial Council resulted. But would the super-sobersided, humorless, recipients recognize Quigley's ironic touches! Would they, not knowing Quigley, risk putting any but the most serious construction on his words? Here, in any event, is the Quigley letter in its entirety:

14th April, 1981

Mr. Andre Laframboise
Acting Commissioner for Federal
Judicial Affairs
Lord Elgin Plaza
66 Slater Street
20th Floor
Ottawa, Ontario
K1A 1E3

Dear Mr. Laframboise:

On March 18th last I forwarded to Mrs. I.R. Fox my account of expenditures for the fiscal year ending March 31, 1981 under Section 20(1) of The Judges Act as amended by Bill–C–34. That account was certified by me in the following words:

"I hereby certify the above account correctly shows the amount of actual expense incurred by me for *the fit and proper execution of my office as a judge*, and that I am not entitled to be reimbursed therefore under any other provision of the Judges Act."

Sometime thereafter I received a copy of a letter written by the Chairman of the Canadian Judicial Council under date March 25, 1981 wherein the Executive Committee on the Canadian Judicial Council attempted to interpret S.20(1) of the Judges Act. Without entering into the propriety of that action, let me at the outset, completely disassociate myself with the view therein expressed in particular the statement... "we do not think that *personal items such as shoes...* should be included in the items to be covered by the $1000.00 allowance."

While I respect the right of any member of the judiciary or any group thereof to express an opinion on what he or she or they consider to be necessary expenditures for "the fit and proper execution of (one's) office as a judge" it is *my certificate* under Section 20(1) that is attached to my account and not someone elses.

Any binding legal interpretation of Section 20(1) would of course have to be made by The Federal Court in the first instance in any suit brought to recover what a particular judge has certified as being an actual expense incurred by he or she for the fit and proper execution of his or her office as a judge.

On a more practical level, it is beyond my comprehension how one could logically come to the conclusion that while shirts, blouses, tabs, cuff-links, collar stubs, vests, gowns, trousers and skirts are considered proper attire for a judge, shoes are not.

As an ex-member of Her Majesty's Canadian Forces (World War II) let me point out that those who held no commission (my status) were provided not only with a uniform but also with black boots. Commissioned Officers were granted a money allotment to purchase a dress uniform and no prohibition was placed on the use of these monies insofar as the purchase of footwear was concerned—only on the acceptable style and color. Army officers invariably purchased dress pebble-grained brown oxfords; Air Force Officers dress black shoes and Naval Officers black Wellingtons. In each case it was to enhance their respective images as officers and gentlemen.

On all Navy, Army and Air Force establishments routine inspection was made, often daily, to ensure the proper neatness and adherence to dress regulations. Let me assure you, such inspections did not stop at the trouser cuff, nor at the bottom of puttees or bell-bottomed pants. Boots and shoes had to be regulation and polished to a high gloss.

I have been sitting in the Courts of this Province for over 23 years at four different levels, and I have witnessed a general carelessness amongst members of the bar in adhering to traditional standards of dress. Even in times of affluence it is astounding to see how many counsel persist in wearing light-colored trousers and brown footwear. On a few occasions, I have observed other members of the judiciary wearing brown shoes, or black shoes in need of repair. A few have worn frayed vests, gowns and shiny trousers. Some members of our Court have openly criticized these breaches of traditional decorum. I do not intend to breach it myself.

In their personal lives the tastes of judges relative to the matter of clothing varies with the sex, age, degree of color-blindness and one's general ability and/or desire to coordinate a wardrobe. When not fulfilling judicial duties judges wear loud or subdued jackets, slacks, skirts, dresses and suits. Their shirts, ties, blouses, and sweaters are as varied as the general populaces.

Some wear caps, tams, fedoras, Homburgs, sunshades or out west—Stetsons. Others may go bareheaded or wear toupees.

Footwear may consist of blue suede, brown suede, black and white, brown and white, saddle shoes, boots, casual loafers, hush puppies, scampers, sandals, sneakers, or out West cowboy boots.

But however one's subjective tastes may vary in the matter of personal clothing, it has always been recognized that members of the bar and judiciary while about their official duties and in particular while conducting trials in Court, should, if they are exercising their office in a fit and proper manner, be attired in proper clothing. In my view, any footwear other than good dress black shoes would be improper, and even though I have always leaned toward brown or various shades thereof in purchasing my own personal wardrobe and other than black to compliment the same, I deem it necessary to provide myself with dress black shoes as a part of and to complete my judicial attire.

I have always considered that a good pair of dress black shoes was as essential to the proper attire of a judge, as white shoes are to a nurse, ballet slippers to a dancer, logging boots to a forester, hockey skates to Team Canada, or bare feet to a freckled faced youngster in summer.

I refer once more to the letter of the Executive Committee of the Canadian Judicial Council and am impelled to say, with deference, that I cannot accept the view therein expressed that shoes, being a "personal item" should not be included as a Section 20(1) re-imbursable expenditure but trousers meet the criterion. My judicial trousers cover a much more "personal" part of my anatomy than do my dress black shoes.

While equity at one time was said to have been administered according to the length of the Chancellor's foot, that appendage I am sure was always covered by slippers of the finest leather and embellished with the purest silver buckle.

My certificate was not executed by me carelessly and I do not expect it, my independence as a judge, nor my responsibility to exercise my office properly to be challenged on the basis of some gratuitous opinion advanced by others.

Yours very truly

FRANK H. QUIGLEY

All of this brings us back to those felicitous phrases—"representational allowances" of the Alberta law and Mr. Chrétien's "representational expenses." It is axiomatic that justice must not only be done, it must be seen to have been done. Judges, ergo, must not only *be* judges they must be seen to be judges, hence judicial decorum and rules governing the appearance of judges, and the emphasis of basic black in judicial appearances.

One curious aspect of the controversy is that it took no cognizance of the massive infusion of women into the legal profession in the last twenty years. Instead it served to emphasize that the law is a bastion of male chauvinism. The women judges, essentially, must garb themselves in male costumes in order to perform their judicial duties. Certainly there is no record of the Canadian Judicial Council going into executive session to design an appropriate feminine costume for women judges. Moreover, the steadily increasing number of women entering the profession must conform to male canons of taste and behaviour in court. Which brings to mind the well-known case of the young Calgary barrister who was ordered out of a judge's presence because she was improperly accoutred.

This case happened back in the miniskirt era when hem lines rose almost to the hipline, and the young woman lawyer in question naturally dressed as fashion dictated. On the day in question she had to make a brief appearance in court on a motion of some kind and tarried too long at lunch. She had barely time to rush into the court house, grab her gown, and make her way into court. In the rush, she neglected to complete the buttoning of her gown. As she turned before the judge the gown parted, revealing an extraordinary stretch of calf and thigh. The angry judge ordered her from the courtroom with a stern rebuke for appearing before him in such inappropriate dress!

When the executive of the judicial council was at work defining the outside limits of representational expenses they managed to ignore the existence of female judges. If they had thought about the women judges they would have had to confront the shoes problem head-on, but they would have become involved in an even trickier question of differentiation between personal garments and representational garments. To wit: women's hosiery.

By any canon of modern English usage, a pair of women's pantyhose must be defined as personal.

And yet———

In the day to day practice of their profession, women barristers are seldom notably different from women accountants, physicians, or computer operators. They dress as the dictates of fashion prescribe. Women's fashions are traditionally big on colour co-ordination, particularly when it comes to shoes and hosiery. As a result, many women's closets generally contain five times as many shoes as men's. Some women habitually spend ten times as much on hosiery as men do on socks.

It is difficult for many men to imagine anything more personal to a woman than her shoes and stockings. But is there a practicing woman barrister anywhere in Canada who would be found dead in a pair of black shoes and black stockings except in a courtroom? Obversely, would a woman judge, traversing a courthouse corridor on her way to her bench not be regarded as positively gauche if the feet beneath her black robes were clad in high-heeled yellow spiked pumps and matching yellow pantyhose? But if the woman judge were required by "representational" considerations alone to purchase black shoes did the purchases not qualify as the required "reasonable incidental expenditures that the fit and proper execution of her office as judge"?

But would the purchase of a pair of plain black shoes have been enough? Suppose for the spring assizes the woman judge's street wear ensemble had featured bright spring colours, light lilac, perhaps, with shoes and stockings to match. Would the substitution of the black shoes have been enough? With a flash of unroyal purple still apparent between shoe-top and judicial gown? Surely the purchase of black stockings would not only have been justifiable it would have been, representationally, imperative.

And if Canadian taxpayers became required by any logical interpretation of s.20(1) of the Judges Act to provide pantyhose for women judges, what becomes of the argument that men's shoes are strictly personal and non-expensible?

Whether the Quigley correspondence or the sudden realization that there were also women judges caused the august executive of the Canadian Judicial Council to make another run at the interpretation of the law is not a matter of record. But what has happened is that the judges who include the cost of black shoe replacement in their accounts are now being reimbursed.

To all this a footnote should be added which, incidentally, shows that the federal government is more trustful toward, and generous with, its judges than Alberta is with its. Instead of permitting its judges to do their own shopping for their representational enhancements, the Alberta government does the shopping in bulk and makes payment in kind. All this dates back to the dawn of Alberta history and the pioneer police magistrate system. That was a time when lawyers were scarce in the remote regions of the province and laymen functioned as magistrates. To establish some kind of demarcation between a local implement dealer acting as chairman of a school board and the same person sitting as magistrate, a system of supplying magistrates with black gowns to be worn over street clothes was devised.

Ultimately, the magistrate system was replaced by the appointment of provincial judges, but the system of government supplying the gowns was continued. Indeed when lawyers replaced farmers and small town undertakers, and judges replaced magistrates, then shirts, tabs, and vests were also supplied as replacements for the items that wore out. To get new ones, judges are required to return their old items to the government, presumably for inspection and ultimate disposal. As of the spring of 1985, provincial judges in Alberta are not provided with shoes, ladies' pumps, or stockings.

# Chapter Eleven

# Remembering a Super-Intellect and an Underdogs' Champion

The vintage years for Calgary barristers were clearly the first half of the twentieth century. Those were the years in which the barristers dominated the profession and the solicitors laboured in near-anonymity. And not only in Calgary. The stars of the profession in Winnipeg were Isaac Pitblado, E.J. McMurray, Hart Green, A.J. Andrews; in Saskatchewan there were Murdo MacPherson, John Diefenbaker, and Robert Milliken. Edmonton was the stamping ground of George Steer, A.S. Woods, and Neil Maclean. Calgary had a full roster of eminent solicitors, of course, like J.E.A. Macleod, O.H.E. Might, E.J. Chambers, and Alex Hannah. But it was the barristers— R.B. Bennett, A.A. McGillivray, A.L. Smith, McKinley Cameron, Sam Helman, whose deeds of derring-do, legal and otherwise, are best remembered by their heirs, assigns, and successors in both branches of the profession. They were the leaders of the partnerships that bore their names, a condition that would undergo a complete reversal in the next thirty years. Glancing over that list of all-stars, it is difficult to imagine a more disparate cast of characters. All, in their own special ways, dominated whatever courtroom they entered with their presence.

While Sam Helman was thoroughly at home in a barrister's role, he, of all the group, probably shifted into the solicitor's role with the greatest of ease. He was, by all accounts, the most cerebral of the five, a fact that may have detracted from rather than enhanced his courtroom performance. He had a passion for the printed page and when a childless marriage freed him from the time-consuming responsibilities of parenthood, he gave free rein to that passion. The pursuit of legal precedents into the dimmest reaches of history fascinated him, a fact which at times may have mitigated his effectiveness. As a contemporary put it, Sam Helman was the past-master of the overkill. "He never knew when it was time to shut up and sit down with his case won. If the citation of three or four precedents was sufficient, he had difficulty contenting himself with seven or eight."

There was one quality which Sam Helman and McKinley Cameron shared equally. That was an overweaning dedication to seeing that justice was done. In the days before legal aid became a legal profession growth industry, impoverished clients could always count on Cameron and Helman. And not only in the lower courts. Cameron probably took more cases to appeal for impecunious clients that any other lawyer in Alberta history. There was the time when the Alberta attorney general drew blanks in his effort to find a lawyer to take the case of a convicted murderer to the Supreme Court of Canada, until he came to Helman and J.V.H. Milvain. Taking the case cost them two weeks away from their offices without remuneration. But they took it, lost it, and their client went to the gallows anyway.

Helman's weakness for becoming involved with lost causes gave rise in later years to some wondering about his super reputation as a barrister in view of his rather mediocre won-lost batting average. One explanation was a clientel with a surplus of Cuthbert Harrys. Though a successful businessman, Cuthbert Harry was a character of sorts. He had a thing about the colour brown: he always dressed in brown—shirt, tie, suit, socks, and shoes—the works. While he had operated a pharmacy in Calgary for more than twenty years, he had maintained his American citizenship and made no secret of his intention of ultimately returning to the United States. By the end of the Second World War, that intention became a confirmed decision.

During the war, Canada had enacted rigid and severely enforced restrictions on trading in foreign currency, particularly American dollars. The country needed all the American currency it could obtain to finance war purchases in the United States. The effect of the regulations was to wipe out access to American currency by individual Canadians, and it all but put an end to Canadian travel south of the line. It also meant that when Canadians did get their hands on American money they squirreled it away against the time when the controls ended and travel again became possible.

While most wartime regulations were phased out after the war, exchange control in attenuated form remained until 1950. In the interval, oil was discovered at Leduc, there was a massive influx of Americans into Calgary, and a good deal of American money circulated in the area. This was manna for Cuthbert Harry who had decided the time had come to move back to the United States. Not content simply to hoard the currency that floated into his store, he pestered his tourist customers to exchange their American money for his Canadian money. By the day of his departure in 1950, he had more than eighteen thousand dollars in his possession. As it was still unlawful to take more than one hundred dollars in American currency out of the country, Harry had his wife secrete his money in her bra before hitting the road for California.

Meanwhile, stories of Harry's efforts to pry American money out of his customers had reached the RCMP. So had the news that he was going back to the United States. The Mounties at the border-crossing station at Coutts-Sweetgrass were alerted to catch him in the act of violating the foreign exchange regulations. As days lapsed into weeks, however, directives of all kinds piled up in the Mounted Police files in the Coutts customs house and vigilance naturally lapsed. When Mr. and Mrs. Cuthbert Harry eventually turned up to fill in the required exit forms, the agent on duty glanced at them and made the understandable mistake of transposing Cuthbert Harry's given name and surname. After checking their car over, he waved them on their way with a friendly, "Good luck, Mr. Cuthbert."

Cuthbert Harry was making his way through the American customs and immigration before his name suddenly rang a bell in the Canadian office.

"Hey," shouted the Mountie on duty, "Their name's not Cuthbert, that's the Cuthbert Harry we're supposed to catch with the American money." He rushed for the telephone and the American customs stopped Harry in his tracks.

"Sorry to trouble you Mr. Harry, but the Canadians were just on the phone and they've got a couple of questions they forgot to ask you to fill in their forms. Would you mind going back?"

Harry U-turned back to Canada.

The first question was, "How much American money are you taking with you, Mr. Harry?"

Well, as a free-born American, Cuthbert Harry was not about to have his rights infringed by any officious Canadian.

"It's none of your goddam business how much American money I've got," he replied.

It was quickly demonstrated that it was very much the business of the Mounted Police and the Canadian customs. The Harrys were seized bodily, stripped, and searched, and Harry's $18,000 cascaded from his wife's bra. They were formally charged and returned to the Lethbridge jail for incarceration. A telephone call to Calgary brought Sam Helman into the case. The prosecutor, Max Moscovitch, was instructed by the Ottawa authorities to demand the imposition of a $10,000 fine, failing which, Ottawa would seek an order to have the entire $18,000 confiscated.

Harry was caught cold without a shred of defense. When they got before the local magistrate Helman entered a guilty plea and the crown prosecutor asked for the imposition of the $10,000 fine. Helman said, "My client says that is in order."

By this time most of Canada's wartime austerity programs were being phased out and the currency restrictions were one of the last to go. Aware of the situation, the magistrate came to the conclusion that the size of the fine consented to by the accused was out of all proportion to the seriousness of the offense. He said so.

"I'm going to impose a fine of $2,000 which appears to me to be more than ample," he said.

Propelled by the vision of the government's threat to confiscate the entire bankroll, Sam Helman leaped to his feet.

"Your Worship, may I have an adjournment to discuss a matter with you in your office." So both counsel and magistrate left the courtroom and they told him of Ottawa's instruction to the prosecutor. The magistrate fussed and fumed but in the end agreed to impose the required penalty. They returned to the courtroom, Harry was ordered to his feet and the magistrate sentenced him to a fine of $10,000, or a year in jail.

Now it was Harry's turn. He stood there for a moment considering $10,000 *or* a year in jail. "I'll take the year in jail," he said.

Helman again got to his feet.

"Your worship, may I have another adjournment?"

It took all Helman's power of persuasion to convince Harry to pay the $10,000 fine and continue his journey back to the States with what he had left.

Any lawyer with a clientel composed mainly of Cuthbert Harrys would have had trouble maintaining a winning average. Fortunately for Helman he had, over the years, accumulated a full complement of other types of clients, the Canadian Pacific Railway for one, the City of Calgary for another, Premier E.C. Manning for still another. He had taken the landmark Borys case, which involved the definition of gas and oil in mineral rights cases, clear to the Privy Council and won it for the CPR. Premier E.C. Manning, thanks to Helman, emerged from a royal commission investigating his government with his reputation intact. And Helman's influence on public utilities regulation in Alberta was important as a result of his long involvement in the defense of the interest in Calgary consumers.

Helman's practice of the law in Calgary spanned precisely fifty years, from his arrival from Winnipeg to join A.A. McGillivray in 1921 until his retirement in 1971. McGillivray had come west in 1907 from Nova Scotia following his graduation from Dalhousie where he had been a classmate of McKinley Cameron's. Calgary, in 1921, was very much the drowsy, branch plant, branch office market town, with a thriving wholesale district that supplied southern Alberta, a thriving meat packing industry, and the locale of the western region headquarters and shops of the CPR. Southern Alberta was not an overly litigious area, certainly, but McGillivray nonetheless soon achieved more than a local reputation in criminal law, mainly on the side of the prosecution. (He was the prosecutor in two of the decade's most famous cases in southern Alberta. The first was the Picariello-Lassandro murder trial described in chapter 4, the second was the so-called Carbon murder case described in chapter 3.) Naturally, when the Turner Valley oil boom developed, the firm, like all the other Calgary lawyers, became mildly involved with the oil promoters. In between, McGillivray found time to run for the leadership of the provincial Conservative Party and to get elected to the legislature in 1925.

Sam Helman's parents were part of the first wave of Russian/ Jewish refugees who reached Winnipeg in the 1890s. After graduating from the University of Manitoba he moved to Calgary where the office of McGillivray and Tweedie stood open for him.

As the firm reached the end of the decade, both partners could have looked back on the decade with reasonable satisfaction. Although the Wall Street crash had reduced the value of the shares of its oil company clients by two thirds, the outlook for 1930 looked reasonably rosy. As a result, McGillivray gave up the leadership of the Conservative Party and retired from active politics at the next election to concentrate on his law practice which was probably fortunate given the way things turned out.

On a trip to Toronto, McGillivray had unexpectedly been retained by the firm of Solloway Mills and Company, the largest mining brokerage firm in Canada. The stock market crash in October brought government agencies into investigations of the brokerage business across the country. Though the investigation in Alberta was just the beginning, McGillivray Helman were retained by Solloway Mills to act in case anything came of the investigation. Even if nothing came of the inquiry, the account of the largest brokerage firm in the country was a good one for any office to have. And that was not all.

On November 30, 1930, a telegram arrived in the McGillivray Helman office from A.J. Andrews of Winnipeg. It reported that a client of the Andrews firm, one Harry Bronfman, had been arrested in Montreal on two charges laid by the attorney general of Saskatchewan in connection with Bronfman's operations in the liquor export business in 1922. One was concerned with the alleged bribery of a customs officer and the other with a wilful attempt to subvert justice in a bootlegging case. If McGillivray would accept a retainer on behalf of Bronfman, would he proceed to Regina immediately to consult with Andrews and P.N. Robertson of Regina in preparing Bronfman's defense? McGillivray would, and did, and thereby involved himself and Helman in the simultaneous defense in two different provinces simultaneously of two of the most spectacular cases in the history of prairie jurisprudence. Having a millionaire client to defend in criminal court was an experience as yet unknown to the members of the Calgary bar. Having two such clients, Bronfman and Solloway, put the McGillivray Helman firm in a class by themselves.

One of them, the Bronfman case, was responsible for the creation and widespread circulation of one of the most enduring myths in Canadian legal history, the legend of the grand drunk of Lyman Duff, justice of the Supreme Court of Canada. But of that, more anon.

Harry Bronfman was a hotel owner, patent medicine bottler, and car dealer in Yorkton, Saskatchewan, when Prohibition came in in 1916. When the First World War ended he converted his bonded warehouse in Yorkton into a blending plant in which he bottled whiskey, rum, and gin for export to the United States. Ultimately he had a string of export warehouses across southern Saskatchewan selling liquor to American rumrunners. There was, of course, some leakage from the export houses into domestic consumption, for enforcement of the prohibition law was notoriously lax in Saskatchewan.

In 1922, a couple of undercover agents succeeded in buying a bottle of whiskey from the manager of Bronfman's Moose Jaw store. Charges were laid and the government proceeded to confiscate the entire stock of liquor in the store, worth thousands of dollars. But when the case came to trial the undercover agents could not be found and the charges were dropped. Then rumours spread that Bronfman had arranged their absence by sending them on extended vacations as guests of his hotels in Winnipeg and Fort William.

At around the same time a couple of American rumrunners who had loaded up at Bronfman's Beinfait warehouse got lost enroute back to the States. They were arrested by a Canadian customs official in Manitoba. They were taken back to Beinfait where, in a three-cornered conversation between the customs officer, the rumrunners, and Bronfman, the latter was alleged to have offered the customs officer a bribe to drop the charges and let the Americans take their liquor home. Though the customs officer tried, he could never get his Ottawa superiors to lay charges against Bronfman. But word of his struggle got nosed abroad and so did the story of the disappearing liquor agents.

Fingers of suspicion were pointed at the Liberal Government in Saskatchewan and the Liberal Government in Ottawa. Opposition demands for the prosecution of Harry Bronfman became a political cause célèbre in Saskatchewan. In the 1925 provincial election, the Conservatives charged the Liberals with being in cahoots with the bootleggers, and claimed that the reason they did not prosecute Bronfman was that the trial would reveal government culpability.

When the Conservatives, with the help of the Progressives, unseated the Gardiner Liberals in Saskatchewan in 1929, one of the first acts of the new regime was to lay charges against Bronfman of "wilfully attempting to obstruct, pervert or defeat the course of justice by causing Douglas Readman and Herbert Clement to refrain from giving evidence," and of attempted bribery of the customs officer.

Bronfman, meanwhile, had taken his profits from Saskatchewan to Montreal to construct a distillery and a string of huge export warehouses in the Maritimes and Ontario, along with a mansion in Mount Royal. On the late afternoon of November 28, 1929, two RCMP constables from Regina appeared on Bronfman's doorsteps with warrants for his arrest. He was permitted to make a phone call to his brother and then taken in custody and hustled onto a train for Regina. This procedure was adopted, it was later explained, because Saskatchewan authorities feared that the federal department of justice would interfere on Bronfman's behalf if it got wind of the prosecution being undertaken. Over the previous six years, after all, federal authorities had refused to lay charges under the Customs and Excise Act in connection with the bribery allegation. The new Saskatchewan attorney general had dodged the Customs and Excise Act and laid the bribery charge under the Criminal Code. Arraigned on December 3, 1929, Bronfman was released on bail and returned home pending preliminary hearing, which was set for January 18.

Meanwhile his defense team went into executive session and came up with a plan to short circuit the Saskatchewan courts entirely and take the case directly to the Supreme Court of Canada. This would be done by a habeas corpus action attacking the prosecution on several technical grounds, including the statute of limitations and provisions in the Customs and Excise Act which required that charges of attempted bribery of officials be laid under the Customs Act. This defense required that Bronfman be in custody, so when he was committed for trial on January 18, 1930, with the trial date set for February 17, Bronfman refused to post bail and was returned to the Regina jail.

In the meantime, while McGillivray was in Regina for the Bronfman committal hearing, word came from Calgary that Alberta had ordered the arrest of I.W.C. Solloway in Vancouver. McGillivray fired off a heated, telegraphic blast to Premier Brownlee for reneging on his promise to advise him if action was to be taken against Solloway and Mills. Then McGillivray and

Helman caught the train for Ottawa to apply for a habeas corpus hearing for Bronfman. Supreme Court Justice Lyman Duff heard McGillivray's petition on January 22 and agreed to hear the habeas corpus petition on Saturday, February 1.

Meanwhile, Bronfman was still in jail in Regina and for the February 1 hearing, had to be moved from Regina to Ottawa. That required that Sergeant A.G. Champion be ordered to Regina with a writ to be served on E.C. Gregory, the Saskatchewan attorney general, and Warden Charles Gleadow of the Regina jail, ordering them to produce the body of Harry Bronfman before the Supreme Court of Canada.

While Bronfman was enroute east in custody of Sergeant Champion, his defense team had added Eugene Lafleur of Montreal to plead his case before Justice Duff. This he did at great length. Duff reserved judgment until the following Monday. Duff then refused to quash the charges and Bronfman was remanded for trial in Saskatchewan and released on bail immediately.

Let's run through those dates again because they are important evidence that the legend of the grand drunk of Lyman Duff is whole-hog myth. Bronfman was arrested in Montreal on November 28, arraigned and released on bail in Regina on December 3, appeared for preliminary hearing on January 17, committed for trial and took up residence in the Regina jail on January 18, so that habeas corpus action could be taken in Ottawa. That action occurred on February 1 and Duff's decision was delivered on February 3.

And now the myth which has circulated in legal circles in both Manitoba and Alberta for many years: This version has it that Bronfman was arrested shortly before Christmas of 1929 and when he appeared in Regina, with the same defense team, he refused to post bail so that his lawyers could proceed immediately with their habeas corpus action before the Supreme Court of Canada.

Long before Lyman Duff had been elevated to the Supreme Court, he had built a reputation as a first class drinking man in Saskatchewan. He heard the habeas corpus application, and appeared to be on the verge of granting the application, and vacating the charges, when he had second thoughts and said he would sleep on it and deliver his judgment the next day. But instead of sleeping on the judgment, he went off to a pre-Christmas celebration at one of the embassies, fell off the wagon with an awesome splash and did not resurface until after New Year's. In the meantime, McGillivray and the other counsel were marooned in Ottawa, chewing their fingernails off at the elbows. Their millionaire client was sequestered for two weeks in the Ottawa jail with the flotsam and jetsam of the Ottawa-Hull underworld.

On his return to sobriety, Justice Duff discovered his Bronfman case and was shocked by the realization he had kept Bronfman in jail unnecessarily over the entire holiday season. And what would the reaction be if, after all this time, he found for Bronfman? How could he possibly justify such behaviour? Obviously he could not. So he solved his hangover problem by denying the application and sending the case back to Regina for trial.

That is the myth. Who started it, how it got started or where, is unknown. But surprisingly, as late as 1985, it was still floating into the conversation when the names of Duff or Bronfman came into juxtaposition. The facts and the legend both agree, however, that Bronfman went back to Regina and to trial on February 17, 1930.

While McGillivray was at work at the Bronfman trial, Helman was acting for the Solloway Mills defense preliminaries in Calgary. When the Alberta government's brokerage investigation was winding down, a blanket search warrant was obtained and sheriff's deputies descended on the Solloway Mills office and carted off all the documentation they could find. (See Chapter 6) That completely disrupted the brokerage office and made it impossible to transact any business for its clients. Helman prepared an appeal to the Alberta Court of Appeal to have the search warrant quashed and get the firm's books back. Helman argued the appeal while McGillivray was in Estevan defending Bronfman on the customs officer bribery charge. The Appellant Court quashed the search warrant on March 17.

Was there ever a legal office faced with simultaneously defending two millionaire clients on two such disparate charges, in two such disparate jurisdictions as Calgary, Alberta, and Estevan, Saskatchewan? While Bronfman had surrounded himself with the finest legal talent available in western Canada, it was McGillivray who was the combination quarterback and ball carrier of the Bronfman defense in all three Saskatchewan trials. And when Solloway Mills went to trial in Calgary, he was again front and centre. In the latter case, however, it was Helman who did the bulk of the preparation of the Solloway defense.

In the first Bronfman trial, despite McGillivray's two-hour address, the jury could not agree. So a new trial was ordered for June, which would put it plumb in the centre of the Solloway trial. Ultimately, the Bronfman retrial was put over until September. From Regina, McGillivray went to Estevan to defend against the customs officer bribery charges. Here he was able to produce high officials from the customs department in Ottawa to contradict some of the claims made by the main crown witness, and Bronfman was acquitted. At the retrial in Regina in September, he was also found not guilty.

Then, again according to legend, with the highest fee ever paid in a criminal case in western Canada—fifty thousand dollars—

McGillivray returned to Calgary and the Solloway Mills defense. Here, after a preliminary hearing that took a week in March and a trial that took three weeks in June, the verdict went against Solloway. There are no legends afloat of the fee McGillivray and Helman earned from the Solloway Mills trials. That it may well have exceeded Bronfman's is indicated by Solloway's own statement that the trials in Calgary, Vancouver and Toronto cost him more than a million dollars. Of that amount six hundred thousand dollars was for fines; the balance was for legal fees and expenses. The Calgary trial was the longest of the three.

Whatever the fee, McGillivray must have felt by the end of 1930 that he could now afford to take an appointment to the bench. On May 9, 1931, he was appointed to the Appellate Division of the Supreme Court of Alberta, where he served until his death of a heart attack on December 12, 1940, at the age of fifty-six.

McGillivray's decision to accept a judgeship left the field wide open and the one who next came to be regarded as the outstanding trial lawyer of his time was undoubtedly A.L. Smith. Certainly Dean W.F. Bowker, lately of the Institute of Law Research and Reform, and the authority on the history of the Alberta bar, who had seen all the most eminent in action during the interwar years, chose Smith as the first among Alberta trial lawyers.

Among his other singularities, Arthur Leroy Smith was probably the only matured child prodigy among his Calgary contemporaries. Born in Regina in 1886, the son of the town's first mayor and resident tinsmith, he graduated from high school at fourteen and had a second class teaching certificate at fifteen, all the while spending his summers punching cows on a Manitoba cattle ranch. While breezing through the University of Manitoba to a B.A. degree at nineteen, he played professional hockey for the Winnipeg Rowing Club, as well as lacrosse, a game that seems to have combined the more robust features of soccer, rugby football, and a soupçon of Irish hurling. At the University of Manitoba, he won the governor general's medal and a Rhodes Scholarship, which he turned down in favour of pursuing a law degree at Osgoode Hall. He played professional hockey with the Toronto Argonauts, with St. George's while at Osgoode, and when he returned to Regina to complete his articling, he played for the Regina Capitals.

In 1910 Smith moved to Calgary and the firm of Walsh and McCarthy, and was introduced to the great Paddy Nolan whom he came to regard as his patron saint and legal role model. One time, early in Smith's career, he was offered a chance to act as Paddy's junior in a rather serious preliminary hearing. The Crown introduced a professional witness—a doctor—and it was obvious that the case would hinge on his testimony. While Smith sat nervously at his side, Paddy seemingly napped with his head in his arms on the desk until suddenly he sprang to life, quickly wrote a brief note, and then settled back in a doze. Smith edged the paper along the desk to find out what Nolan had decided would be the basis for cross-examination. The note read: "The son of a bitch is wearing a celluloid collar."

While Smith's career as a professional hockey player was over at twenty-four, the rink-rat in him was never completely sublimated. He turned to refereeing amateur hockey in Calgary and was soon a prominent participant in the Calgary sporting scene, particularly as a curler of more than local repute. It was probably this identification with sport that led to his first big case, the defense of Arthur Pelkey and his manager, Tommy Burns, in the manslaughter trial that arose out of the death of Luther McCarthy in a heavyweight boxing match in Calgary.

By the simple process of knocking out all rival claimants, Tommy Burns had succeeded to the World Heavyweight Champion's title in 1905, following the retirement of Jim Jeffries. He held the title until 1908 when he was knocked out by Jack Johnson, a black man. That a black man should hold the title was regarded by racist America as an affront to the whole human race. There began a search for a great white hope who would beat Johnson and restore white supremacy. But as fast as new white hopes appeared, Johnson disposed of them with his fists.

One such hopeful was Luther McCarthy, an American who had had his first fight in Calgary and then had considerable success in the United States, defeating several so-called contenders. Tommy Burns, having retired from active fighting, found his way to Calgary where he became a fight promoter and sponsor of a great white hope of his own, Arthur Pelkey. He matched Pelkey against McCarthy for the White Heavyweight Championship of the World on Victoria Day, 1913, in Calgary.

The fight took place in the outdoor arena Burns had built in Manchester. It lasted less than a round. McCarthy was knocked to the canvas and never got up, dying of a hemorrhage of the spine caused by a dislocated neck. The police immediately arrested Pelkey and, although a coroner's jury found him blameless, he was nevertheless charged with manslaughter and brought to trial in June 1913. It was not the most difficult case Smith ever had, but his courtroom performance stamped him as a comer in Calgary legal circles.

In 1921 Smith made his first run for Parliament as a Conservative and was beaten. In 1926 he established his own firm, with W.G. Egbert and his younger brother, Clarence. He was also appointed the agent of the attorney general in Calgary and was ultimately involved in the prosecution of the Solloway Mills case. Like most Calgary lawyers, Smith was deeply involved in the oil boom that hit Calgary in the 1920s and like most lawyers, accumulated a box full of oil stock certificates of dubious value rather than certified cheques for work performed.

While Smith was the agent of the attorney general in Calgary for fourteen years, his most prominent cases, those on which his reputation was based, came from his private practice. Of these he would probably have put the Powlett damages suit at the top of the list, followed very closely by the Ramberg mercy killing.

The Powlett case went back to the days when initiation horseplay was very much a part of the university life. Newly registered freshmen had to survive a week of sometimes brutal, mostly only embarrassing, hazing by the sophomore class. It was all part of the rite of passage from teenage to adult life and was tolerated if not sanctioned by most of the institutions of higher learning. The University of Alberta, where the events took place, was one of the institutions that actually sanctioned the practice. Initiation week was under the control of a four-person initiation committee which was elected from the preceding freshman class by the students council in June. A member of the senior student body was also elected to supervise the program of horseplay. It was the job of the supervisor to confer with the members of the committee and discuss their program with them and then meet with the provost of the university. The provost was not informed of the details of the program but was responsible for enforcement of the behavioural rules at the university.

Among the two hundred freshmen registering at the University of Alberta in September 1932 was Armand Powlett, the son of a well-known Calgary lawyer of the Conservative persuasion. Instead of hero-worshipping such idols as Babe Ruth, Lefty Grove, Howie Morenz, or Percy Williams, young Powlett's icon was the Right Honourable Prime Minister of Canada, R.B. Bennett. He had worked for Bennett during the 1930 election and whenever the prime minister returned to Calgary, young Powlett was on the station platform to welcome his idol. Aside from an off-pattern and exaggerated interest in politics, Armand was a bright, outgoing, gangling, and thus less than perfectly co-ordinated, nineteen-year-old.

On his first night in residence, as an introduction to freshman hazing, Powlett along with the other freshmen in the dorm had been taken to another residence. There they were forced to shed their pyjamas and take turns dragging each other down the halls by the feet. When the sophomores had had enough of this entertainment, they doused the freshmen in cold showers and allowed them to return to bed. So far so good.

The next day, after registration, the sophomores picked up the freshmen and escorted them to the basement of Athabasca Hall for more hazing. On the way each was asked a stereotype question with a set answer. The question was, "What is the highest form of animal life?" The required answer was, "A sophomore." Instead of giving the required answer, Powlett answered, "R.B. Bennett," and despite continual harassment as the question was repeated he continued to answer the same way.

At Athabasca Hall the names and addresses of the freshmen were taken down and each assigned a number. Powlett was 213, and he was singled out for special attention for his refusal to give the required answer. The entire freshman class was forced to disarray their clothes and then submit to having their hair cut in outrageous patterns. Powlett, as he persisted in his refusal, was given a second haircut, and had "R.B. Bennett" inscribed on his forehead in India ink. Then he was given another lengthy interrogation, forced into another cold shower, removed to an upper corridor and ordered to be "skin-assed" the length of the corridor five times and "hot-handed." The first was a repetition of the previous experience of being stripped and dragged nude on his buttocks the length of the corridor. The latter described the freshmen being forced to crawl, still nude, on their hands and knees through the widespread legs of a half dozen upper classmen. As one passed through, each sophomore spanked him smartly on the buttocks, then ran to the end of the line to administer a second spanking. Then he was again cold-showered and ordered to his room.

That night Powlett was again taken from his room to a mock court being held for freshmen. He was charged with the crime of preferring R.B. Bennett to sophomores and was presented with a recantation which he had to sign. It ended with some such statement as, "and may The Almighty, whose only son is no longer R.B. Bennett, strengthen me in my recantation." After the mock court, one of the students noticed Powlett walking around in a daze and talking incoherently. He took him to his room. The next day one of the sophomores called Powlett, gave him some money and a package and ordered him to go to the post office, get some stamps and mail the package. Later he was seen wandering around the campus with the money in one hand and the package in the other, in a state of confusion, and was again taken to his room. Later that evening, after attending a lecture, he was again seen wandering aimlessly. The dormitory janitor, alarmed at his behaviour, sat with him for awhile, then he reported Powlett's condition to the provost.

The next morning a doctor was called to Powlett's room and the young man was taken to the infirmary. He was later transferred to the university hospital and placed in the psychiatric ward. He was diagnosed to be insane, was kept in the hospital until November 27, 1932, when he was transferred to the Homewood Mental Hospital in Guelph, Ontario.

G.H.Q. Powlett on behalf of himself and his son sued the

university, its board of governors and senate for damages. The case was heard by Mr. Justice William Ives in 1933. A.L. Smith and Ronald Martland appeared for the Powletts, and S.B. Woods, S.W. Fields, L.Y. Cairns, and H.A. Dyde for the defendants.

The trial was noteworthy on several counts. Judge Ives arranged for a panel of six psychiatrists to sit in the jury box throughout the trial and have access to all the medical notes available from both the university hospital and the Homewood sanatorium. Doctors who treated the young man at Homewood came to Calgary for the trial, testified that young Powlett was now fully recovered but should be kept in the protective environment of the hospital for some additional time.

The psychiatrists in their testimony, disagreed. The specialists retained by the university contended that young Powlett had a schizoid personality; they identified his trouble as schizophrenia which only developed in schizoid personalities. One of the defense specialists, under cross examination by A.L. Smith, admitted that the kind of excitement young Powlett had experienced could have accelerated the insanity. The next day, under orders from another defense pyschiatrist, he recanted that opinion. Powlett's panel, under Smith's questioning, made point by point rebuttal of the schizoid-schizophrenia link as it applied to Powlett. Such patients, they said, never made the kind of recovery Powlett had made and they swore his childhood behaviour was not that of a schizoid personality.

Judge Ives, in what was probably the longest judgment he ever wrote, found for the Powletts and against the university on all counts. He awarded them $6,840 special costs, including the maintenance of young Powlett for an additional year at Homewood, $50,000 in damages, and costs of the action including discovery. (On later appeal, the Alberta Court of Appeal sustained Ives by a three to two vote, but reduced the damages to $15,000.)

For those who knew Ives professionally his lengthy judgment was a somewhat puzzling departure from his usually laconic, oral judgments delivered from the bench. There is an oft-repeated story about the Cowboy Judge from southern Alberta and his first cattle drive in the Porcupine Hills: The foreman, in a seemingly innocent inquiry to Ives about his skills, discovered that young Ives "could do just about anything." Thereafter Ives found himself doing just about everything, and thus learned a truth that would last him a lifetime: keep your mouth closed.

The hard work drove him from the cattle range back to the McGill law school and he returned in 1901 to take up a practise in Lethbridge on the way to his eventual role as chief of the Trial Division. His judgments were short, to the point, and rarely reversed by superior courts, so this rather emotional judicial decision in the Powlett case came as a surprise. But, to those who knew him personally, the pathos of his participation in the trial was obvious indeed. Only recently Ives' own adolescent son had committed suicide and his marriage had foundered to the point of separation. Surely the trial had been a difficult ordeal.

Spectators at the Powlett trial saw Smith at his best in cross-examination, and at his best he was unsurpassed in Canada. Indeed, Ronald Martland, who recalled the case many times in later life, expressed the opinion that Smith's performance was comparable to the great cross-examinations of Lord Birkenhead, Sir Edward Carson, and Marshall Hall. Smith had a field day with the psychiatrists, with the university provost, and with the freshmen who had gone through the initiation with Powlett and had considered it great fun. When Smith was through, there was not a shadow of doubt in Ives' mind about where the blame for Powlett's condition lay.

In contrast with the work Smith had to do in preparation for the Powlett suit for damages, to say nothing of the lengthy siege of courtroom labours, Smith's other most noted human interest involvement was one which he could have won even if he had gone duck shooting, the defense in Alberta's only mercy killing murder trial. The accused were Victor and Dorothy Ramberg who lived in the village of Keoma, thirty miles north east of Calgary, where the husband operated the Alberta Wheat Pool grain elevator. Smith represented Mrs. Ramberg and J.T. Shaw appeared for the husband.

The Rambergs' firstborn son was in every respect a normal baby until he approached his second birthday. Then the parents noticed that he was bumping into things a he toddled around the house and was more and more frequently seized with fits of crying for no reason they could discover. They began a lengthy series of medical consultations with Calgary doctors, with inconclusive results. The crying became more extended until the young couple was kept awake nightly for hours on end. Ultimately, one of the baby's eyes began to swell and another hurried visit to Calgary for medical attention was made.

The examination of the child's eye revealed extensive cancer which had spread to the other eye and was diagnosed as spreading through his body. While the surgeon recommended the removal of both the child's eyes, he could hold out no hope for recovery. Nothing could be done to assuage the child's pain other than keeping him completely sedated twenty-four hours a day which would have meant, of course, that he would have eventually starved to death.

The Rambergs refused to permit the operation and went home with their son, determined to put an end to his suffering. The next morning the father attached a hose to the exhaust of his car and pushed the nozzle through an opening in the bedroom window.

The mother sealed up the cracks under the bedroom door, and when her husband started the car, took her son in her arms and held his face to the hose nozzle. Then she signalled her husband that the baby was gone and he went out and turned off the car. After placing the baby in his bed, she left the bedroom and collapsed on the kitchen floor. Her husband, returning to the house, went into the bedroom where he too slumped unconscious to the floor. Mrs. Ramberg recovered first and was able to answer the door when a neighbor called. Together they pulled Mr. Ramberg from the bedroom but he remained unconscious. Eventually the neighbors got the Rambergs, with the baby into a car, and drove them into Calgary to medical attention—and the police.

The Rambergs were charged with murder and went to trial on December 10, 1941, before Mr. Justice Shepherd and a jury. The trial ended quickly the next day with the acquittal of the accused. In his address to the jury, Smith dwelt at some length on the need for legislation to remove from the Criminal Code such cases as that before them. It was, he said, outrageous that decent people like Victor and Dorothy Ramberg, who loved their son and could no longer bear to see him suffering, had to be classed with murderers and cut-throats. Perhaps this case, he said, the first of its kind in Canada, would result, as it should, in the law being changed to provide for machinery that would treat such problems as that posed by the dying Ramberg baby. The jury took just enough time to leave the court room, take a vote, and return with an unanimous verdict acquitting the Rambergs of the murder of their son.

In contrast, there was no such emotional super-charging of the case that not only brought Smith one of his fattest fees but profoundly affected natural gas safety procedures in Alberta for all time to come—the Corona Hotel case. It was lengthy, two weeks before the trial court, and was before the courts, off and on, from January 1934, until the Judicial Committee of the Privy Council had its final say in October 1935.

It began with the explosion and fire that destroyed the Corona Hotel in Edmonton following the rupture of a gas main in February 1932. The hotel janitor, going to investigate a hissing sound in the basement of the hotel, lit a match. He escaped with his life but the hotel went up in flames. In addition to the hotel owners, more than ninety others filed claims for damages against the gas company and its insurers, the London Guarantee Company. All claims went into limbo until the courts decided who had been responsible for the fire—the Northwestern Utilities Company which owned the broken gas main, or the City of Edmonton, whose excavations near the main had disturbed the surrounding earth, causing the line to subside and a weld to break. The plaintiffs in the suit against the gas company were represented by

S.B. Woods and five other lawyers; A.L. Smith and Ronald Martland of the Milner firm represented the gas company, and S.C.S. Kerr appeared for the insurance company.

Martland long relished one happy memory of a particular moment of cross-examination. "We called a welding expert from the United States who knew his stuff and gave excellent testimony. He was then cross-examined by Mr. Woods, who, unfortunately for him had his guidance from a local technical school teacher, and he had been told that a double weld—that is, a weld which is made on each side of a plate, is stronger than a single weld from one side. The cross-examination was the classic example of one question too many:

'This was a single weld on this pipe, wasn't it?'

'Yes, Mr. Woods, yes.'

'Why wasn't there a double weld?'

'Mr. Woods, when they develop a welder who can climb into the inside of an eighteen-inch pipe and weld, you will have it, you will have it.'"

The gas company won the first round in the trial before Justice Frank Ford. He ruled that the city, in the course of constructing a new sewer line, had excavated beneath the gas line and subsequent subsidence resulting from the excavation had caused the break. The Alberta Court of Appeal thought otherwise. It ruled that while the city did excavate for the sewer line, the gas company was aware of the construction work being carried on around its gas line and was duty bound to take whatever action was needed to protect its line. The case then went to the Privy Council which found that the city's conduct had caused the break in the gas line. But in conveying a dangerous substance like gas through its pipelines, the gas company was under duty to take care of the plaintiffs.

The Judicial Committee ruled that if the gas company did not know of the city works, their system of inspection must have been deficient; if they did know, they should have been on their guard. In any case, the committee felt it was their duty to the respondents, at the lowest, to be on the watch and be vigilant and they had not even pretended to have done as much as that.

The case was a landmark in the law of negligence and has since been cited in the main works on the subject. In this case, Smith was on the losing side, but his performance in the original trial was outstanding in the cross-examination of the many technical witnesses called to testify. Out of the case, the gas company learned that concern for customer safety had to be made a categorical imperative. It immediately introduced an odiferous substance into its gas which made it possible for consumers to identify gas leaks. It installed an inspection system of its lines, together with a system to keep track of all construction in the vicinity of its lines.

A.L. Smith's last case equalled in poignancy any that had gone before, even though in substance it hardly rated with the others. This was the case of the bank robber who zigged when he should have zagged. It occurred in the early postwar era when Smith was a member of Parliament and as a result had little time to devote to his law practice. This case began one morning soon after the main branch of the Bank of Montreal in Calgary opened and a young man appeared with what was later determined to be a toy gun, pointed it at a teller, and demanded her money. The teller filled a bag with cash and pushed it across the wicket. The robber grabbed the bag and fled. But instead of escaping through the main entrance to melt into the crowd on the street, the robber rushed through a nearby door that took him down the stairs into the basement. He was trapped until the police arrived and arrested him.

When the circumstances of the case were explained to Smith, he came back to Calgary to defend the bank robber. The young accused had enlisted in the RCAF early in the war and married shortly before his departure for overseas. A son was born in his absence. The young man won his commission in the air force and became a co-pilot on a Lancaster bomber. On a raid on German installations in Norway, the plane was badly damaged and the pilot ordered the crew to abandon ship. On the parachute jump, one of the jumpers pulled his rip cord too quickly and the billowing parachute became entangled on the undercarriage of the plane. As the co-pilot watched in horror, the entangled jumper was slowly beaten to death against the exterior of the plane.

Ultimately the plane made a crash landing in Sweden where the crew was rescued, hospitalized, and interned, but the experience of watching his buddy being battered to death unhinged the co-pilot mentally. When he returned home he was unable to hold a job to support his family and was refused assistance by the Department of Veterans Affairs (DVA) whose officials ruled his mental instability was outside their jurisdiction.

Smith pleaded the accused guilty of the bank robbery charge before the magistrate Harry Rose and embarked on a detailed plea of extenuating circumstances. He began with the production of the pictures of the accused's wedding, various shots of a bright and handsome young man in his early twenties. Next he brought out snapshots taken during his active service in England, pictures again of a man as normal as any of the hundreds of thousands of other service personnel in England. Then came the pictures of a hollow-eyed, emaciated, spooklike creature in the Swedish internment camp. The Swedish doctors had done what they could for his body, and by the time he returned to Calgary he had put on weight and seemed as good as new. His mind was another thing.

The mental scars were still there, and despite the preference which servicemen received from employers, he had extreme difficulty in keeping a job. He applied to the DVA for assistance, when he ran out of resources; he was cold-shouldered away. Eventually, when the family was down to its last bottle of milk and half loaf of bread, he went out to rob the bank.

This was the raw material for what the court reporters called the most masterful plea of extenuating circumstance they had ever heard, one in which Smith turned his attack on the way in which the DVA officials had been derelict in their duty to an injured Canadian hero. The several DVA officials in the court room became cringing targets of Smith's invective. In the end, Magistrate Rose put the fellow on suspended sentence and remanded him into the custody of the Department of Veterans' Affairs for treatment.

Perhaps less dramatic but equally successful was Smith's handling of Guy Weadick's lost-cause-of-all-lost-causes suit against the Calgary Exhibition and Stampede. The Stampede became an integral part of the Calgary Exhibition in 1923 when Guy Weadick was hired as its impressario. Weadick was an old cowhand turned vaudeville-rope-trick-artist who staged the first Stampede in Calgary in 1912 and returned in 1919 to organize the Calgary Victory Stampede to mark the end of the Great War. In the meantime he had purchased a ranch west of Longview and added some rodeo touches to the Calgary horse shows. One of the frequent visitors to the Weadick ranch was A.L. Smith, who had once been a working cowboy himself.

In 1923, when the exhibition was casting about for something new to attract crowds to its summer show, it hired Weadick to promote and stage the Calgary Stampede. Ever cautious where money was concerned, the exhibition board did a very special deal with Weadick. It would pay him five thousand dollars to stage-manage the Stampede. He would begin work on January 1 and be through when the Stampede finished. If it was decided to continue the Stampede the following year it would notify him prior to January 1. He would repeat the performance on the same terms. So for the first few years the letters went out and Weadick came back on staff after a six month hiatus.

By 1928 there was no doubt in anybody's mind about the permanency of the Stampede. So the deal was varied to this extent: If the Exhibition did not notify Weadick in writing that his services were no longer required, he could count on returning each year. Then came the Great Depression, and in 1932 the Exhibition board drastically cut back the prize money offered for the Stampede events. The board was told by Weadick that they were ruining the show, that the cowboys would never compete for the money being offered. Weadick was wrong, the cowboys even increased their participation. During the 1932 show some bitter arguments continued between Weadick and several board members, and when the show closed the general manager, E.L. Richardson, was instructed to notify Weadick that his services would not be required for the 1933 show.

Weadick was outraged and promptly sued for damages and retained his old friend A.L. Smith to act for him. The Bennett firm had acted for the Calgary Exhibition and Stampede for many years, and E.J. Chambers of Nolan, Chambers, Might, and Saucier was instructed to defend. On the surface, the defense seemed impregnable because it conformed so strictly with the contract. But when the case eventually got before Mr. Justice Ives everything came unstuck. Witnesses for the Stampede insisted on carrying the defense away out into the loading chutes, as it were.

During this semiarid stretch of Alberta history, the Stampede maintained a quasi-secret "snake room" in the Palliser Hotel where booze was purveyed to visiting celebrities and local politicians. One of Weadick's duties was to greet the celebrities and socialize with the high and the mighty. It was a duty he had assumed at the beginning and performed with enthusiasm. In 1932, however, he seemed to get deeper into the sauce than usual and was occasionally heard bad-mouthing the directors for their chintzy action in cutting the rodeo purses. On the final night of the show, he turned up considerably the worse for wear and floundered around on the stage disrupting the prize-giving ceremonies. The Stampede witnesses insisted on making Weadick's behaviour a contributing cause for his dismissal.

When the suit was heard by Mr. Justice William Ives in 1934, Smith concentrated all his attention on the misbehaviour of the defense. So did Ives in his judgment. He held that the Stampede board was providing the booze that Weadick was expected to dispense in its hospitality suite and if, in doing his job he occasionally became somewhat boisterous, even out of control, how could his employers have reason to complain? He awarded damages of $2,500 and costs to Weadick.

Everett Chambers, who regarded the decision as utterly perverse wrote the Stampede board urging that the decision be appealed. But the board, seemingly affected by the adverse publicity the suit had engendered, decided to put up and shut up. Thereafter Smith regarded winning the Weadick case as one of the highlights of his long and illustrious career.